Factual Television Producing

This book is an unvarnished look at how to originate, pitch, sell, and produce factual television programming for global broadcast television networks and streaming services.

Grounded in firsthand experience, this essential "how to guide" walks readers through the crucial steps in the factual television process while unpacking valuable insights to successfully producing and delivering projects on time and on budget. With over 20 years of experience in the TV documentary arena, Executive Producer Dylan Weiss shares how to break into the industry, originate your own documentary ideas, forge a path forward through the creative process, prepare your concepts for commissioners, and then pitch them to networks, broadcasters, streamers, and distributors around the world. Industry voices are layered throughout sharing their experiences from each stage of the process. These interviews include top executives from Disney, Investigation Discovery, National Geographic, and many more.

This is an ideal resource for independent documentary producers looking to create and pitch their work to top television networks and streaming services.

Dylan Weiss is a documentary filmmaker and President of Cry Havoc Productions, where he has overseen over 100 hours of factual programming for a wide range of pan-regional and global networks, including the National Geographic Channel, National Geographic International, Discovery Networks International, Smithsonian Channel, Science Channel, and Animal Planet.

Factual Television Producing

A Hands On Approach From Concept to Delivery

Dylan Weiss

NEW YORK AND LONDON

Designed cover image: © Cry Havoc Productions

First published 2023
by Routledge
605 Third Avenue, New York, NY 10158

and by Routledge
4 Park Square, Milton Park, Abingdon, Oxon, OX14 4RN

Routledge is an imprint of the Taylor & Francis Group, an informa business

ISBN: 978-1-032-27324-2 (hbk)
ISBN: 978-1-032-27323-5 (pbk)
ISBN: 978-1-003-29228-9 (ebk)

DOI: 10.4324/9781003292289

Access the Support Material: www.routledge.com/9781032273242

Typeset in Univers
by Apex CoVantage, LLC

Contents

Introduction

What exactly is a *factual television producer*? The term "producer" gets bandied about an awful lot these days, yet its definition remains elusive. That's partly because being a producer means different things in different creative industries. There are producers in nonfiction television, narrative television, film, still photography, web video, corporate video, and a host of other outlets.

In the world of factual television, a producer is almost always the driving force behind a project. They're the creator, organizational wizard, main number cruncher, and the person who oversees the project from start to finish. A factual television producer's role can overlap with our vision of what a TV director does, *plus* they're responsible for coordinating and supervising all facets of production, from originating the idea through final delivery. If you think of each program or series as a small business, a factual television producer is the CEO who does everything possible to ensure success.

What factual producers craft is the ultimate democratic creative enterprise. Viewers vote on the work with their remote controls every single minute of every single day. There are no questionable outcomes, just cold hard ratings and viewership. In the end, you can either be judged because you create something and put it out into the world or be ignored because you left your brilliant idea alone to wither on the vine.

The ones who truly make it in the factual television game enjoy the process as much as the outcome. There are few feelings as absolutely magical as seeing your finished program bounce back via a satellite or beamed through the internet via a streaming service as it entertains and enlightens viewers across the globe.

Creating a factual broadcast program or series is also a unique creative endeavor that offers the power to share knowledge, entertain viewers, and sometimes even change the world. Factual television can bring light to darkness and help empower the powerless.

These programs often share new insights and offer a peek behind the scenes in the places that you normally can't go. They spread insight and offer a different prism through which one can view our world in new ways. At their very best they can afford audience members a way to escape whatever ails them, and at their worst they're the gossipy watercooler conversation that binds our culture together.

As a factual storyteller harnessing the power of a documentary-style project is an addictive, invigorating, and deeply fulfilling pursuit – yet the process of crafting one from start to finish can be a daunting journey that's full of potential landmines and seemingly unscalable mountains.

Creating successful content requires dedication, perseverance, mental toughness, a strong sense of purpose, and, above all else, a relentless ability to believe. In yourself. In your idea. In your team. In your project. In your process. In your dream.

Do it successfully, and it'll lead you to a rich life full of curiosity, adventure, brilliant image-making, and powerful storytelling. You can find yourself waking up as the sun rises over the Serengeti, Ancient Rome, magical parts of Southeast Asia, or even glorious racetracks all over the world. Telling stories for a living is the ultimate gift and something worth cherishing every step of the way – even when the journey gets tough.

As little as 10 or 15 years ago the phrase *documentary filmmaker* held a very specific meaning, often describing a passionate director who aimed to tell a personally relevant story from a highly specific point of view in a 90-minute format intended for a theatrical audience. Today, that definition has evolved. We now live in an always-on multi-platform visual content-driven world where the distinction of what constitutes a *true documentary* continually expands by the day. What once was the purview of a few hardcore *documentarians* fighting for their cause has now evolved into the underlying connective tissue of an entire nonfiction programming industry. It's a universe that ranges from theatrical films and Occudocs all the way to reality competitions, lifestyle programs, and factual entertainment series. Every year new programming emerges that redefines our documentary understanding a bit further. As the lines that define what constitutes a documentary continually evolve, so too does our ability to consume the resulting content. The modern theatrical experience might be waning; however, television and streaming have become the benefactors, if not saviors, of the documentary genre.

So why should you care what I've got to say about factual television producing?

Glad you asked.

I'm an award-winning factual TV producer who's built my entire professional career one fast lap around a racetrack at a time. For the past 20 years I've been fortunate to chase fast cars and crazy machines all around the world while creating factual content for a wide range of global and pan-regional broadcast networks, including Animal Planet, National Geographic Channel, Discovery International, Smithsonian Channel, American

Heroes Channel, Motor Trend, and Science Channel. My work has been seen on the largest factual television networks by *hundreds* of millions of people and distributed in nearly every country in the world. If your cable system gets a signal, chances are you've had an opportunity to watch my programs and series on a variety of global networks.

Since graduating from the University of Southern California's Cinema-Television School in Los Angeles, I've successfully navigated the world of factual content while running my own factual production company called Cry Havoc Productions. I've been extremely lucky to be able to blend my personal passion for fast machines with a natural inclination toward heady engineering and my professional fascination with the television industry. It's been a wild ride to say the least, full of incredible highs and crushing lows, but I wouldn't trade it for anything in the world. *Well maybe a brand-new Lamborghini and some open roads in Northern Italy, but who wouldn't, right?!?*

Now I'd like to share some of the lessons that I've learned, some of the tricks of the trade that I've discovered, and some of the hidden steps in the process so that you too can create your own on-screen documentary magic for broadcast networks!

In the pages that follow I'm going to use the terms *documentary* and *programming* rather interchangeably given the rapid transformation within the factual industry. This will undoubtedly upset some purists; however, I hold a very expansive view of factual content and believe that the tenants of great documentary filmmaking can be found across a whole myriad of specific genre definitions. The lines that used to separate narrative-driven personal documentary films and easily digestible nonfiction programming have become extremely blurry these days. Even though they sit at opposite ends of the *very same spectrum*, they actually employ a nearly identical production process and even often end up sitting right next to one another on the same network and streaming platforms. Therefore, I'm going to use the word *filmmaker* in a very broad and inclusive context meant to highlight whoever is the driving force behind the production, regardless of whether that's a director, producer, or writer.

What follows is a blueprint to originate your own factual programming idea, go about selling it to a broadcaster or streaming service, and how to go out and produce it. While most of my career experience comes from handcrafting automotive and engineering content for broadcast, the lessons learned, tips, tricks, and techniques are applicable to all manner of factual programming creation. These skills superseded any one specific genre or type of production and even my own background in episodic work.

The processes described can be applied to any type of factual content creation you can imagine, and by the time you finish reading this book, my hope is to.

- arm you with the knowledge to go out into the real world and create content for mass distribution on a global scale;
- have an open and honest discussion about what it's like to be a professional factual producer;
- encourage anyone with a documentary idea to go tell their story on the grandest scale possible.

My particular path has bent in a certain way; however, yours can head in any of a number of different and equally exciting directions. Anything is possible, and wherever your interest lies you can forge your own factual-producing destiny if you so choose.

It's entirely up to you and your imagination.

These are the tricks, hacks, and processes that have helped me, the insights I've gained over the years, and the things that I'd do differently if I were starting out now.

Hope you enjoy the read!

Chapter One

Breaking In and Getting Started

In its simplest form producing documentaries is an occupation built on four basic tenets: telling great stories, crafting amazing visuals, making things happen, and problem-solving.

Whether it's finding funding, securing talent, or simply gaining access, your job is to connect the dots in order to bring people, places, and networks together for the sake of a single story.

You sit at the intersection of great ideas, incredible determination, and fortunate opportunities.

In many ways you're both a detective and a straight-up hustler, first uncovering a unique subject matter and then transactionally finding a way to convince someone to *pay you* to film it.

Bringing your vision to the screen is an arduous journey that requires relentlessly pushing forward in the pursuit of getting your project made.

Your currency is story, access, and talent.

Do it successfully and the power of the documentary genre can unlock infinite possibilities.

Through a tremendous amount of trial and error and hundreds of thousands of hours spent perfecting the craft, here are a few core beliefs that I've honed during my career that might help make your journey a bit easier and perhaps more rewarding.

DOI: 10.4324/9781003292289-1

Why We Create Factual Television

Creating content for broadcast, or streaming, often starts as a hobby, then perhaps morphs into a dream, before finally, if you're lucky enough, becoming an occupation. Some factual filmmakers aim to tell stories that they feel are important. They may be doing it not for the money but rather because it's their calling in life to bring these tales to a wider audience. On the other hand, there are those among us that not only want to tell visual stories but also get paid to do it. Neither route is better or worse; however, the main thrust of this book is aimed at helping you take your passion for filmmaking and finding a way to transform it into a professional career that's full of amazing sights and highlights.

A factual filmmaker's life is full of travel, unique opportunities, surprising journeys, and a constant state of inquisitiveness. It's a brilliant recipe to live a fulfilling and unusual life. Deciding to become a factual producer sets you out on a nonstandard life journey where you'll stand apart from others. When you're in your twenties, you'll see your friends land exciting jobs while you're still broke and hustling. It helps to measure your life in decades, not years. The glory of television is easy to see; however, the industry has challenges that you have to learn to overcome too: internal and external politics, salary concerns, lengthy hours, extreme pressure, subject and talent issues, longevity concerns, as well as continually evolving technological hurdles. The positives far exceed the negatives as long as you never lose sight of just one thing – *the joy of creating on-screen magic.*

If you live and breathe factual television, if the visual language lies deep in your soul, and if your days begin and end with new ideas emerging for new stories to tell, then this might just be your path in life. It's a powerful trek full of wonder and accomplishment.

Most educators have now come to the conclusion that everyone learns differently, and there is no one way to learn how to do something. Nowhere is this truer than the factual television arena. It is both a personal journey and a group activity all rolled into one. You can't take a single course or read a single book and simply know it all. Instead, you need to find inspiration, nurture it, and avail yourself of industry-specific processes, terminology, and workflows in order to succeed. You have to become a giant sponge that soaks up every bit of knowledge around you and then finds creative ways to put it to use in new ways.

The First Rule Is There Are No Rules

At its core creating factual programming merges great images with critical sound as a means to convey a story, or narrative, to a wider audience – yet ironically that's actually the easiest part of the process!

As you endeavor to explore how to bring a project to life, you'll quickly find that there are a myriad of supposed rules put in place by those who've come before you.

Twenty years after starting my own independent production company (indie pro co), I've come to the conclusion that there's only one rule worth remembering.

There are no rules.

In fact, if you look around our society rule-breakers tend to be the ones that create the greatest change. They're the ones that alter the game in the most meaningful ways. Yet from a young age most people are encouraged to color inside the lines and follow a traditional path.

Instead, I suggest you allow your creativity to run wild and open yourself up to the magic of the unknown. There is a great power that lies in the brilliance of naïveté. Use it to your advantage.

The truly successful producers don't let anything stop them on their quest to see a project through, including conventional wisdom or old school rules that harken back to outdated times. Instead, they look for new angles, new approaches and new ways that might give their project an edge.

There's No One Way to Do Anything

A lot of people in our society work 9-to-5 jobs with strict protocols about how to go about their company's business – producing documentaries is a different beast.

When it comes to how one actually produces a project – *there's never just one way to do anything.*

This is the cardinal rule of television, and it is especially true when it comes to the knowledge dropped below. What follows is a highly personal collection of steps that have worked for me over the years. Other producers might do things in an entirely different manner, and that's equally worth exploring. I suggest that you learn as many of those tricks of the trade as well. You can never glean enough insights or learn enough alternative ways to do something in order to perfect your craft.

As a young Padawan producer you should seek guidance and knowledge from as many different and distinct sources as you can. The best content creators openly lift ideas from all corners and find what works best for them.

I'm always on the hunt for better methods, new approaches, and easier ways to get things done. Greatness is a continual quest to hone your skills in as efficient a manner as possible. The less you have to think about doing a task, the more spontaneously inspiration can strike.

Always Be Creating Content

Creativity is a producer's most cherished skill set, and it often comes at a price. It's not easy to be creative, and many people like to tell you about the obstacles that stand in your path. Whether it's writer's block or another impediment, it's easy to put off being creative for another day. Unfortunately, that doesn't help you get better. As Henry Ford once said, "Obstacles are those frightful things you see when you take your eyes off the goal". Our society tends to believe that inspiration is this quasi-mystical force that strikes in a hot flash, out of the ether, and knocks divergent thoughts together in such a powerful new way that you instantly see a brilliant new idea emerge.

Certainly, we've all experienced these moments of divine intervention, when a great idea just hits us. However, I'm a firm believer that creativity is also a skill that you can cultivate day by day and hour by hour.

True creativity is forcing yourself to do something of value when it feels damn near impossible to get anything of substance done. When the real creative warriors face a motivational challenge, they roll up their sleeves and double down on the task at hand.

Sitting around waiting for a lightbulb moment stagnates your potential growth as a creative force.

You're far better served to remember your ABCCs:

- **A**lways
- **B**e
- **C**reating
- **C**ontent

The more you flex your creative muscles, the better your ideas, concepts, and projects will become. The more repetitions you have, the stronger your skill set will grow and the more productivity you'll be able to harness. Your work will become more nuanced, more powerful, and more insightful too.

Without a doubt creativity is the lifeblood of the factual industry; however, the dirty little secret is that being creative begets more creativity. You need to be a terrific self-starter and get comfortable finding your way through the labyrinth-like darkness that comes with a new project. Every day you've got to push a bit more. Every day you have to ask yourself *how I can get better*?

In the end, motivation is like a fire. Once you start it and if you can keep it burning, then you'll always be able to cook a creative meal.

Don't Settle for No

At no point in humanity's history has creating content been easier. The tools of television are more democratized today than at any point ever before, and the ability to self-distribute is a true game changer. People consume media in ways that were entirely inconceivable just a decade ago.

However, to succeed professionally as a factual content producer you have to use your wits to create engaging programming that speaks to an audience, and if you believe in it – truly believe in it – you can't let anything stop you from telling your story.

No matter how many times someone tells you something can't be done, or a network execs passes on your project, you have to find the inner strength to get back up, dust yourself off, and look for another path forward.

Fortune might favor the bold in the real world; however, in the factual arena fortune favors the persistent.

There are hundreds of thousands of people who say they want to produce television but then give up at the first sign of trouble. Don't be that person.

Be brave. Be bold. Believe in yourself. Believe in your idea.

When I first started out, a lot of the people in the industry offered very concrete ideas for how a young filmmaker like myself should get their foot into the proverbial door. Teachers, current professionals at the time, and even former factual producers all tended to gravitate toward the particular path that worked for them – which makes great sense since it was based on their personal experience. The info was solid, if not practical advice. Yet their suggestions also rarely left much wiggle room for the new or unknown. It is far more powerful to ask, "Why not me and why not now?" and then forge your own path forward.

If the history of Hollywood and the entertainment industry at large has taught us anything, it's that the newest thing always starts as an avant-garde off-shoot but eventually takes over and becomes the norm.

Parents who grew up listening to classical music had children who listened to Elvis. When those folks became adults, their kids listened to the Beatles and the Rolling Stones. The children of the 1990s were into Grunge fans, and their parents absolutely hated it. Yet today those Grungers have families of their own and kids who listen to something else completely.

Like many things in the greater entertainment industry, the key to breaking in and *actual factual television producing* is to appreciate that there's *no one predetermined path you have to take.*

The best producers treat the process of creating factual television like a Silicon Valley entrepreneur goes about getting a start-up off the ground. They constantly keep their eyes open for emerging trends, relentlessly rethink their approach, and constantly pivot toward new opportunities. They ask themselves, "What would this look like if it were easy?" and then build toward that goal. If it turns out to be a closed route, they turn right around and push in another direction entirely.

You see this online too. We now live in a creator-driven culture, where unique content is king, and it often takes YouTube channel operators several tries to find their audience. Ultimately, whether you're an Instagram influencer or a hardcore filmmaker, the ability to tell meaningful stories is a prized profession with a healthy amount of competition.

To break through you need to harness your unique voice and learn how to film your subjects.

Becoming a professional producer is asking for a world of negativity to be hurled at you on a regular basis. Sometimes you've got to create hundreds of pitches and proposals just to get one project off the ground.

That means you're going to hear the word "no" an awful lot. Even the best producers get rejected often. The trick is to find a way to divorce yourself from the concepts. They're not rejecting *you*; they're rejecting the *idea*. You must find a way to develop a protective layer around you and your creativity.

The best course of action in this crazy business is often to chase your dream relentlessly without judgment or internal fear. That's often easier said than done but is crucial to your survival. There are enough negative outside influences already. You can't allow yourself to crush your own dreams. You have to be your biggest champion, your biggest advocate, and your bravest self.

You have to believe!

So put all of your energy into applying your skill and desire toward the path set before you and never take "no" as the final absolute answer. Continually push the envelope for what you believe in, be prepared to do the work, and prepare yourself so that you can make the most of your opportunity when it comes. As they say in the tech start-up world, "The days are long, but the years are short".

The challenge a factual producer ultimately faces is to simultaneously have the confidence to go after what you want while also having the humility to accept the difference between what you know right now and the willingness to build your skills in a way that connects the two.

You can't care what others think of your vision. Instead learn to accept that it's ok to not have all the answers, let your imagination flourish, follow the paths that interest you the most, stay curious, and feel free to "experiment, fail, learn, rinse, and repeat".

Victory isn't one day or one program; it's about building a meaningful career that you absolutely love.

And it can be done if you're brave enough to try.

Nobody Is an Overnight Sensation

If there's one thing that Hollywood loves to continually perpetuate, it's the myth of the overnight sensation. Our ad-infused six-second pre-roll attention span culture craves hyping the instant success archetype. We celebrate the idea of raw talent trumping hard-won knowledge or experience. Yet the truth is that it rarely if ever happens that way.

If you read the industry trades or follow factual producers and production companies on social media, it often appears that selling and producing documentary-styled television programs look easy.

What you don't see is the arduous trek that these well-established producers and bigger production companies took to their overnight success. The folks who run those companies ate glass and barely made the rent for a very long time.

As a society we tend to over-index on our starting benchmarks – the perceived *overnight success* – and we mistake them for meaningful predictors of long-term achievement. Producing, like entrepreneurship, is a massively long walk. The secret is to patiently and consistently craft a solid foundation for sustained success.

The majority of claimed "overnight" success stories are revisionist history that reframe lengthy struggles to get to the top.

- The pilot for *Seinfeld* tested terribly. Execs called it a "dagger to the heart".
- *Cheers* was almost canceled after its first year.
- *Stranger Things* was passed on 15 times before Netflix bought it.
- *Survivor* was passed on by every major network multiple times.
- The major over the air networks all passed on *The Sopranos*.

Little about the TV industry is fair. It never has been. It never will be. Don't be a victim. Don't fall into the trap. Instead, use each "no" as a battle cry to find the one person who says "yes".

Find a way to channel negativity and use it as a motivation. Make a secret oath to yourself that *you'll show these folks your idea was worthwhile.* It doesn't matter if you have to restart. It doesn't matter how long it takes, or if you can't find funding.

Just. Keep. Going.

Learn to love the grind and be at peace with the process. Don't worry about whether you're on the right track. Don't fret if you're not making enough progress. You can't be easily dissuaded nor allow yourself to give up at the first sign of trouble. Focus on what is right in front of you and what you can control right now.

There are so many variables in the factual television industry. As a creator you can only control what lies before you. A fear of failure often means you're on the right path and about to do something bold. Stay focused on making great programs, telling great stories, and delivering projects on time and on budget to buyers.

The pursuit of perfection is not a sin.

None of us creatively might reach perfection, but we can aspire to find it in the work we can control day in and day out.

Fast-Tracking Your Knowledge

The quickest path to gaining a foothold is to watch every factual film or program that you can get your hands on – including the ones from genres that don't initially intrigue you.

Every finished piece of content is a teacher. The more films or factual episodes that you can consume, the more you'll begin to appreciate the subtle nuance in the factual film-making language.

Factual television producing isn't always about reinventing the wheel. In fact, that's rarely what most networks are looking for at any given moment; instead, the best path forward is often to showcase your proficiency at telling factual stories using well-established tropes and techniques found in other contemporary programming.

For instance, it's hard to have a home renovation show without a reveal of some kind at the end. It's equally challenging to create a hosted car show without any onboard direct address to camera considerations. In the blue-chip nature genre, we've grown accustomed to seeing magnificent aerial establishing shots and surprising close-ups of flora and fauna. These are just some of the many contemporary parts of the factual filmmaking visual language.

Deconstruct what you see on screen and try to work those elements into your own work.

Creativity and the Process

Television is one of the great creative multidisciplinary enterprises. It combines art, knowledge, and technical savvy with a clear and distinct vision. Yet it's not a business of unique singular voices furiously scribbling away in their lonely writer's garret. Instead, TV is a creative venture that requires leveraging the vision and talent of multiple people. The oddity of the factual slice of the TV landscape however is that the process shapes your team's creativity. What the audience sees on screen is one-fifth inspiration and four-fifths protecting the vision. The vast majority of the creativity comes at the beginning of the adventure, when you're envisioning your project, writing the treatment for it, crafting your shooting script, and going through the initial rough cut edit. Everything else is an actionable defense intent on ensuring your work survives.

Mastering the craft is a muscle that you have to train additively over time. You don't wake up one morning as Steven Spielberg, Ken Burns, or Thom Beers. You have to continually refine and add to your skills, no different than a weightlifter slowly building their strength day by day. Each creative rep will earn you a bit more confidence and fuel your mastery of the process. Put in the effort early and reap the rewards endlessly. There are a limitless number of factual stories waiting to be told.

All of that content is beamed, broadcast, or downloaded directly into homes and businesses across the country and the world thanks to a rapidly changing distribution landscape. Forty years ago, broadcast television was largely dominated by the big three free over-the-air channels, ABC, CBS, and NBC, as well as a handful of small UHF stations (Ultra High Frequency Over-the-Air stations). In the 1990s cable television emerged as a direct competitor to free-to-air networks, offering better quality and more channels for a fee. Like most emerging technologies, it took a while for cable broadcasters to find their way; however, by the dawn of the 2000s the system had exploded into a 500-channel universe full of choice. There were now networks dedicated to all kinds of specific interests, including travel, food, home renovation, worship, music, and sports. It was the dawn of niche programming for very highly defined audiences. Today, these niche channels are under pressure, along with all the original traditional broadcasters, by another new piece of emerging tech – streaming services. First popularized by Netflix, streaming is the newest transformative technology to alter television content distribution; however, it almost certainly won't be the last. Between linear television networks, newfangled streaming services, and online video distribution, there are now more ways to get your project seen than ever before in human history. *There's literally never been a better time to be a factual producer.*

A Dearth of Content

The downside to all of this new consumer choice is a frustrating lack of diverse content. Broadcast networks and factual television channels are remarkably conservative entities. They look for *the best business cases* with the most potential upside to capture viewers, earn ratings, and ultimately garner the most advertising revenue. They know exactly how much they're willing to spend per hour of finished programming, they know precisely how much ad revenue they'll be able to generate against it, and they usually have a very strong idea of the return on investment (ROI) for every new project. While factual producers like taking risks, networks like sure things and easy bets.

This isn't a new phenomenon. In 1961, newly minted Federal Communications Committee chairman Newton Minow stepped up to the microphone at the National Association of Broadcasters (NAB) and laid out a clear vision for the future of factual entertainment.

> When television is good, nothing – not the theater, not the magazines or newspapers – nothing is better. But when television is bad, nothing is worse. I invite each of you to sit down in front of your television set when your station goes on the air and stay there, for a day, without a book, without a magazine, without a newspaper, without a profit and loss sheet or a rating book to distract you. Keep your eyes glued to that set until the station signs off. I can assure you that what you will observe is a vast wasteland.

Today's wide range of factual filmmaking runs the gamut from cheap-as-chips mindless lowbrow entertainment to high-end visual treats that illuminate the far corners of our universe and perhaps beyond. Factual network exes are fond of telling producers that they're looking for the next big thing; however, if you look at what they ultimately program their channels with on a day-to-day basis it often feels like a derivative of another show or program that you've already seen. After the amazing success of *Deadliest Catch*, it didn't take long until there were over 50 series set in Alaska. Ask an average TV viewer which network broadcasts any of those wilderness shows, and chances are they can't even tell you. This often leaves new producers in a bit of a quandary: Do you follow the herd and create derivative programs and series, or instead, do you forge your own path?

A lot of copycat programming today is being filled by the "mini-major" studios; these are production companies owned by larger corporations that own a handful of production outfits across the globe. They do an incredible amount of business with the big global broadcasters and create hundreds of hours of programming per year. These larger concerns are part of the global factual ecosystem, and their scale helps assuage any concerns that a network might have during the development process. They're well staffed and well resourced, and because they're part of larger corporations, there's no fear that they'll go out of business halfway through production or deliver an unairable program.

On the other hand, bravely going in your own direction and developing your own unique programs or series can be tricky as well. While the market claims to want the newest and freshest ideas – that's not exactly what they actually buy. Often pitching an idea that hasn't yet become a mainstream trend can be met by concerns that the concept won't rate well enough to merit being greenlit. It can feel like an unmovable rock that meets an unstoppable force; however, the really good producers find opportunity in the crevasses by creating new factual categories or genres.

The Evolution of Nonfiction Programming

Documentaries have been evolving ever since the dawn of cinema. The earliest examples were short newsreels, instructional pictures, and recordings of current events. Many credit Robert Flaherty's *Nanook of the North* as being the world's first true documentary film. Produced in 1922, the picture chronicles the harsh conditions that Canadian Inuit Eskimos endure living in the Arctic. The project opened up a new world to viewers, yet it also highlighted the continual tug of war that all documentary filmmakers face between journalistic truth and constructed storytelling. Flaherty aimed to tell a true story but also staged several scenes to *tell* what he felt was a better story.

Traditional Documentary Film: A point-of-view-driven narrative-based film. The most celebrated are feature film length and often are created by a filmmaker who feels extremely passionate about a specific subject and wants to bring awareness to that topic by sharing it with a larger audience.

In the early 1990s film critic Bill Nichols proposed that there are six basic documentary modes (or "genres").

Expository: These docs feature an omnipresent, omniscient, and objective presence, typically expressed by narration that presents the subject. The filmmaker does not appear on camera, nor is a viewer readily aware of their creative hand in the film.

Poetic: A nonlinear film that highlights feelings, mood, and tone and often features a juxtaposition of imagery. These are nonnarrative films that put the onus on striking visuals and artistic style.

Participatory: These films are defined by the interaction between the documentary filmmakers and their subject. They often showcase the filmmaker's version of the truth, and many of the filmed interactions support the filmmaker's point-of-view.

Observational: A cinema-verité documentary style that attempts to discover the ultimate truth by acting as a fly-on-the-wall. Ob doc filmmakers capture reality without interrupting or altering the story as it unfolds.

Reflexive: These films focus on the relationship between filmmakers and the audience and often feature a behind-the-scenes element.

Performative: A film that focuses on a filmmaker's personal involvement with a subject as a jumping-off point for a larger discussion.

These six genres are the backbone of not just cinematic documentary storytelling *but also factual television*. Ever since the first over-the-air TV signals were broadcast, documentary-styled programs have been a key component of television. However, in modern times **Nonfiction Television**, or factual content, has evolved well beyond its traditional formats. Today's factual genres and subgenres are constantly being mixed together and hybridized in new ways to create fresh categories of nonfiction entertainment.

Here are a few of the key mainstream factual genres.

Docu-series: A long-running television program that truthfully sheds light on a situation with real people and events. Key examples are *Frontline, Planet Earth*, or *30 For 30*.

Occudocs: Occupational documentary-based programs that follow a host or talent as they do their profession: for example, *Dog the Bounty Hunter, Bear Grylls*, and *Mike Rowe on Dirty Jobs*.

Celebrity Docusoaps: Similar to the more expansive docusoap genre but featuring celebrity subjects. These are often heavily orchestrated and/or scripted. For example, *The Kardashians, The Osbournes*, and *Real Housewives*.

Occusoaps: Occupational documentary-based programs that follow a crew of people as they work: for example, *Gold Rush, Storage Wars, Axe Men*, and *Fish Tank Kings*.

Docusoap: A documentary-style entertainment series that revolves around the real lives of regular people. Examples are *American Chopper, Cake Wars, Bridezilla*, and *Duck Dynasty*.

Docu-drama: A project that features dramatized reenactments of actual events. Examples are *Killing Kennedy, Real Stories of the E.R.*, and *I Shouldn't Be Alive*.

Do-It-Yourself: A host or hosts take the viewer through the process of some kind of improvement. Typically, best used in the home renovation space on shows like *Flip or Flop, Extreme Home Makeover*, and *House Hunters International*.

Factual Entertainment: A bit of a catch-all category for programming that exists to be fun. Examples are *Myth Busters, Top Gear, Queer Eye*, and *Antique Roadshow*.

Competition Reality: Programs where real people compete for prizes: for example, *America's Next Top Model, Last Comic Standing, Top Chef, Big Brother, Survivor*, and *The Bachelor*.

Studio Game Show: Shiny floor studio shows in which people play games or answer questions in order to win prizes: for example, *The Price Is Right*, *Deal or No Deal*, and *Wheel of Fortune*.

Food/Cooking: Typically, hosted programs that feature information about how to cook: for example, Julia Child, Emeril, and Rachel Ray.

Travel: Programs that revolve around a host or talent traveling to new places. *Anthony Bourdain* is the gold standard of this genre.

Talk: A host interacts with guests and entertains: for example, *John Stewart, Colbert,* and *The Tonight Show.*

Current Affairs: Serialized news programs that use long-form storytelling. Examples are *60 Minutes* or *Nightline.*

Panel Shows: Programs that feature several guests who debate topics.

Inside of each of these factual genres sit a multitude of off-shoots that have organically grown in new ways, often altering each genre's idiomatic style of storytelling. Yet at its core all factual programming share one thing in common – the roots of today's factual programming go back to traditional cinematic documentary storytelling.

A Multitude of Platforms

The dearth of content is exacerbated by the explosion in distribution currently underway. Today, there are more possible outlets for factual content than ever before, and each comes with its own set of unique requirements and funding potential.

Free-to-Air Networks: These are the original over-the-air television channels, or *Broadcast Channels*, that distribute their content for free and derive revenue primarily from advertising. These networks have considerable audience penetration, or *reach*, and can be seen in nearly every household in a country. For example, ABC, CBS, NBC, and Fox can reach an estimated 300 million American households and therefore can afford extremely robust programming budgets. Generally, these nets don't air any content with explicit sex, violence, or profanity.

Cable Networks: The vast majority of cable networks, sometimes referred to as *linear networks*, emerged during the cable's rapid growth over the past quarter century. At one point there were upward of 500 different channels broadcasting content; however, today, this number is beginning to dwindle as the business case for traditional cable has begun to erode. Cable nets drive revenue through carriage fees, which is what the nets charge a cable system for the right to carry their channel, as well as generating revenue from advertising. The largest linear networks, such as Discovery Channel, History Channel, the Food Network, or Animal Planet, reach just over 90 million homes in the United States and produce thousands of hours of new programming annually. Small linear networks such as the Science Channel, Cooking Channel, or Motor Trend are only available in 60 million homes, so their programming budgets are considerably more restrained. Because cable networks are for pay, they're afforded more latitude when it comes to graphic sexual or violence content, though family-friendly networks still adhere to a very strict code for their content.

Satellite: In the United States satellite systems like DirecTV and Dish arrived about a decade after cable and offered yet another way for viewers to watch their favorite networks. However, overseas satellite became the dominant distribution system platform partly because it's easier to download a satellite signal versus rewiring an ancient city. Satellite services can be both distributors as well as programmers too. In certain countries, like the UK, Sky is a service and offers their own channels.

Streaming Services: When Netflix pivoted from being a rental-by-mail DVD service into a **Subscription Video-on-Demand** service, or SVOD, they ushered in a new era of entertainment. Viewers no longer needed to wire their house for cable; instead, they could use the home's internet to stream their favorite movies and shows to their TV screen. Today, SVOD is quickly becoming the dominant *premium* distribution platform for home entertainment. Today, Netflix has around 220 million subscribers globally or nearly twice the audience of a traditional domestic U.S. broadcast network. Every week it seems a new network conglomerate announces a new service; however, unlike Netflix, which is a modern tech company, most of these companies are straddling two worlds as they try to continue to ring the register on their legacy linear channels while at the same time building up new streaming options. To bridge the gap, a number of networks have turned to **Advertising-based Video-on-Demand**, or AVOD. These services replicate the free-to-air business model because they don't cost consumers anything and instead generate revenue with traditional commercial breaks and advertising. **Free Ad-supported Streaming TV**, or a FAST Channel, is a new off-shoot of the AVOD movement and typically is run by a substantially smaller company than a traditional broadcaster. The premium nature of streaming offers the most freedom in terms of format and content.

Internet Video: As Netflix exploded onto the content creation scene, at the same time "new media" emerged online. What was "new" is now normal, and YouTube is the de facto online video standard for global viewers of user-generated content, or UGC. Initially, this home-brewed content was rough around the edges but now runs the gamut from home videos to super-polished programming that gives any traditional broadcaster a run for its money.

The total number of potential distribution platforms continues to grow, and regardless of whether it's transmitted via a free-to-air network, a linear channel, a cable or satellite system, or streamed, the global hunger for quality content seems destined to continue unabated in the foreseeable future.

Two Factual Routes

Factual programming blends art and commerce in a beautiful way, yet when it comes to professionally producing it there are two distinct types of producers.

Route 1: Those who film their project and then hope to find a home for it later on.

Route 2: Those who find the funding and distribution first and then go make their film come to life.

There's nothing entirely wrong with either approach; however, it's effectively an art versus commerce debate, and from my standpoint if you want to be a professional, then you've got to get paid.

I'm a firm believer that selling your idea is just as important, if not more important, than your actual final piece of content. Commissioners come and go, networks continually change their mandate; however, if you want to make a career out of this occupation, you have to earn a living.

Working on spec and looking for distribution later might be creativity fulfilling, but it's not a great way to pay the bills. Filming factual content is far more than a calling; it's a way of life, and it should be compensated accordingly. What I want to share with you in the coming pages is how to get paid to create factual content and do what you love.

Inside the Industry With Matt Taylor, The Walt Disney Company

Matt Taylor is Vice President of Factual Programming for The Walt Disney Company. He's responsible for leading the content strategy under the National Geographic brand and providing the strategic direction and framework for all markets in Europe and Africa, with direct operational responsibility for the UK and Ireland. Matt works across platforms, including linear channels, branded VOD services, and digital platforms, as well as with the DTC programming team.

- **What advice would you give to a smart and inquisitive film school student entering the "real world"?**

Get as much experience as you can. Whether that's in the field or in the offices of a production company. Say yes to any role and soak everything up. Producing great content takes the combined effort of many talented people – all of whom you can learn a lot from. Ask a lot of questions. As best you can try to understand the process from pitch to finished product and figure out where you want to be in that process.

- **How would you suggest a young factual filmmaker begin their producing career if their goal is to eventually create original programming for a global network like the National Geographic Channel?**

Knock on the door of as many production companies that already work with Nat Geo (or the leading factual and FTV broadcasters) as possible. Most production company websites will outline the broadcasters they work with most often. Try and get an internship, junior role, or even just work experience with one of them. Getting a foot in the door will expose you to what it takes to produce content for Nat Geo.

- **You commission hundreds of hours of programming per year. When you're making greenlight decisions, how do you determine whether to move ahead with a project or not? (If helpful, it could be best practices for pitching or drafting treatments, any places that people usually drop the ball, sizzle reel suggestions, etc.)**

Here are a few points, in no particular order. The most important thing for me as a commissioner is the audience. Will a project appeal directly to the desired audience? There's no point commissioning a really great female skewed program for a male skewed audience. Ask the broadcaster what they are looking for. You might not have something quite right the first time around, but you could come away with some really great leads. A good sizzle won't get you a commission alone, but it may get a commissioner interested. Sizzles are an art in itself, but the key again is to know your audience. Make sure the sizzle is not only impactful but clearly gets across the idea you want to pitch. I sometimes like to watch a sizzle before reading the treatment to gauge whether I can understand the idea from the sizzle alone. A sizzle that is all style and no substance can do more harm than good.

- **What is the best investment in yourself that you've ever made?**

The best investment I made was to move to different countries with my job. Not only was it an amazing life experience, but learning about different cultures and their individual viewing habits helped me to better shape my understanding of content. Each country tackles content in different ways, and each country digests it differently. Understanding the differences helped me to focus more on delivering the right content to the viewer. In my experience working for an international factual broadcaster, there always tends to be a sweet spot between content that's too local or too international. Finding it definitely takes a lot of trial and error, but living and working in these countries have made a huge difference.

Chapter Two

The Eight Factual Steps

Ask most aspiring creatives what goes into crafting a factual television program, and they'll almost always immediately zero in on production and editing. Yet those are just two of the nine distinct steps in the factual filmmaking process.

- Idea Creation
- Crafting a Presentation
- Pitching Your Idea
- Selling Your Idea
- Pre-production
- Field-Production
- Post-production
- Delivery and Exhibition

In its simplest form creating a factual program or series requires you to come up with an idea, give it life by filming someone or something, finding its voice through script writing and post-production phase, and then sharing it with an audience once it's finished.

Idea Creation: Every great program or series starts with a very basic idea. It might be a fleeting thought that comes out of nowhere, or it might be a subject that you've been obsessing over for ages. In the pages that follow we'll discuss ideating.

Crafting a Presentation: Shockingly, most onscreen creativity begins ages before you pick up a camera. To bring your brilliant idea to life, you'll need to craft a compelling presentation (or "deck") to share with network execs and potential funding opportunities. In the chapters that follow we'll take a deep dive into how to craft a killer presentation.

Pitching Your Idea: A great presentation gets you in the door, but eventually you'll need to persuade someone to fund your vision. This is the subtle art of pitching, and a few pages from now we'll discuss how to put your best foot forward.

Selling Your Idea: Awesome ideas can get network execs excited; however, you still need to close the deal and sell your concept. Not everyone is a born salesperson, nor

DOI: 10.4324/9781003292289-2

do you have to be, as long as you follow some industry best practices, which we'll explore in the chapters that follow.

Pre-production: Selling a brilliant idea is a terrific win, yet it doesn't amount to much if you can't prepare to shoot it. Pre-production separates those who do from those who dream. We'll detail how to go about it and some tricks of the trade that will make your life easier.

Field-Production: Finally, it's time to break out the cameras and hit record! Yet film-making is rarely that simple. The field-production phase is invigorating yet challenging. In the pages that follow we'll reveal how to stay on top of the process and keep your wits as you capture your vision.

Post-production: Great films, programs, or series come to life in post. Scripting and editing are the cornerstones of the televisual language. They are the tools that create the art of compelling storytelling. Several chapters from now we'll explore how to find your way through the post-production stage and level your production up a notch or two.

Delivery: Factual broadcast television productions are meaningless unless the project hits the airwaves or internet. To do that you've got to keep your eye on the ball through-out the delivery process. We'll find out how to stay on track of mastering and delivery, as well as how to craft final network legal binders.

Exhibition: After all, eight steps here are completed, you can finally exhale! It's time to sit back and watch your handcrafted hard work pay off when your project is beamed or broadcast to millions of viewers potentially around the world.

Love the Process

If you're into multitasking and juggling a lot of different balls in the air at the same time, then you'll find that producing can be its own kind of addictive drug.

You feel an incredible sense of wonder and accomplishment when you transform the briefest of ideas into an actual television program. From the initial conceptual phases to its eventual sale, and from the field production to the actual scripting and editing, creating factual content is a giant and continually morphing Rubik's Cube–type challenge.

There are a thousand pressure points however if you learn to love the process of problem-solving; you'll find that none of them are really an impediment to crossing the finish line. When you've got a bounce in your step and are eager to move the project forward in a meaningful way, there's literally nothing that can stop you!

One of the greatest parts of having a hand in every phase of a film is that your role constantly changes. When you're all tapped out writing treatments, it's time to sell. When the sale has gone down, it's time to get into the field and film. When the field production is wrapped up, you're back scribbling away and eventually it's time to dive into the footage before you begin cutting small sequences together, which slowly become large acts, and eventually once you have enough of those, a full show.

It's a brilliant symbiotic system that requires coordination, synchronization, and pacing so you don't burn out. Plus, the drive to see the thing through. If you can learn to appreciate the magic in the chaos, you'll never look back.

Chapter Three

Idea Creation

Ideas Are Everywhere . . .

Inspiration for the next great factual program or documentary exists everywhere; they surround us, are inside of us, and often float right past us during our daily lives.

Great factual producers keep their eyes and ears open, are a student of the world around, and, above all else, are curious. *Ask yourself why? And how? And where? And what is interesting to you?* Read everything that you can get your hands on. Devour the internet. Consume as much content as you can on any given subject and become an expert.

If you're intrigued by something, chances are others will be as well. Research it with abandon and dive deeply down the knowledge rabbit hole. Ultimately, ideation is a lot like writing. The more you do it, the better you get at it. Reps sharpen the blade.

Once you unlock the creativity and begin thinking about potential factual topics, you'll find that ideas will populate your mind throughout the day. The various corners of your life will soon become fodder for curiosity and inspiration.

Usually, the most powerful concepts are also often the simplest – I'm not suggesting that they're simple programs to make, but rather that the initial core of the idea is concise, to the point, and seems relevant for the time. The easier you can explain the idea, the better it is.

For example, if you say you want to create a series about *the ins and outs of the fashion industry* that's very broad. However, if instead you say you want to *explore the fashion industry by highlighting each fabled brand's five key designs and five key historical moments*, that's instantly accessible and easy for both network execs and viewers to grasp.

Curiosity is a social binder as well. Have as many conversations with equally inquisitive and like-minded people as possible, and think about what you're interested in that you don't see on the television screen today.

DOI: 10.4324/9781003292289-3

Be open to accepting ideas from every corner of your team – great ideas can come from anywhere and you almost certainly don't have exclusive access to all the brilliant concepts available. The more open you are to collaboration, the more invested your team will ultimately be and harder they'll push on your behalf.

The best ideas have yet to be conceived. The best treatments have yet to be written. The best documentaries have yet to be made. It's never too late to get into the game. The most interesting parts of our world have yet to be explored.

Don't Self-Reject

It's not uncommon for young content creators to often focus so much on breaking in that they unconsciously limit their own potential by coming up with ideas that are *too small.*

Surprisingly, it takes nearly the same energy to research, develop, and nurture an idea for a full series as it does for a one-hour special, yet only one can grow into multiple seasons and higher budgets.

The same is true for the episode count in a series, it's incrementally more work to develop extra eps and offer a higher volume project. Yet the end payoff can be substantially larger thanks to the financial economies of scale you can unearth when you produce more content.

Don't predetermine your ceiling. Pitch the biggest and boldest ideas that you can think of right now. A network can always scale you back, yet in my experience they'll seldom if ever tell you to make the idea or a budget *bigger.*

If you don't think you deserve a series, when in doubt pitch it. If you don't think you deserve a big budget, ask for it anyway. Don't set limits on yourself or self-reject your own ideas in advance of sharing them.

Once you find a compelling idea, it's time to turn that thought into an actionable concept. The more you do it, the sooner your actions become habits. Great habits build great skills, self-belief, and self-reliance. These attributes quickly put you on the path to finding your producing destiny. No one is going to do it for you or just give it to you. You must make your own momentum if you want to jump into the factual industry. So, dream big, bet big, and be bold.

When it comes to advancing your ideas, you also must be somewhat ruthless when determining which concepts to spend your time developing. You can have thousands of great ideas, but only a handful will pop and get made.

In the world of finance this is known as the *Pareto Principle*, which states that 80% of the results come from 20% of the action. Factual programming ideas are the same. Most of your success will come from a small handful of great ideas. However, to generate those few remarkable concepts, you need to be constantly ideating and finding new ideas to present to networks.

An Eye Toward Accessibility

There are all kinds of factual programs waiting to be made and broadcast. The amount of genres and hybrid formats seems almost limitless as new categories constantly emerge. It is an ever expansive and yet constantly morphing form of storytelling.

Most networks define a project's success by quantifying how much viewership it receives compared to the overall potential television audience. This is stated as a number and often referred to as the *ratings*.

A project's ratings are a numerical representation for how much mass acceptance it sees during the broadcast. The higher the rating number is, the better the project is perceived to have done and the more viewership it captures.

In the United States the population hovers just over 328 million people; however, not everyone has a television set. There are *only* about 121 million TV households spread across the country.

The traditional "Over-the-Air networks" like ABC, CBS, and NBC reach nearly 98% of all viewers, while the big "pay networks" like the Discovery Channel or the National Geographic Channel reach around 87 to 90 million homes. The smaller cable networks like the Smithsonian Channel or Reelz can only be seen in roughly 30 to 40 million homes. Interestingly, not all networks "receive ratings". Some have such small market penetration that it's not even worthwhile to tally their total viewership.

Production budgets tend to directly correspond to a network's potential "household reach", or the total number of potential homes the channel can be seen in. The larger the possible viewership equals, the more money a network typically has to put into its productions.

If your end goal is to garner as high a rating as possible, it's often in your best interest to appeal to as wide an audience as possible. This means you need to come up with an idea that is as *accessible as possible*.

One-Offs versus Mini-Series versus Series

When you're ideating, one of your first tasks is to determine what kind of project best fits your concept. There are three basic types of factual programs: one-off specials, mini-series, and series.

Special: Often described as a 1 × 30 or 1 × 60 (1 program that fills either a 30- or 60-minute programming slot), a broadcast special is a rare occurrence these days. However, they used to be a prevalent part of each network's schedule. One-off docs are typically based around current events (e.g., disaster specials or royal family stories) and are built to stand on their own. You don't need to have seen any other episodes to follow the story, and the entire narrative arc is contained in the one program. Networks used to like to start new producers off with one-off specials because they were an easy way to give a new storyteller a chance while not putting the entire broadcast schedule at risk. Today, however, there are very few one-hour special programming slots available as most networks have moved to high-volume repeatable programming. Streamers on the other hand often are more inclined to fund or acquire one-hour specials since they're freed from the traditional programming schedule constraints.

Mini-Series: As one-off documentaries have gone out of vogue, a new type of "short order" documentary project has emerged – the four or five-part mini-series (sometimes referred to as a 4 × 60 or 5 × 60 *limited series*). These projects split the difference between traditional high-volume commodity-type series and highly crafted bespoke one-hour specials, offering highly contained stories spread over a handful of episodes and built to be highly bingeable. The best examples of this form of programming suck viewers in and are a highly "sticky" type of entertainment that allows a viewer to consume the whole series over the course of a night or two – the perfect storytelling format for the streaming age.

Series: The holy grail for most networks are high-volume repeatable series that generate amazing buy-in from their audience and generate high ratings. Series train the audience when to show up and help reinforce what makes a specific network unique or special in a very crowded marketplace.

Long-running series essentially become their own business ventures as well, creating stars out of the talent, in-demand merchandise, and lucrative off-screen opportunities.

Network ad sale teams love series because the time it takes to sell commercials in a one-hour special or limited series is usually fairly similar to the effort required to sell ads in a multiple-episode series. So, from their point of view, it's far more financially rewarding to fill the schedule with known quantities.

The more eps a series has, the higher the financial commitment required by the network, and thus the more risk attached to the project. This helps to explain why so many series are made by the same handful of production companies. They're known entities, and while every show they produce might not be amazing from start to finish, they'll all deliver on time, usually on budget, pass network QC, and consistently hit the air.

Ideas Are Everywhere, Talent Is Not

While ideas are often omnipresent, finding great talent for them is not. If you scan a broadcast schedule or a streamer thumbnail carousel, you'll find two basic types of factual television programs; those that are talent driven and those that are narration led.

Classically constructed factual programs or documentaries are built around key interviews and images, and use a narrator, often referred to as *the voice of God*, to push the story forward.

Most contemporary factual networks will air this style of programming at some point in their broadcast schedule; however, the vast majority of modern factual television is now talent driven. Stories or series that see a host, or possibly multiple hosts, drive the narrative from start to finish.

This could be a pair of home renovation experts, a group of people living in a house together, a celebrity chef, or perhaps a Hollywood A-lister out on an adventure. The beauty of having talent front your project is it gives the audience someone to relate to and root for (and sometimes even root against). The beauty of talent for a producer is that it can elevate an idea and transform it into something markedly bigger and better.

The tough part is that finding great talent is *really hard*.

Especially unknown talent that leaps out at you on screen. Some networks or streamers like showcasing fresh faces that have never been on screen before, while other nets prefer professional talent that's worked in TV previously. This is why you tend to see a lot of the same presenters (like Mike Rowe or Richard Hammond) over and over in different programs on different networks or streamers.

To find fresh new faces many producers will cast a very wide net. Some production companies have submission portals built directly into their websites, while others try to leverage social media and craigslist ads or even hire people to spend all day scouring the internet looking for potential personalities. YouTube, Twitter, TikTok, Snapchat, and Instagram have all become fertile ground for finding new unseen talent.

If you're looking for more traditional talent, your best bet is to connect with a talent manager or agent. They usually have a roster of clients that they can suggest for various projects and genres. The trade-off with professional talent tends to be the cost of their talent fees.

Regardless of which type of talent you zero in on, once you settle on a particular person it's time to lock them down for the project. To do this you need to get them to sign a **Shopping Agreement** prior to pitching an idea that you've attached them to.

A shopping agreement is a basic contract that states that the talent is giving you the right to sell an idea that they're involved with. Typically, it does not include rates or payment info. Generally, that will all be negotiated later once you know what network is interested in the project. Rather at this stage everything is done *in good faith*. The key is to have a clause in the contract that spells out you're the only producer allowed to pitch a series based on a specific type of idea with them involved. (Some agreements can be *even more exclusive* and state that a producer is the only person who can pitch *anything* involving a talent.) The shopping agreement is a crucially important step to prevent another producer from swooping in at the last minute and signing your fresh face after you've discovered them. Locked-in talent becomes yet another selling point for your project. The more buttoned up your project is and the easier you can make life for the network execs, the better your odds become of landing a deal. If you can offer them a compelling turn-key package with all of your talent in place, that makes a far more compelling case for your idea.

There are two basic types of talent-led programs.

Talent for Hire: This is perhaps the most common form of talent-driven programming, where a producer or production company hires talent to front their series. The talent generally has a specific rate based on shooting days or overall deal length and is not involved in the creative process. They are simply a gun-for-hire whose job is to *present* the story to the audience.

Talent with Buy-In: On the other end of the spectrum sits talent that's fully bought into the project. They tend to be an equal part of the creative process, often coming aboard early in the ideation phase and typically sharing in the financial success of the program.

Many years ago, we filmed an observational documentary-styled special for Animal Planet about competitive poultry showing. We followed five chicken breeders through a season of chicken shows leading up to that year's Grand National event, when the *Best Chicken of the Year* would be crowned. The network loved the early cuts of the program and thought it would be great to add a celebrity talent for the finals. After a bit of discussion, we settled on the idea of adding Hollywood actor Fred Willard as the host.

He had just had a leading role in Christopher Guest's mockumentary film *Best in Show*. Fred was a gun-for-hire who shared his thoughts and experiences at the finals with the audience but didn't engage in any creative aspects of the overall project. He showed up on finals day and jovially interviewed countless chicken show participants, cracking one-liners throughout the finals.

Access Docs

If you can't find great talent, your next best bet is to secure amazing access that allows you and your crew to go beyond the normal locked doors of a highly known company, institution, entity, or inside a well-known person's life. Ultimately, access is another form of currency that a great producer mines and trades.

Any aspiring producer can do this right out of the gate. You just have to have the gumption to pick up the phone or send an introductory email and make your case for why a program, or documentary project, is worthwhile for the subject's consideration. The more persuasive you are, the further you'll get.

Broadly speaking, there are two kinds of access-driven programs.

Self-Secured Access: The most typical access-driven path is when you convince another party to let you inside to film. This will then open the doors elsewhere for funding and distribution.

It took a lot of back and forth, but back in the early 2000s we were able to convince the powers that be inside of California's Transportation Department to let us film a one-hour engineering special on the agency's Bay Bridge rebuild. Caltrans had determined that the Eastern span of the bridge that connects San Francisco to Oakland wasn't seismically fit to withstand a major earthquake. So, they began the arduous process of planning how to build a new bridge next to the old bridge with minimal traffic disruption. Once we secured the access, we were able to go to the Science Channel and get them to commission a one-hour special on the incredible engineering taking place.

When securing access, it helps to have a strong body of work to showcase to the prospective subject. In our case, it has greatly helped to call up *Car Brand X* and say that we'd just filmed at *Car Brand Y* or to share a video link to a finished project with their crosstown rival. However, even if you don't have the perfect credit list or reel to send, you still can tweak how you present your previous work to make the case more compelling. For instance, when I pitch non-automotive brands for access, I don't highlight all of our decades-long car work but rather focus my presentation on how we've successfully showcased dozens and dozens of Fortune 500 brands. It's a small difference that can go a long way and a great example of how a bit of *spin* can be a powerful tool in a producer's toolbox.

Access Comes to You: The other route to access-driven programs is when the subject *comes to you.* Often a company or person reaches out to you directly after seeing your previous work and suggests that they have a compelling story worth telling on screen.

This is a powerful path forward because the subject's buy-in and motivation is crystal clear. They want to be filmed, which means that the only convincing you have to do is at the network or streaming service level.

This happened to us many years ago.

In 2005 the Bugatti supercar brand shocked the world with the introduction of the Veyron. Nearly overnight the machine rewrote the supercar rulebook. The initial version featured an 8 liter quad-turbocharged W16 cylinder engine that made an absolutely mental 1,000 horsepower. The car was faster than anything the world had seen in a production car, launching from naught to 60 in under three seconds and hitting an insane 253 mile per hour top speed.

It was like no other car on the planet and a tour-de-force engineering exercise that helped coin a new automotive term – *the Hypercar.*

When the machine dropped, it captivated both car fans and ordinary viewers across the globe. The machine was featured several times on the BBC's Top Gear program, but no one had filmed a truly in-depth factual program about the vehicle.

Knowing that we're naturally inclined toward engineering, three years later the National Geographic Channel asked us to produce a one-hour special about the Veyron's creation. We filmed for well over a month all throughout Europe. Every single frame was perfect. The resulting film was absolutely epic by any measure and did extremely well for Nat Geo. It literally was shown all over the world and stayed in constant rotation for many years.

In fact, the film did so well that a *decade* later Bugatti reached back out and asked us to visit their engineering headquarters in Wolfsburg, Germany. I very distinctly remember taking a seat on a transcontinental flight with no real idea what I'd find on the other side of the Atlantic. Little did I know what would happen next.

On our first day on the ground we were shepherded into a secret design facility far away from prying eyes and shown the not-yet announced prototype for the *Chiron.* It was Bugatti's multimillion dollar follow-up to the Veyron and the world's next great hypercar.

The brand wanted to know if we could help them tell their story once again. It took a little bit of time and a unique deal structure to get the job done, but a year later *Bugatti Super Car* debuted on the National Geographic's International channels to rave reviews. However, the key to the program's success was that Bugatti *came to us* and asked our help in telling their story.

Inside the Industry with Winona Meringolo, Investigation Discovery

Winona Meringolo is Senior Vice President of Development for Investigation Discovery. ID is the preeminent true crime destination, ranking #1 for women 25 to 54 years old (W25–54) and people 25 to 54 years old (P25–54) in Total Day and #1 length of tune in cable for people 25 to 54 years old (P25–54). ID is available in more than 160 countries and territories (including the United States), delivering over 650 premiere hours a year of mystery and suspense programming that fully immerses and engages audiences.

Meringolo provides leadership and creative direction for the network and is responsible for the conceptualization and development of several hit ID series, including but not limited to Evil Lives Here, Body Cam, People Magazine Investigates, American Monster, Village of the Damned, See No Evil, Dead of Winter, Dark Waters, Lake Erie and Someone You Thought You Knew. As Head of Development for American Heroes Channel, Winona oversees the strategic vision of the network, as well as development of numerous programs, including fan-favorites UFO's The Lost Evidence, America: Facts vs. Fiction, Hitler: The Definitive Guide, and Blood and Fury: America's Civil War.

- **What advice would you give to a smart film school student entering the "real world" who wants to get into producing their own content for a company like Discovery?**

Be patient. There's tremendous value in forming an array of relationships – think long term, don't get consumed by the immediate pay-off/what can you do for me right now, and think it's not worth your time to invest in relationships, it is. Be open to partnering on projects, it might be the first opportunity to get your project made and learn from someone who has more experience in the business. Stay in touch with people and see how you can bring them value – don't make it all about what you need/want.

- **How would you suggest a filmmaker begin their producing career, and what is the best way to grab a network's attention if you have no previous track record?**

Experience and networking. Gain experience through reputable production companies and/or by working with filmmakers/producers who will build your skill set – all while you work on your projects. Don't get tunnel vision about only working on and selling your projects, you can learn from others while you work on your projects. Network with filmmakers, agents, and execs – don't be hierarchical.

- **What are the most important skills that a producer should learn?**

It's about the audience! Creative flexibility is critical. The needs of the audience and the "buyer" – for example, streamer, cable/network, podcast, film studio – are ever changing. Be consistent and dependable, ask questions, be willing to adapt, and work to anticipate the needs of your client.

- **What do you look for in a producer or production company?**

Collaboration, innovation, creative and strategic foresight. Fire in the belly. Intentional passion!

- **When you were initially starting out, what was the best piece of advice that one of your mentors shared that has had the greatest impact on you and/or your career?**

Think about your audience first and foremost, not about yourself. This is a small business; you'll remember how people treat you, and they'll remember how you treat them.

- **Today, you commission hundreds of hours of programming. When you're making a greenlight decision, how do you determine whether to move ahead with a project or not? (If helpful, it could be best practices for pitching or drafting treatments, any places that people usually drop the ball, budget/schedule concerns, advice that might help inform how discussions go in the room, etc.)**

My decision for a greenlight is completely different from other networks and/or streamers, thus the importance of building and fostering relationships and maintaining continual communication. The reasons for greenlight are constantly shifting – for example, budgets are expanding or contracting, volume of content in a specific sub-genre, focus on streaming versus linear. My network might greenlight after significant paper development, while another network might require a "proof of concept" tape because they're a more character-driven network. The conversations can shift weekly, monthly, and/or quarterly; it's imperative for producers and filmmakers to keep a steady conversation drumbeat with their network/streamer/agent contacts so that they can adapt to the ever-changing needs of the platform, thus increasing their chances for greenlight.

- **How does the split between streaming and linear television affect your programming decisions?**

The decisions come down to several factors—for example, competitive projects, budget available for streaming versus linear content, volume of slots available in any given year allotted to streaming and linear content, performance.

- **Once you decide to move ahead with a project, what are you looking for in the initial kickoff call with a new producer and/or production company? Any words of wisdom for how a producer should interface on that call? Any suggestions on what not to do?**

A network and/or streamer has hundreds of hours of content in production at any given time. They have established standards and practices to streamline processes, create uniform efficiencies, and keep communication reliable. The initial project kickoff calls typically introduce the network team – for example, development and production team assigned to the project – to the production company team. We go over the topline network process – specifically post greenlight through production (processes: episode outlines, scripts, number of rough cuts, fine cuts, network note process, etc.). The network team fields questions from the production company to further clarify the process and help move the project forward. What not to do: dictate how the project will run and who you'll be hiring.

- **How do you determine the success or failure of a new project and whether you wish to work with a producer again?**

I determine success and failure by several factors, some of which include the following: Did the audience respond to the content? Did the content rate? Did the content provoke a conversation/make people think? Did the team challenge themselves/try something new? If the content didn't rate well, I don't consider that a failure; instead, what did we learn from the audience's response to the programming? What could we do differently?

With regard to wanting to work with a producer again, I consider:

- Did they deliver on the creative we developed and greenlit?
- Did we need to make changes during production (adapt because of access, characters, and/or any other number of reasons that impact the creative and production)? How did the producer respond to making changes? How flexible and creatively inventive were they? Are they problem solvers or problem creators?
- Did they produce the content within the agreed-upon budget? If not, why not, and what happened?
- Were they good partners?

- **What is the best investment in yourself that you've ever made?**

What's been most beneficial for me is being open to change and taking risks, knowing each time that I'm going to bet on myself. I've always known that I'm willing to start from the beginning. When I left LA (after 5 years in film) and went to DC (to pursue a career in TV) I was willing to start at the bottom all over again. I've never been afraid of hard work because I know that I'll master the tasks, learn new skills, meet new people, surpass whatever expectations are identified, and move my career forward.

- **What is the worst advice that you continually hear people giving new or young producers?**

Chase the title. Netting flashy titles quickly often offers the CliffsNotes to the roles and responsibilities you need to know. Take the time to learn, build, and develop the skill sets that will make you an expert at your craft; there's no short-cut. Figure out who will teach/mentor you – who will give you the opportunities that will challenge you and the opportunities for growth.

Chapter Four

Crafting a Presentation

Coming up with an idea for a factual program or series is just the first step – and a hugely important one – but it takes a whole lot more to bring that idea to life!

To sell your brilliant idea you're going to need to present it to others who can fund your vision.

And to do that you have to find a way to communicate what is inside your mind to others.

DOI: 10.4324/9781003292289-4

Presentation Materials

Great producers don't just think of amazing ideas; they also arm themselves with the right types of materials to convince a potential buyer to greenlight their project and pay for it.

Typically, there are three key elements to a pitch presentation.

1. A written treatment (which is known as "a deck")
2. A demo reel that helps visualize your concept (known as a "sizzle reel")
3. A verbal presentation (your "pitch"!)

While these are the basic required pitch elements, every producer thinks differently and creatively develops whatever assets they believe might intrigue a buyer the most for their idea.

If you're pitching a baking show, perhaps it's worth sharing some of your star chef's tasty treats, while on the other hand if you're presenting a fashion show, it might be helpful to share a dress sample.

Nothing is particularly out of the box if you think it'll help development execs remember your project and champion your cause.

When you're crafting your pitch, you should start by asking yourself, if you were in a development executive's shoes, what would you want to see, and what would be a differentiator?

No two producers attack the problem the same way.

It All Starts With the Pen

Factual TV is a visually rich medium; however, it all starts with the written word. The power of the pen (or currently the word processor) is paramount to your success. Great films start with great writing and documentaries, or factual programs are no different. To perfect your craft, you must harness language and use it to describe your vision.

Treatments run the gamut from highly intriguing one-pagers that captivate a prospective buyer all the way to 30-page in-depth mini-novellas or even 100-page series bibles that spell out every step of the project. It's up to you to find the perfect way to describe your idea and unleash your creativity.

Some producers have hard-and-fast rules about how they build their presentations, while others feel a project out and then put together the different types of materials that they think are right for each specific idea.

A lot of producers also test their treatments, or decks, with a game theory-like approach where they constantly try subtle tweaks to their presentations in order to see if they can find "the secret sauce" that convinces a network or service to say "yes" more often.

When you hear similar feedback about an idea, oftentimes it's because it's not well explained or thought out in your deck.

Creating a Treatment

Writing is a way of life and not just a skill that you build. It begins with seeds of inspiration, grows over long walks and deep conversations, and comes to life when you finally put words on a page. Celebrate it, champion it, and harness it to your advantage.

Great treatments begin with terrific research. It's the fuel that powers the forge of storytelling and an essential part of the process that helps focus your ideas, broaden your understanding, and lead you toward your film or series point of view.

When you finally land on your first great factual idea, it's time to put the concept down on paper. Often, it'll take several attempts to get it just right, so you should welcome the art of revision. What you're aiming for is a clearly stated concept that's simple enough for a child to grasp and compelling enough to leave the reader asking, "what happens next?".

It helps at this stage to ask yourself, "have I seen this before?" and to separate your idea from the competition, pre-thinking every angle of the story, and the practicalities involved in turning it into a living breathing program or series.

While conceptualizing your treatment, it helps to give some thought to a few key descriptive industry buzzwords that can help quickly describe your idea to others.

Self-contained: When a story resolves itself within a single program that can stand on its own. Most cable networks feature a strong lineup of self-contained programs that can run anywhere in the schedule.

Arced: When a storyline continues from one episode to the next, incentivizing the audience to watch the programs in order to follow the narrative. Most over-the-air broadcast shows are arced. *The Bachelor, American Idol, and Survivor* are all great examples.

A program or series can be *either* self-contained or arced, yet both can feature **Formatted** elements. Are there any structural components to the project that repeat in every episode?

As you work through the process of crafting your treatment, it's crucial to find your own voice. Words bring ideas to life, and you need to write with the same kind of passion that you *feel* for the material. Some producers try to write as entertainingly as possible. Others focus on the facts or structure. Some play around with the format and even write in potential dialogue. There's no one way to do it. You just need to find *your way to do it.*

Ultimately, networks want to know that they're in good hands, that you can tell a great story, and that you really know your stuff.

Don't Self-Limit

Hollywood writers are often given the advice to *write what they know* when they're breaking in, and sadly the same is often true in the factual world.

A lot of committed producers continually produce pitches solely on the subjects they're the most comfortable with. However, if you only develop pitches inside your wheelhouse, then you'll never stretch yourself or raise your professional ceiling.

Don't limit yourself to the knowledge that you already possess. Push yourself to explore divergent areas of interest and seek out the hidden curiosities in our world. The more inquisitive you are, the more the market will reward your interest in learning new things. If you put a cap on your own potential, you'll never grow. Avail yourself of every opportunity to stretch, and your options and potential projects are limitless. Keep pushing yourself to feel uncomfortable. The more discomfort you feel, the more growth you're experiencing.

The most interesting people tend to live the most varied lives, and in factual programming the most powerful storytellers tend to equally stretch themselves to the max.

Celebrities can be **insane**; Their **lives are wild** and **adventurous**, their homes and cars are **over-the-top**, and they've got **money to burn** and **famous friends** to join them. Plus, they **throw some** utterly **amazing** (and often completely out-of-control) **parties** too -- So if you want to make it in Hollywood you've got to learn from the best!

Acting is actually only half the battle. To be a real star, you know the front page of US Weekly variety, you've got to be a Diva *on and off the screen*. True A-Listers take years to cultivate their skills and hone their star-studded antics, but here at the Hollywood Celebrity Club we'll pull back the curtain and share the most scintillating secrets of the trade! It'll puff up pompous tail feathers in even the most even keeled individual.

Ripped straight from the Headlines, stolen directly from the gossip rags, and pulled right out of the supermarket tabloids comes ***THE HOLLYWOOD PLAYERS CLUB***, a self-contained 10x60 series that **showcases how to truly live the La-La Land lifestyle** and become the most famous, or perhaps infamous, Celebrity possible!

From epic Meltdowns or bloody Feuds to passionate Affairs or hardcore Parties that never end, our blockbuster how-to guide will breakdown the very best ways to become absolutely iconic! They say that imitation is the sincerest form of flattery — but why duplicate the past when you can learn from it and do it even better? Part Cruise with a dash of Clooney, and a touch of Pitt with a little Redford thrown-in for good measure, the Players Guide will selectively dissect the stars that we know and the moments that we remember...

Like a paparazzi retracing an A-lister's steps, in each episode we'll strive to uncover the scandalous moments, drill down into the most salacious details, and rewind the tape on some of our favorite star's most memorable bits of glitz and glamour, in order to craft the perfect artisanal how-to-become a celebrity recipe. Using a combination of expertly presented insights, user generated content, and memorable archive, we'll present the perfect mixture for Stardom and revel in the missteps of our favorite stars, their surprising scandals, and even their most heartfelt scenes. All to find out exactly what it takes to become a true Hollywood Player!

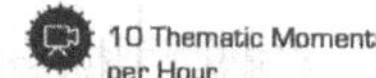

Expert Insights & Gossip

Chart a Path to Stardom Thru the Stars

Unique Points:

Evergreen

Snackable

Scalable

Cry Havoc Productions, Inc.

FIGURE 4.1 A Sample Documentary Series Treatment.

What Goes in a Treatment?

Treatments are your opportunity to share the great idea that's been rattling around inside your head for ages with an audience that can potentially fund your work.

Like many parts of the TV industry, there are numerous ways to approach a treatment; however, I've found that it is best to break a presentation down into six specific sections.

- An Overview
- Project Logline
- Run of Show (also called *Narrative Beats* or an *Act Structure*)
- Episode Breakdown
- Episode Outlines
- Producer and Company Overview

General Overview: I like to open each pitch with an exciting and captivating description of the project. Think of this section as your teaser. You want to hook the reader, so they continue through the remainder of the document. When you send your presentation to a development executive, you literally have no idea who else is going to read it.

Project Logline: Next, you want to summarize the general overview section in a succinct sentence or two. Later this will be invaluable as a quick means to explain your project via phone or embedded in an email.

This is your **High Concept Line** and or Silicon Valley elevator pitch. Be direct, to the point, and hopefully engaging enough to make the reader curious to see what comes next.

Format (sometimes called "Run of Show"): As you move into the heart of the deck, it's time to highlight the basic structure of an episode. Every network has a different structure for their programs. Some broadcasters use four-acts in an hour-long program, while others might use six-acts for the same 60-minute program slot. A lot of European networks tend to gravitate toward a four-act structure and a 44-minute total content running time. (The remaining 16 minutes are filled by commercials.)

Episode Breakdown: After the Run of Show, some producers like to craft a simple episode description. I'll do this if the idea warrants it; however, most of the time I try to keep the treatment deck as tight as possible and jump to the next item on the list.

Episode Outlines: If you're pitching a series, you'll want to highlight the different subjects for each episode. It can run the gamut from a few simple sentences to an entire page per episode.

Producer and Company Overview: Finally, you'll want to end each presentation with a brief biography or credit list that tells the reader about yourself. Even though you've contacted a specific network executive, you can't assume that they'll tell their colleagues everything about you. So, you want to use this section of the deck to humble-brag a bit about yourself.

Brevity Is Its Own Reward

When you come up with a terrific factual idea, you'll invariably have *a lot to say about it.* While writing it up, it's easy to have a massive brain dump as you bang out a novel-length proposal. Try to temper that enthusiasm. TV is a business built on fragments of thoughts and well-honed copyrighting aesthetics. The shorter and sweeter your deck is, generally the better it'll be received.

The art of selling is really the art of seduction. You want to engage the buyer, intrigue them, get their mind to spin up with the possibilities. Development teams are often overloaded and underpowered. It's incumbent upon you to pay attention to the time commitment that you're asking from whomever reviews your presentation. The longer the required reading time, the easier it is for them to pass. Instead, try to whet their appetite and leave them wanting more.

Over the years, I've tried a wide range of different types of treatments and have found no matter how great the idea is, it's always the tightest descriptions that sell. Ultimately, if a network execs is keen on your idea but wants more info, they'll ask for it. My advice is to err on the side of brevity.

Crafting a Deck

Factual programs and series are a visually rich medium, yet amazingly for a long time, crafting a presentation to sell them only *required a rudimentary* Word document.

Not anymore.

Today, producers are asked to supply a visually rich *deck*. The term "deck" harkens back to presentations made on old slide projectors before it was eventually co-opted by Microsoft's PowerPoint presentation software.

Even though the term goes mainstream thanks to PowerPoint, these days producers use all kinds of graphical tools like Photoshop or InDesign to bring their creative visions to life. Personally, I prefer to use online tools that are easily shareable, such as Prezi or Adobe Spark. Ultimately, it doesn't matter what software you use to create the deck if the resulting presentation is visually rich and dynamic.

If you need to count on someone else's imagination for your proposal to work, then you're probably already out of the running. You simply never know how someone else will interpret your idea, so it's best to lay it out in as clear a manner as possible. Assume that the reader has no knowledge beyond what they see on the slides. Readability is also tremendously important. You want to make sure that you give your idea the best chance to be seen.

Cutting a Sizzle Reel

Once you have a deck, it's time to create a sizzle reel. This is a short one- to three-minute video dazzler that showcases what your project is about in broad strokes.

Every producer goes about crafting their sizzle reels differently. Some replicate network promotional spots for their proposed project, while others might go out and film a short segment that showcases their idea. Bigger production companies might spend thousands of dollars on their sizzles, while small indie producers keep it cheap and cheerful. There are no hard-and-fast rules when it comes to creating a sizzle reel. You must do whatever serves your story best and get the point across as quickly as possible within the realm of whatever is feasible for you at the time.

There are some producers who feel their greatest strength is in-person presentation, so they'll film themselves pitching their project directly to camera. In their mind this takes the development execs out of the equation and allows them to speak directly to the decision-maker – even if they never get into the room with them!

Back in the day you'd show a sizzle reel during an in-person meeting with a network executive, and you'd instantly know if they were keen on the project or not based on their reactions.

These days it works a bit differently. Most network exes prefer to be sent links in advance before deciding whether to discuss the idea further. This means you never know if you've got their undivided attention while they're watching your reel. Nor do you know what kind of mood they're in while viewing.

Both Vimeo and a private YouTube link are great video-hosting platforms. Personally, I like Vimeo since it's a highly secure system that also offers great viewing analytics. You can log in and see not only if the video was viewed but also where, when, and how long the viewer watched. With a little bit of sleuthing, you can usually figure out who might have viewed your sizzle if you've shared it with multiple nets.

Just like your treatment, the point of the sizzle is to leave the network viewer wanting more. You want to pique their curiosity and ensure that they're never bored.

Importance of Titles

Having a great title on your treatment, deck or sizzle is often half the battle.

Just like a casual TV viewer who's sitting at home flipping through a complex programming grid while trying to figure out what to watch next, development execs have limited time and an abundance of proposals being sent their way. Presenting them with something catchy right at the top is extremely helpful if you want them to fully dive into your idea.

A great title can sell an idea all by itself. You need something catchy and hookable that describes your series idea. As the Brits are fond of saying, you want the series "to do what it says on the tin". The better your title is and the quicker it can convey what your project is about, the better your odds to land the sale.

Interestingly, the title that sells a project and the title that hits the air can be two different things. During my career, I've found that a project title is one of the few places that a network can really exert its own creativity *after* greenlighting a project. So, it's helpful to not become too attached to your project's brilliant name. We've had countless projects renamed by executive producers, marketing team members, or ad sales folks. It's all part of the process.

In fact, many years ago we pitched a one-hour special to Animal Planet about competitive poultry showing. We followed several chicken breeders around the country as they prepared for the national finals in a dog show-like national chicken competition – sort of like the Christopher Guest mockumentary movie *Best in Show* only with poultry.

When we initially pitched the film with the title *Showcocks*, it was a fun double entendre that caught people's attention. The network greenlit the project chuckling through the whole process. However, Animal Planet is a G-rated network, and they were never going to broadcast a program with the word "cock" in the title. So, it wasn't exactly shocking when the marketing stepped in and renamed the project "Fowl Play" – an equally smart title but far less potentially offensive.

Inside the Industry With Michael Welsh, Executive Producer

Michael Welsh is an Emmy, Peabody, BAFTA, and DuPont-Columbia award-winning executive producer, showrunner, and writer who has worked with the industry's top networks and producers on over 800 hours of programming in all genres of television and documentary. He spent eight years as an executive producer in production and development at the National Geographic Channel, where he oversaw *Battleground Afghanistan, Drugs, Inc., Alaska State Troopers, Inside Nature's Giants, Expedition Wild,* and *Witness Katrina.*

- **How would you suggest an aspiring producer get into the factual industry if their goal is to create and sell their own content to a global broadcaster or streamer?**

My suggestion for an aspiring factual producer whose goal is to sell their own content to a global broadcaster or streamer would be based on their level of experience. For example, if they're new to the industry, I'd suggest they start by working at a production company to learn the ropes and build a portfolio of ideas and projects they can develop, sell, and produce through that production company. Later, once that producer's established a reputation in the community and with different network execs, they can branch out to working with larger, better established production companies or to selling their ideas on their own. I'd strongly recommend hiring an agent as well once you've established a foothold in the industry.

- **What do you think are the keys to a successful producing career? (If it's helpful are there any traits or core tenants that you feel aspiring producers should hone, any tips or tricks that you feel are helpful to utilize, etc.)**

I think the key to a successful producing career is to be willing to do it all and work in different genres. By that I mean, regardless of whether you want to be a producer or an editor, writer, or director, learn (or at least have a basic understanding of) how to shoot, edit, write, produce, and direct. Watch a lot of content to see what's in the competitive landscape that you can learn from, emulate, borrow, or make better. Read and watch the news to see what stories can naturally jump from the written word to a visual medium. Most importantly, don't pigeonhole yourself to one genre (e.g., natural history, crime, science) because it'll limit your versatility in the marketplace.

- **When you begin developing a project, what are your initial steps, and how do you know if the idea is going to resonate with a network or streamer?**

Truthfully, when developing a project, you never know for sure if your idea is going to resonate with a network or streamer. To get a handle on whether it might, be sure to familiarize yourself with the various outlet's types of programming so you can better target your idea. And start by developing ideas that aren't too laser-focused so there's greater opportunity to shop them to multiple outlets at once. I would recommend, as a rule, that if you can't find at least three potential outlets for your idea, it's too narrow and won't be worth your time and ROI in the end. The truth is, there are a lot of good ideas, but that's not enough – you need a home for your good idea.

- **There's a lot of different ways to create a pitch deck or treatment (e.g., it should be short and sweet, it should be 20+ pages long to showcase your knowledge). Are there any hard-and-fast rules you live by?**

This is a generalization, but by and large, the folks looking at pitches have short attention spans. Part of that is because they're seeing so many pitches, they're looking for/needing something that'll cut through the noise and grab them. The current school of thought is to create a short, pithy, and visually interesting deck that lays out story and style in a contemporary medium like Prezi or Square Space. That said, as someone who focuses on story, I tend to overdevelop my ideas by writing long-form pitches that clearly demonstrate how the story will play out and be executed, both visually and narratively. I'm not sure I'd recommend this execution though because the ROI is bad if the idea doesn't go anywhere. I'd recommend generating a mix of ideas that are both topical and evergreen so you're not expending all your energies on subjects that are going to be quickly dated as well. Also, try to create some sort of sizzle reel if you're able because again ours is a visual medium at its core.

- **You've sold factual ideas to both linear broadcasters as well as streamers. In your mind, is there any difference between the two? Any advantages or disadvantages working for one versus the other?**

I don't think there's a huge difference between linear broadcasters and streamers when it comes to selling factual content. Both have specific needs to meet their respective target audiences. And in terms of advantages or disadvantages, when it comes to working with one versus the other, I think it's a draw.

- **A lot of aspiring producers have trouble determining their worth in the marketplace. How do you negotiate with a network or streamer so that you have enough budget to produce the project you're envisioning and can make a living doing it?**

Unless you have a one-and-a-million ideas or exclusive access to a subject matter, the market sets the value of a project. It's best to come in with a target cost per hour (CPH) (e.g., $125K, $250K, $350K) based on what's being produced in the marketplace and try for that as your CPH, knowing what it'll take to make the show and have some take-home at the end of the day.

- **You spent many years on the network side as an executive producer and buyer where you saw a lot of pitches from outside producers – any best practices when it comes to pitching that you gleaned from that time?**

Know your pitch backward and forward when selling it so that you can speak to both the project's strengths and its potential challenges. Don't be too derivative. Know your network execs style and tailor your pitch to them (i.e., if they're only interested in sizzles, have a great sizzle; if you need, they'll read a treatment, write a treatment). Be able to tailor your pitch on the fly if that's what the room's telling you; have a firm direction on how you see the project playing out, but try to solicit the network execs opinion on how it could best be tailored/tweaked to meet their audience's needs.

- **How would you describe the freelance life that goes along with the TV biz?**

I'd describe freelance life in the TV biz as a hard, never-ending hustle. You've got to keep moving, have lots of irons in the fire at all times, and constantly work your contacts. Don't get complacent. If you're not working, develop a new idea. Read. Watch – or at least sample – shows, even the ones you don't like. Plan on bursts of 24/7 work followed by extreme fallow periods. Find a Zen place with this rhythm, or you run the risk of burnout.

- **How has failure, or apparent failure, helped shape your career?**

It may sound Pollyanna, but failure or lack of success – whether the rejected pitch or the show-running gig that may have not gone as well as hoped – only makes you stronger. Learn from your misses or mistakes. Try to have a colleague or associate in the business who can honestly tell you how you might do it better or change/up your game. Learn from it.

- **What is the best professional investment in yourself that you've ever made?**

I'd say the best professional investment I've made in myself is learning the different steps of the industry – going from Production Assistant (PA) to Associate Producer (AP) to executive producer (EP)/showrunner, etc. If you take the time to learn the ropes, it'll help your career in the long run. Also, taking a job as a network exec helped give me a more complete understanding of the industry as a whole – by that I mean, not just how to make a great show creatively, but what it takes to bring that show to fruition on the business side of TV.

- **What is the worst advice that you continually hear people giving new or young producers?**

There's no "one" or "right" path to take. Some major in production in undergraduate, some choose film school, some learn on the job. Tailor your path to your own desires and interests.

- **When you were starting out as a producer, what salient advice did one of your mentors share that has had the greatest impact on you and/or your career?**

Learn as much as you can. Don't pigeonhole yourself. Be careful not to burn bridges.

Chapter Five

Pitching Your Idea

The art of pitching is a producer's lifeblood. As they say on Wall Street, *You eat what you kill*. The same applies in factual TV.

There are lots of different pitch methods and no one "right" way to do it. It's not an easy skill to learn or master, but a crucial part of the job. In fact, some might say it's the entire gig. Those that pitch, sell projects. Those that don't, end up leaving the industry.

DOI: 10.4324/9781003292289-5

So What Is a Pitch?

Pitching lies at the heart of great producing. It's the mana that runs your producing life, an inescapable part of your daily existence and perhaps the most important aspect of the gig.

Nearly every day you'll end up pitching someone or something, so get ready to get your hustle on. At its core level, pitching is how you sell your idea, gain access, hook talent, and cut deals. Know what you want out of each conversation before you start, and try not to over sell either yourself or the idea. The trick is having the self-awareness to understand how you best communicate and to use that knowledge to your advantage.

In the context of selling a factual program or series, the art of *pitching* refers to how you go about convincing a broadcaster or service to commission (or buy) your idea.

Every network runs differently, but generally the person you'll be trying to sell your programming idea to is a network or streaming **Development Executive**. They act as the network's "buyer" and listen to hundreds if not thousands of pitches every week as

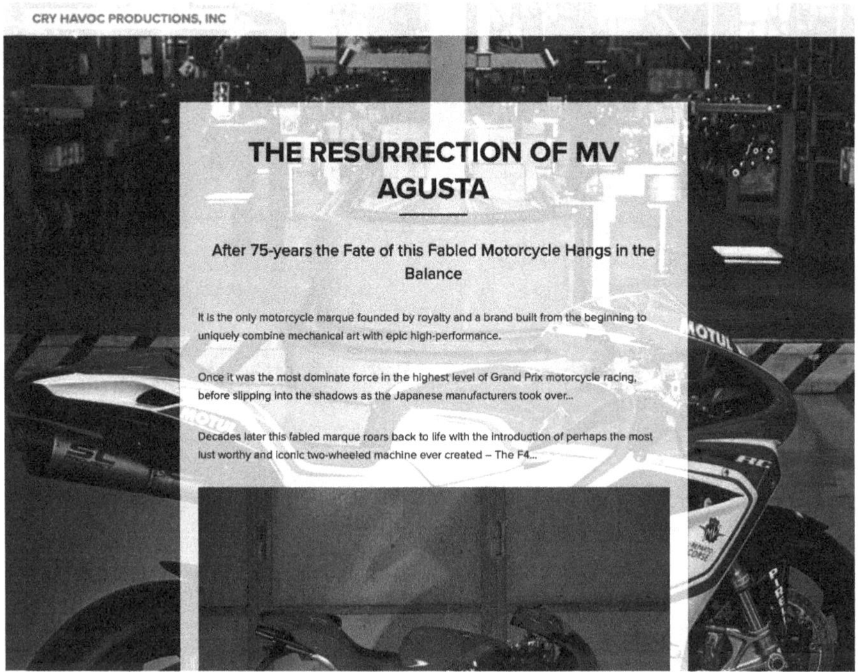

FIGURE 5.1 An Online Treatment Deck

well as countless variations of the same idea. Your job as a producer is to convince this person that your concept is a can't-miss project.

Typically, you start by giving a short verbal presentation on the phone or via a videoconferencing application and then follow the discussion up by sending additional materials via email, which include a written proposal or deck, and often a sizzle reel.

If the development executive likes your idea, then they'll take it to the network's development team for consideration. Should the entire group get excited about the concept, then it'll get pitched by the development team to the network's head of programming. In the end, if you want to find funding for your project, you've got to pitch.

It's the crucial step that makes or breaks your idea. To do it successfully, you need to know the story that you're trying to tell inside and out, and you've also got to put together a collection of materials that help illustrate your vision to potential buyers.

The Gift of Conversation

Before you pitch a prospective network development executive, it helps to elicit feedback from those around you so that you can hone your approach.

Great pitching often starts with great conversations. They're the cornerstone of producing. The more you talk to people, the greater the number of ideas that will emerge. Not all of them will be awesome, but as the sample size grows, so too does the number of potential winners.

When you're alone, your ideas are like lonely and unexcited atoms. They move slowly and only sparingly bounce off other thoughts. However, when you converse with a great number of people, it's like heating a beaker in a science lab and watching the water begin to boil. The more conversations you have, the faster and more energetically the atoms bounce off one another . . . until not one idea arises but several all at the same time. Don't be precious with your ideas; share them with as many folks as you can and see where the discourse takes you.

These early conversations also give you an opportunity to practice your pitch and perfect your storytelling for it. Each discussion will help inform you of the missing links in the presentation. As you describe the concept, try to pay attention to whether others can follow your description of the concept. What are they missing? What aren't they picking up that you think is self-explanatory? Ask your audience if they're confused at all, or if there are any portions that don't make sense. The more feedback you receive, the better your final presentation will become.

I don't usually get too hung up if one person has an issue with an idea, but if multiple people point out the same flaw, then it's time to take notice. Often, we celebrate the lonely artist who goes off into the woods to create their masterpiece; however, the reality is that most of the time creativity is a social beast. It needs to be fed interaction to grow into something remarkable and worth pursuing long term.

The Right Person to Pitch

Getting your foot in the door to pitch a broadcaster or a streamer is one of the trickiest parts of a producer's job. Most network execs typically will only take pitches from producers they know or agents they trust. This creates a unique insider echo-chamber that's full of the same faces and ideas. It also might explain why you see so many iterations of the same type of shows with the same faces repeatedly.

Some networks and services have pitch submission portals on their websites that allow anyone to send their materials through. They're impenetrable digital fortresses intent on placing a large moat between aspiring producers and development team members. I've never made a sale through a portal without knowing someone at the network first, nor have I ever heard of someone selling their idea via a portal submission. One gets the sense that they only exist to limit potential legal liability for unsolicited submissions.

So how do you find the right person to pitch your great program or series idea to?

It starts with researching prospective buyers at various networks and streamers. You can skim IMDb or deep dive into various industry trade websites like Realscreen or Television Business International (TBI). You can also attend festivals like Realscreen, Banff, or Sunnyside of the Doc or markets like MIPCOM. Personal introductions are by far the best way into a network. If you can strike up a relationship with someone who already has network contacts and then ask them for an introduction to a development team member, you'll instantly improve your chances. A word-of-mouth introduction is the best route in the door, and if someone who knows you and your work can vouch for your skills, it can make all the difference.

I've been very fortunate to make multiple sales thanks to some very kind introductions made by others. I'm grateful for their help and the willingness of other industry colleagues to connect me to new potential buyers. Whenever someone kindly makes an introduction on my behalf, I like to follow up via a second email so as not to clutter the mutual acquaintance's inbox.

A few suggestions for that private note.

- **Remind the Recipient Who Introduced You:** Reference the warm intro that your mutual acquaintance shared.

- **Reiterate Credentials**: Hopefully your mutual contact already praised your previous exploits; however, whether they did or not, it's worth briefly refreshing the recipient's mind as to why you're worth their time.
- **Offer Help:** You must assume that every vulture out there is asking for this person's time and trying to *sell them* on an idea. Tell them how you can *help make their life easier.*
- **Make the Ask:** Concisely lay out why you're contacting them and your aim.
- **End on Action:** Finish your note with an actionable event. Don't leave things open-ended. Instead, ask to schedule a phone call, hold an in-person meeting, or connect via a video chat.

Like most business-to-business conversations, personal introductions are powerful. However, they're not the only way to get your foot in the door. If you don't share a mutual connection, that begs a very simple question: *How do you find the correct point-person to contact at a network?*

A Fragmented Playing Field

These days the visual entertainment marketplace is more fragmented than ever before, and the result is that the end consumer is being offered an incredible amount of nearly limitless viewing choice; they can watch traditional free-to-air broadcast networks, scope out linear cable nets, turn on a streaming service that operates over the internet, fire up an iPhone app like TikTok or Facebook, or just scour the internet looking for random videos. It's an amazing amount of opportunity surrounded by a vast sea of mediocrity.

For a factual content creator, and more specifically a producer starting out, this means there are more potential homes for your projects than at any point in the history of the entertainment industry. That's pretty awesome, right?

Historically, viewers have tended to gravitate repeatedly to the same eight to ten channels, or digital locations, repeatedly. Through the decades networks have become increasingly more niche in their offerings. Some nets have gotten so good at replicating their past programming success that it's hard to tell where one program ends and another begins; the style, pace, and substance are nearly identical no matter what time of day you tune in.

Streamers have upped the ante even further thanks to their ability to digitally track viewing habits. Companies like Netflix and Amazon have tremendous data sets at their disposal and can use artificial intelligence algorithms to reasonably predict the kinds of new programs that their viewers will watch.

It's a far cry from back in the day when you could develop a doc or series idea and reasonably assume that you might be able to sell it to six or eight different networks. Today's networks and streamers are so hyper-defined that generally you must craft custom proposals for each network that you pitch, and sometimes even each person that you pitch inside of a company. Ultimately, there might only be one or two logical homes for any given idea.

If you don't know anyone who can offer a personal introduction to a network or streamer development executive, then you've got to get a bit craftier and find your inner *hustler*.

One successful route is to attend conferences like Realscreen, London Content, Banff World Media Festival, The World Science Congress of Factual Producers, or any of the other myriad of factual festivals. Networks send their development team members to these events to look for new programming ideas as well as finished programs that they can acquire for less investment. They're essentially the factual television versions of the *Sundance* or *Tribeca* film festivals. You can also attend programming markets like MIPTV or MIPCOM, though they tend to be more transactional and focused on finished content.

The downside of these festivals and markets is that they tend to cost quite a bit to attend. If you feel they are too expensive, then the next best thing is to keep your eyes and ears open for news about a network's development team and then try to track down the key players on *LinkedIn*. You can use tools like Rocketreach to find a LinkedIn profile's professional email address and then send them a traditional cold call email.

Finally, there are services that sell contact information for various network development and commissioning team members. Peter Hamilton's *documentarytelevision.com* site is a go-to resource for these lists. It's an easy and efficient way to nab a whole slew of network contacts all at once; however, if you're reasonably savvy online, you can often find all of this info on your own for no out-of-pocket expense. Google Search can be a powerful friend for your digital snooping.

Unfortunately, cold call emails are *extremely hard*, and their hit rate is fairly low. However, they're worth your while because one never knows what is going on at a network or service at any given time nor what direction they might be moving in. Nor do you know what will happen when you send your introductory email. Perhaps lighting will strike!

You're the hunter (the emailer) and they're the prey (the recipient). The worst thing that anyone can say is *no*, and once you realize that, you're almost invincible.

Here are five key steps for generating actionable cold call emails:

- **Grab Their Attention:** Use a catchy title or highlight a potential shared contact. I'm very fond of titling an email *Per (Name of Mutual Acquaintance) – A (Insert Your Production Company Name) Intro*. It's short and sweet and instantly tells the recipient why they should read further.
- **Keep It Short:** Get right to the point. Don't be wordy.
- **Share Your Commonality:** Briefly tell them how you're tangentially connected (mutual acquaintances, shared experience, you went to the same university, etc.)

or highlight recent successes. Help them understand why this note is worth their time.

- **Don't Assume:** Don't jump to the conclusion that they're the correct person to email about a new idea or to pitch. Ask for their help finding the right person to talk to. At this stage you're trying to forge a relationship, not make a sale.
- **Make Your Ask Clear:** Be clear and specific about what you want.

Be respectful of the network development team member's time. They're getting hammered all day long with hundreds of requests and no doubt being pulled in a thousand different directions by a million different producers. Don't be one more pain in their ass.

Sending an email is easy. Feeling a ping of regret and stopping a sent email from arriving is hard. So always think twice before hitting send. Your first gut reaction is usually correct. If you think you're being too friendly via email, you probably are. If you're writing in anger, it'll show. If you're being too cute, you are.

One of the best pieces of advice I ever received was being taught to re-read my emails out loud prior to hitting send. You can often hear grammatical issues far easier than you can find them by reading. Take a beat before hitting send and make sure it's exactly the tone you want to put forth.

Everyone is so used to instant communication that they feel compelled to fire off emails instantly with little oversight. However, each and every interaction you have represents you and your craftsmanship. Little details might seem minor, but they offer a window into how you'll produce. Strive to be perfect. Know that nobody is. A lot of hustle, a bit of persistence, and a dash of perseverance go a long way when you're trying to reach the correct person at a network to pitch.

Development Discussions

Once you've connected with the appropriate development person, you need to get the conversation going in earnest, and regardless of whether you're pitching a linear broadcaster or a streaming service, the process is identical. Development people are the conduits for new proposals. Their job is to filter out the noise and take only the best of the best to the commissioning team. You'll rarely if ever know the true commissioners – at least not until you've done a project or two for a network. So, the development person is your key to unlocking the network's funding.

When you talk to them you have to appreciate that what a network wants is a moving target, and it morphs as the channel adds shows or series to their lineup. What you want to do is cultivate a relationship with the development team member so that when they take your great idea into the larger team meeting, they passionately pitch it for you.

Yes, that's right – *you pitch someone at a network so that they can pitch it to their bosses.*

This is yet another reason that your message must be crystal clear. Otherwise, it's in danger of being misconstrued or misunderstood by the larger group. The more you talk with a development team member, the more you'll realize how their mandate keeps shifting or altering. This can offer clues to what they're seeking and the genres or subjects that they're having trouble successfully filling.

Stay in the game long enough, and you'll soon realize that network mandates change very quickly. Discovery's family of networks is notorious for trying new brands and then killing them swiftly if they don't see high viewership ratings. Discovery is also famous for moving its leadership team around every six to nine months. Their corporate strategy seems intent on giving their management team experience across all their various networks. As a producer you must stay current on who's in charge at any given moment because each new regime brings a subtle direction shift in style, tone, and commissioning strategy.

You must ingest all this info and make strategic bets as to where your time and energy are best served. Sometimes that means doing everything in your power to strike while the proverbial iron is hot; other times it sadly means waiting a specific regime out.

Amazingly, there was a time when factual content was only exhibited within its country of origin. However, those days are long gone. Today, it's a big, big world and content travels literally everywhere!

A lot of young producers solely focus their attention almost exclusively on their domestic television market. I believe that's a huge mistake because there are pots of global and regional funding just waiting for you if you're willing to think beyond your national borders. So don't limit yourself to the obvious networks or just the ones where you live. Every network in every country needs to feed their own content beast, and so many stories are universal. It just takes a bit of ambition, the ability to get out of your comfort zone, and willingness to think globally.

Do I Need an Agent?

Another route that you can take to connect with the correct network contacts is to find an agent to represent you and your work.

Agents are the gears that mesh together to keep Hollywood running, and by extension the greater entertainment industry. Originally, they were primarily focused on narrative films and episodic television projects; however, over the past 20 years as many networks came to the realization that factual series, and in particular reality TV, were cost-effective replacements for high-priced narrative projects, agents worked their way into the factual arena as well.

Today, agents are gatekeepers for big budget productions and connecting (or *packaging*) ideas, producers, talent, and networks.

Unfortunately, landing an agent as a young producer can be tricky. They're hard to gain an audience with and continually are out chasing the newest fads. Usually, you need a big hit or a large online following just to get an agent to take your projects on, let alone submit them on your behalf.

However, agents can be powerful allies and usually have their finger right on the pulse of what networks need this instant. Some agents will also send out intel on network needs at regular intervals as well. This info can be hugely helpful when you're developing new projects and allows you to shape ideas to fit potential homes. Some networks also crowdsource their development needs by asking certain agents to find them specific types of new projects.

I've used agents in the past, and I've made cold calls on my own; neither path is better or worse, and they both have their advantages and disadvantages. The factual industry existed well before agents became hip to it and in some respects goes on just fine without them too. Not everyone needs an agent, nor does every project require one. You can do just fine selling projects without an agent, and having one does not guarantee your success. Agents are a powerful tool in your producing toolbox, but they're not the only way to get something done.

Successfully Making the Pitch

Once you've crafted your proposal, honed your pitch, and contacted the correct person at a network or streamer, it's time to set up a call, video chat, or meeting to sell it.

The key is to remember that presentations are performances, and in order to hook the buyer you need to be compelling and persuasive. If it takes you longer than 30 seconds to describe your idea, then it's

- too complicated.
- or you don't understand it.

So, keep it short and on point, and be ready to answer questions about it.

Here are a few keys to successful pitching.

Never Be Late: A network exe's time is far more valuable than yours, be respectful of it.

Be as Concise as Possible: Brevity is an art, and the shorter your pitch is, the more time you must converse with your potential buyer.

Listen More Than You Talk: Nobody likes an over-talker or someone who thinks of something to say while the other person is speaking and can't wait to drop it into a conversation. Try to listen more than you talk. Every now and then a bit of listening will uncover a new opportunity. Pitching should be a two-way conversation, not a monologue.

Tell Them Why You LOVE the Project: Passion is everything, and if you don't champion your project, no one else will. This is your moment.

Tell Them Why You LOVE the Project For Them: Exes don't want to feel like you're trying to sell them a used car. They want a bespoke experience. For instance, you can reference the net's past trouble in a certain genre and how this could solve that problem, or you can highlight the success of a similar show and how this could keep the same audience around longer.

Give Off Good Vibes: People react well to smiles, yet amazing is we tend not to smile enough. Pitching is a bit like acting, words alone aren't enough. You must be emotionally available too.

Don't Over-rehearse: You need to know your stuff and have a clear vision that you can describe, but you also don't want to sound like an overly rehearsed robot. Don't regurgitate the message so mechanically that it sounds joyless. Joyless = no fun and no fun = no sale.

You'll Know in the First Few Minutes If There's Potential: Remember these are normal people just like you and me, and you have no idea what might be ailing them outside of work or beyond the confines of the meeting time slot. Watch the buyer's eyes. If they wander, you're in trouble. If they light up, you've got them on the hook!

If You're Getting a Negative Vibe, Wrap It Up: Once you feel there's bad mojo during a pitch, it's time to shut it down and head back to the ranch. Overstaying your welcome never turns the tide in your favor and instead leaves the network execs with a poor impression.

Inquisitive Questions Are Your Most Valuable Weapons: On one level, pitch sessions are about selling an idea. On a deeper level, they're an opportunity to connect one on one with a network buyer. Ask pointed questions and try to dig for the buried treasure that lurks beneath the surface. If you're lucky, eventually an execs will walk you through exactly what is working for them, what they're looking for in earnest, and talk to you on a personal level about what they need you to provide them with in order for them to advocate on your behalf. Pitch sessions are a chance to forge strong bonds.

Always Have an Extra Idea Waiting in the Wings: Network directions can change fast – sometimes even between setting up a meeting and having it. So be prepared to pivot quickly when the idea that you walked in the door with fails before you ever get a chance to mention it. A network execs might start your meeting by mentioning that a certain subject is no longer working for the channel. If that topic is remotely similar to your idea, then you're going to crash and burn, so always have one other extra idea up your sleeve. Even if it isn't fully flushed out, it'll require a deft hand to switch gears quickly and quite a bit of thinking on your feet, but every so often the best idea that you'll drop in a pitch meeting is the one you least expect.

Soft Skills: No matter how great your idea is on its own, without tremendous interpersonal skills it isn't going to go anywhere. Learning to "hear" the network and collaborate with them is crucial to advancing your project. Buyers are looking for producers that can work with everyone on their team, take constructive feedback, and proactively problem-solve.

Great pitching, whether in person or through a digital device, is a great dance full of passion and performance. When you make a meaningful connection with someone on the other side of the desk, you'll immediately know it. The vibe is clear and unmistakable. Sadly, so is the opposite – when you hit the deck hard, you'll know it's game over. Savor the good wins. Even if the execs turns down your idea, celebrate that you made a lasting connection.

Sometimes it can feel like playing three-dimensional chess, but you have no idea how an executive's career will unfold. Someone you once had a great meeting with but ultimately passed on your idea might move to a different network and become your biggest fan. You simply never know.

Videoconferencing is the latest technological tool to enter the pitch process. Somewhere between a live pitch meeting and a phone call, the Covid-19 pandemic has rocketed the acceptance rate for videoconferencing, and now it's become a powerful part of a producer's arsenal. I've found Zoom or Teams has made people more approachable and more friendly as we look into each other's homes; however, people's time is still incredibly valuable. Try to keep the off-topic chit chat to a minimum, and remember to get to your pitch as soon as you can without seeming pushy. Too many calls end up being 20 minutes of fluff and 10 minutes of TV talk. Don't be that producer. Get to the point and be succinct with why you've asked for a net execs to fit you into their schedule.

Whiffing a Pitch

Two things are guaranteed to happen when it comes to pitching.

- At some point everyone will perform poorly during a presentation and see their idea go up in flames.
- A concept you feel is a can't-miss project will absolutely be rejected.

It happens to everyone. Without mercy. All the time. Pitching for a living is like getting in the ring with Mike Tyson. You know going in that there's a good chance you're about to get punched in the face. If a network turns you down, it's just one person's opinion. Getting frustrated by the response and taking it personal does no good. There's a big difference between temporary failure and total defeat. What matters is what you do next.

The Follow-Up

Another challenging aspect of the pitch process is the often-interminable wait required to find out if a network is interested in your idea. Back when networks were run by small groups of empowered execs, they used to make decisions very quickly. Now, however the channels are larger, the stakes are higher, and the competition is far fiercer. There are more data-driven decisions, and projects seem to take ages to come to life. For a producer it can be a bit maddening as you wait for a decision. To ensure that your project stays high on the list, you need to correctly follow up.

Ultimately, you must find a balance between not getting lost in someone's email inbox and not being so eager that you send too many follow-ups. Great follow-ups are more of an art rather than a science. I try to be friendly, persistent, and measured without being obnoxious. Being friendly means not emailing someone demanding answers or being a jerk. It also means being conscious of when you hit send or pick up the phone. Don't call or email people right when they get to work or late at the end of a day. It's also bad form to say "I want to follow up" – they know that. Instead, try asking if they've had time to give the project some thought or review it with their colleagues.

As a sidebar, be mindful of time zones and different cultural calendars. Since a lot of my programs have been commissioned by international networks, I've increasingly learned to pay a lot of attention to other countries' holidays or major events. It's never good to email someone in the UK when you know that they have a bank holiday. I do however like trying to tactically take advantage of time zone differences by sending notes late on a Sunday evening so that they'll be sitting at the top of a European broadcaster's inbox on a Monday morning.

These days everyone gets blitzed with a lot of emails, and it's hard to keep track of what you sent to who or when. When you're juggling multiple projects or have several new ideas in development, it's very easy to lose track. My solution is to log all outgoing emails to network execs or potential buyers in a master excel spreadsheet. It's a simple way to keep track of whom I've spoken to about which projects. This way I have a single place to look up what projects I've pitched and to whom, which avoids the possibility of pitching a project to someone who's already passed on it previously.

The excel spreadsheet has a *follow up* column with a pre-populated date formula. Once I enter the email's origin date, the document automatically tells me when I have to follow up. It's simple, it's basic, and it's easy. Generally, I attempt to check-in every two weeks, unless a net execs specifically tells me when they're having their new review meeting.

There are online systems that can help automate the process as well. However, I find doing it somewhat manually helps me remember who I've spoken to and what I need to do next. Ultimately, it doesn't matter how you track your outgoing communications; rather, what is important is that you develop a system and stay consistent. When you do it enough people become attuned to it. Persistence pays off. Great follow-ups aren't normal. Lots of people give up. Or get distracted. Or just don't care. A lot of folks are only in it for the easy wins.

The Sting of Rejection

For every project that pops, hundreds of great ideas perish at the hands of development exes, agents, or distributors. You hear a lot of *no's* before you hear a single *yes*.

You can't take the rejection personally either. You need to delete the word *failure* from your personal framework. When a network *passes* on your project, it's just part of the process. In fact, rejection is how you grow and when the road ahead is unknown, every step requires hope.

When a network passes on a project that you've been discussing with them for ages, always refrain from writing a nasty email response. It might be cathartic, but it won't move the needle. Worse yet it'll irreparably harm your relationship with the team at the network moving forward. It's very a small world these days, and you simply never know where that executive will land next.

The trick is to find a way to channel the negative energy of a *no* into the required motivation to look for an alternative door to knock on instead to find a *yes*. The ability to see the bright side in a seemingly hopeless situation is a core tenant of being a successful producer. If you can envision it, you can make it happen. All great success begins with a tremendous amount of rejection. If you put in the time and the effort to craft a brilliant concept, then there's no such thing as a bad idea, just poor timing or execution.

There are plenty of examples in the entertainment industry where shows or movies took 10, 20, or 30 years to be brought to life. Everyone goes through periods in their life where they don't feel like they're living up to their potential. That's a natural part of human nature. However, if you see yourself as a failure, you'll surely become one. Failure itself is not a crime; however, failure to learn from failure is. Whenever it gets darkest, just keep grinding and moving forward. The best producers never lose their enthusiasm for the process because most of the game is persistence. Develop a love for rolling with the punches and celebrate even the smallest milestones along the way. Little victories help build positive momentum, and one action leads to another opportunity to create. You must create your own terminal velocity even in the face of adversity.

> Never venture, never win.
>
> – *Sun Tzu, a Chinese general, military strategist, writer, and philosopher*

Power of a Deadline

Most sales are a slow grind; however, there are a few exceptions. Our fastest sale was the result of a single phone conversation with a network execs that culminated in a single paragraph pitch.

We gained access to Dodge's Conner Avenue Factory in downtown Detroit, Michigan, where they built their mega powerful Viper supercar. Due to safety regulations, the machine was about to be decommissioned and its facility going to be mothballed for good. We had just ten days before the lights went out. Sensing that it was an epic story about the end of an era and an iconic supercar, we rang Nat Geo's U.S. division and proposed a doc on the car. They instantly loved the idea. Two days later we had a contract and three days after that we were flying to Michigan. The impending plant closure motivated everyone at the network to jump to action as quickly as possible. The resulting doc was great; however, the film's real lasting benefit was the lesson that a deadline (real or imagined) can be a producer's best friend.

The concept doesn't always work, but it can be a powerful motivational force that helps rally the troops at the network level to get into action. It also clearly articulates that there's an opportunity that's about to vanish, which often gives a project another layer of attraction.

While our Viper sale was FAST, the truth is that most of the time you have to prepare yourself for the lag time involved with network decisions. Some nets do rolling commissions, while others wait for specific timing windows when their budgets open up to start planning their future programming. For example, it took nearly a year after our second *Supercar Superbuild* series aired to go into production on our next Discovery International project *SUV Superbuild.* There's literally no rhyme or reason, and all you can do as a producer is prepare yourself for a lengthy ride. This is why it's absolutely crucial to have multiple projects at various stages of development in the hopper at the same time. You need to think in three-, six-, nine-, and twelve-month timelines.

The Middle Ground – A Development Deal

Every so often there is a land that lies in between the sacred go-ahead greenlight and the all too easy to receive rejection. It's called a **Development Deal**.

This is a vote of confidence in your project voiced by the network but not yet a full commitment. Instead, it's a middle ground that allows you to further test out a concept to see if it merits a greenlight.

A decade ago, development teams regularly commissioned **pilot** episodes as a proof of concepts and then tested them in focus groups. However, as network budgets have tightened and filmmaking tools have gotten more cost-effective, this process has morphed into an easier to read short-form version.

Now many networks empower their development teams to spend small sums to test a handful of concepts throughout the year. In effect they're going to the programming casino and placing small bets on dozens of projects to see which hit and which don't.

For a producer, a development deal can be both a blessing and a curse. The good news is that you receive some funding to help realize your concept a bit further and hopefully gets it "over the line" and into production. The downside is that now the IP is tied to a particular network, and you can't easily sell it elsewhere.

Most factual networks will ask for four basic deliverables when they engage you in a development deal.

- **Revised Treatment:** Typically, this is an easy tweak to your original deck that adds or subtracts network concerns.
- **Budget and Schedule**: Documents detailing the cost and timeline for the series.
- **Series Bible**: This is essentially an operating manual for your series. It's a long-form document that spells out the look and feel of your series, drills down into your main characters, describes storylines, and flushes out the program's structure.
- **Tone Tape:** A modern-day short-form pilot. Instead of filming an entire 44-minute episode, the Tone Tape showcases either a solid first act for your project or in some cases the program's entire narrative arc in just 10 or 15 minutes. The goal is to highlight your story and characters so that network exes can get a clear idea of how the project will feel on screen.

Win, Lose, Next

Making deals and securing funding lies at the heart of the factual producing experience. Money is the sustenance that feeds your programming dreams. Finding it, securing it, and repeatedly accessing it are not easy for the faint of heart.

Former Hollywood movie studio executive Lynda Obst famously once wrote "Win, Lose, Next", and it's awesome advice that has served me well over the years. If a negotiation doesn't go the way you want or someone passes on an idea that you love, give yourself a day to feel the sting and then get over it. Twenty-four hours later it's time to move on and proactively look for new solutions and new opportunities. Dust yourself off, get back up and start trying to sling the rock again.

Wallowing in your own self-pity is counterproductive and a waste of time. You can feel angry, but you can't allow that to supersede your motivation. You must continually fight for yourself and your projects. Even if you have an agent or passionate distributor, no one will ever be as great of an advocate for your project as you are by yourself.

If you get turned down, don't sweat it. Just because one net executive didn't grasp your idea doesn't mean it's terrible. Have a little patience, show some perseverance, and keep fighting the good fight. Projects that die abandon you; however, with the passage of time, you ultimately abandon the failed projects.

Mental toughness and mental health are underappreciated components of the factual producing life. Try not to waste time feeling sorry for yourself or your project's rejection. Instead, embrace the challenge at hand and focus on trying to solve your funding riddle in a new way.

The hardest rejections to swallow are often the projects that get the closest to being greenlit without taking off. We've had dozens of potential projects that battled for a final programming slot only to crash and burn at the very last minute. Sometimes, this is due to the competition; other times, it can be outside forces you can't control. The network might have a hole in their schedule, but the time required to create original content might take too long to fill it. Or perhaps the ad revenue projections they were using turn out to be lower than anticipated. Regardless of why the project doesn't take off, the reality is that the pain of knowing you were *this close* is tough.

The truth is that selling yourself and your ideas is *hard*. There have been multiple times where I thought we were down to one last great idea *only to then have a network pass on it.* Each time I thought we were done and destined to go bust, only to be surprised that something else came along that saved the day. There's no way to predict the future or where the producing road will lead you. It's a long and winding route full of surprises.

Serendipity won't always bail you out; however, it helps to be open-minded enough to see new opportunities as they arise. It'll take you ten years of grinding professionally before you really know what you're doing. Ten years to fully grasp the ebbs and flows of the business, as well as to appreciate the vast amount of information at your disposal. However, once the proverbial lightbulb goes on, you'll feel a boundless sense of energy and a security of knowledge unlike any other.

A lot of people initially view pitching as a zero-sum game – believing that if the network doesn't go for your idea, then it was a wasted venture. However, that's far from true. Every presentation you give, every deck you build, every sizzle reel you cut ultimately helps you get better at the sales process. It also reinforces to the network development teams that you're a creative producer worth remembering down the line. It might take dozens of pitches, but eventually a development execs will move your idea to the top of the pile *because of your persistence.*

Everyone questions themselves or their project after repeated rejections. That's human nature. However long term, your desire to succeed must stay one step ahead of your fear of failure.

> Falling down is not a failure. Failure comes when you stay where you have fallen.
>
> – *Socrates*

Inside the Industry with Babette Perry, Innovative Artists

Babette Perry is a partner at Innovative Artists Talent and Literary Agency where she runs the broadcast/hosting division. She was the head of broadcasting at ICM for many years before leaving to run the west-coast broadcasting division at IMG. She specializes in representing entertainment hosts, news and sports personalities, social media talent, and alternative producers. Perry represents Phil Keoghan (The Amazing Race and Tough as Nails), Rachel Smith (Entertainment Tonight), Lauren Lake (Paternity Court), Ollie Pettigrew and Charity Bailey (Right This Minute), Michaela Pereira (Good Day LA), Garcelle Beauvais (The Real and The Real Housewives of Beverly Hills), Jon Fortt (CNBC), Maureen McCormick (Frozen in Time), along with other celebrities such as David Alan Grier, Scott Wolf, and Bill Bellamy. Babette Perry graduated from UCLA as a communications major.

- **What does an agent do within the factual television and streaming space?**

Agents are talking to all streamers, production companies, networks, and syndicators on a day-to-day basis. Nowadays, it's more of a producer's world, so most shows are packaged before they get sent to the networks which we help put together and pitch.

- **How would you suggest a young producer get their foot into the door in the industry? Any tricks of the trade, so to speak when someone is starting out?**

Working at an agency is one of the best ways to expose yourself to the different areas of the industry. The access to information and connections are invaluable. Internships prior to a job are also crucial to learning any skill.

- **What's the best advice that one of your mentors shared with you that has had the greatest impact on you and/or your career?**

To be fearless. Don't ever feel like you must conform to the ways other people do business. And no bad on news on Friday.

- **How has failure, or apparent failure, helped shape your career?**

I don't believe in failure. People don't fail, but they do make mistakes and certain circumstances may have an impact on people. Adversity, however, has had a great impact on shaping my career. Adversity is crucial to learning about yourself and trusting your ability to persevere. Pushing through the toughest moments in my career has taught me to put more trust in myself than others.

- **What do you think is the best route for an aspiring producer to take if they want to eventually pitch, sell, and produce their own content at the broadcast or streaming level?**

If you want to pitch, sell, produce content, you must have something so authentic and unique that no one else has access to it. Whether it's the talent or format you're bringing to the table, there must be intellectual property when selling projects.

Chapter Six

Selling Your Idea

Contemporary Hollywood often recycles the down on their luck salesperson archetype who repeatedly struggles until inspiration strikes and they catch their big break, which vaults them into the big time overnight. It's a well-worn trope that's not particularly tied to reality. Most successful factual producers got to where they're at the hard way, through incremental advances that slowly hone their skills and build their brand.

It's the small sales built over time that trump the one or two massive wins. In the factual producing game, a high-batting average is greater than a solid slugging percentage. The more you get on base, the more you'll score.

If you can continually put yourself out there and be willing to take a lot of rejection, then you're halfway there. The process is all about momentum. Impress an execs in a small way and you'll land a bigger opportunity to prove your worth. There's no greater feeling than having a network call you up to say that they want to move ahead with your project. It's a powerful moment and one that will infuse you with energy while also healing the wounds of any prior pitch rejection all in one fell swoop.

Up until now, getting your project funded has been your main objective; however, that's not actually the real win. The opportunity that now sits before you is the ultimate victory. The chance to recognize your talents and see that your hard work is paying off by having someone else say *we want you to make this for us*!

Continue to do great work, and more opportunities will come your way. Do it right, and what you're doing today will look nothing like what you're doing in ten years.

Like all transactional exchanges, selling a programming idea to a broadcaster or streamer begins with understanding the different types of deal structures commonly used in the factual industry and determining which one best suits your project.

DOI: 10.4324/9781003292289-6

Budgeting

Before a network development team signs off on your project, they're going to ask how much your idea costs. It's a sure sign that your pitch has taken the next step and the beginning of a tricky dance. Now you need to determine what it actually costs you to make the project happen and how to bury a healthy amount of margin into the budget for yourself. Often, this is where making factual content differs from running a consumer-focused brand.

When you run a business aimed at regular consumers, you're pitching your wares to a retail shop at a wholesale price. The shop buys your product and then puts a healthy margin on top of the wholesale price before they sell it to the general public. If successful, everyone makes a bit of mark-up and pockets profit.

When it comes to factual programming, pricing is more of a theoretical exercise. Very few networks will be completely forthright with what they're willing to spend on a project. Instead, they tend to offer vague ranges with the unwritten understanding that you as the producer will find a way to make the project happen for *their price*. Since every project is different, their budgets don't really relate to each other. It's an apple to oranges comparison. So, it's very difficult to suss out what you can actually charge for each program or series.

At a basic level there are the raw costs involved in the production. On top of that however is the cost of your idea – determining what that is worth is not as easy as breaking down a widget into its three or four components and pricing them out separately. Creativity doesn't work that way. You might have thought of this idea in a flash of brilliance, or you might have been chewing on it off and on for dozens of years. Which is worth more?

Good, Cheap, Fast

There are few hard-and-fast rules to factual program budgeting. Every project and schedule is unique. However, there is a well-worn adage in the film and television industry called the production triangle, and it states, *Your project can be good, fast or cheap, but you can only choose two.*

These days nets and streamers increasingly want it all – a brilliant series turned over expediently for a reasonable CPH. Over the last decade there's been a continual downward pressure on budgets thanks in large part to the democratization of the tools, an

FIGURE 6.1 Good, Fast, Cheap – You Can Only Pick Two.

explosion in the number of people seeking the work, and perhaps most notably the nichification of broadcast networks.

At the same time, the immediacy of online videos has heightened the expectation that you can turn an entire series of six, eight, or ten episodes faster than ever before. This has created entirely new cottage industries and crew roles like Digital Imaging Tech (DITs) or Workflow Consultants. Speed is always of the essence. When you're budgeting you have to keep this in mind while determining how you're going to pull your project off. Planning, communication, and finding efficiency in all facets of your project will be your saving graces. The more time that you can spend pre-planning your creative endeavor, the better your chances of success. If you plan poorly, you leave yourself limited options down the line.

Once you're in the thick of it, typically the only way to solve a problem is to throw money at it. Like a sugar high that jacks you up but quickly fades, solving issues with money might fix the immediate problem but often has long-lasting detrimental effects. Money also doesn't guarantee that an issue gets solved well or to a high standard.

Creativity With Numbers

When filmmakers talk about creativity in the factual space, they tend to focus on the visual or narrative aspects of the job. They're solely focused on the mechanics of how to make a great program or series: what camera to use, what lens is needed, how to craft the appropriate look, and so on. Yet I believe that *creativity with numbers* is just as important of a skill to learn and master in your professional life.

In its simplest form a factual program budget encapsulates all the costs involved with your production from start to finish. It's a numerical road map that explains how you're going to capture your on-screen magic. The sooner that you can learn the ins and outs of how to unlock its hidden potential, the greater you increase your odds of success. After all, factual projects are a business, and businesses run on budgets.

Learning Excel, or a comparable spreadsheet program like Google Sheets or Airtable, inside and out allows you to harness the power of a budget and is a great way to cultivate luck. If you aren't a math person, then you should find a trustworthy business partner who is a spreadsheet wizard. Staying on top of the dollars and sense of a production is crucial to your long-term success. Projects that go over budget rarely get renewed, and broadcast channels are extremely cautious to work with producers who can't control the finances no matter how amazing their ideas turn out to be. Of all the creative aspects involved with factual content creation, budgeting is one of the least appreciated and most hidden in plain-sight secrets to the trade.

It's easy to be a producer when you can spend whatever you want, but it's much harder to get the job done when you have to nip and tuck every area of your budget to make ends meet. Harnessing the latent power hidden inside of a budget turns numbers to your advantage.

Every creative decision you make is really a financial decision, and every financial decision is ultimately a creative one.

It's a simple axiom that holds incredible power and one of the most profound professional insights that I've had on the job. Controlling costs and exploiting the value of small savings in multiple line items have allowed us to create great content with less resources. That in turn translates to needing less initial funding to get a project off the ground. There's a tremendous amount of imagination and inventiveness involved in crafting a budget. The sooner you master the skill, the longer your creative runway will become as you squeeze every ounce of possibility out of your funding.

Budgets also reflect your values; if you're an image first producer, you'll dedicate more funds to capturing pictures. However, if you believe in story, you might well spend more time, and therefore money, on research or pre-interviewing.

A well-built budget is also a terrific signifier of your knowledge for the process of factual production and producing, as well as the project itself. The better you know the story, the better you'll build your final budget.

Two Ways to Budget

Generally, there are two methods for budgeting in the factual industry.

Budgeting to a Schedule: A great budget starts with a well-thought-out schedule. You begin by broadly scoping out the total amount of time that you'll need to research, film, and put together your project. Once you've got a broad outline of the required time commitment, you can drill down into more granular details like how many filming days you'll need, how big of a crew you'll need, what the crew's day or weekly rates are, or how many hotel rooms you'll need to support the crew. When you finish this process, you'll arrive at your *total ideal production budget cost*. This is your perfect world scenario and the budget that lets you film exactly the special or series you have in mind.

Budgeted to a Number: Ideally, every network would ask their producers to budget to their ideal schedule and then they'd agree to pay for it no questions asked! Unfortunately, that's not always how it works, nor is it the only way to get the job done. In fact, it's increasingly common for a network or streamer to come right out and state the range they're willing to spend on a potential project. In these instances, you'll have to reverse-engineer your budget and schedule from the proposed total amount of funding and see how close you can get to your idealized plan.

Crafting a Preliminary Schedule

Generally, when I build a schedule, I set out to answer three broad questions.

- How much time does the project require to set up? (pre-production)
- How long will the project take to film? (field production)
- How much writing and editing is required to put it all together? (post-production)

You can easily map out a basic schedule on a piece of paper; however, it tends to go a whole lot smoother inside of a spreadsheet or Gantt chart program.

When I start a schedule, I generally like to lay out the number of episodes across the top and the number of weeks top to bottom in order to really visualize a project's specific needs. Then I dedicate each week to one broad task ranging from research or pre-production to filming or editing. At this stage I don't want to be too prescriptive with the work at micro-level or drill down too far into daily tasks; rather, the aim here is to gain a 30,000 foot overview for the entire scope of work. You know your starting point and you know your destination. This is the route to get from one to the other, and to budget properly you have to know how long the various phases of the project will take. A simple weekly plan typically answers those questions rather quickly.

You'll notice on the schedule in Figure 6.2 that many of the tasks are stair-stepped – this is a visual way to guarantee that no one on your team is double booked during the project.

Week #	Week	Episode 1	Episode 2	Episode 3	Episode 4	Episode 5	Episode 6	Episode 7	Episode 8	Episode 9	Episode 10	Episode 11	Episode 12
Week 06	2/3/14	Production Start Up											
Week 07	2/10/14	Production Start Up											
Week 08	2/17/14	Production Start Up											
Week 09	2/24/14	Production Start Up											
Week 10	3/3/14	Development (Story Outline)	Development (Story Outline)	Development (Story Outline)									
Week 11	3/10/14	Pre-Production	Pre-Production	Pre-Production									
Week 12	3/17/14	Pre-Production	Pre-Production	Pre-Production									
Week 13	3/24/14	Pre-Production	Pre-Production	Pre-Production									
Week 14	3/31/14	Shooting Script Writing	Shooting Script Writing	Shooting Script Writing									
Week 15	4/7/14	Script Writing	Script Writing	Script Writing									
Week 16	4/14/14	FLEX WEEK	FLEX WEEK	FLEX WEEK									
Week 17	4/21/14	INTERVIEWS	INTERVIEWS	INTERVIEWS									
Week 18	4/28/14	RECREATIONS	RECREATIONS	RECREATIONS	Development (Story Outline)								
Week 19	5/5/14	Transcription / Ingest			Pre-Production	Development (Story Outline)							
Week 20	5/12/14	Script Writing	Transcription / Ingest		Pre-Production	Pre-Production	Development (Story Outline)						
Week 21	5/19/14	Rough Cut - Week 1	Script Writing	Transcription / Ingest	Shooting Script Writing	Pre-Production	Pre-Production						
Week 22	5/26/14	Rough Cut - Week 2	Rough Cut - Week 1		Script Writing	Shooting Script Writing	Pre-Production	Development (Story Outline)					
Week 23	6/2/14	RC Review	Rough Cut - Week 2			Script Writing	Shooting Script Writing	Pre-Production	Development (Story Outline)				
Week 24	6/9/14	Rough Cut - Week 3	RC Review				Script Writing	Pre-Production	Pre-Production	Development (Story Outline)			
Week 25	6/16/14	RC #2 Review	Rough Cut - Week 3	Script Writing				Shooting Script Writing	Pre-Production	Pre-Production	Development (Story Outline)		
Week 26	6/23/14	Fine Cut	RC #2 Review	Rough Cut - Week 1				Script Writing	Shooting Script Writing	Pre-Production	Pre-Production	Development (Story Outline)	
Week 27	6/30/14	Final Notes	Fine Cut	Rough Cut - Week 2	PREP WEEK	PREP WEEK	PREP WEEK		Script Writing	Shooting Script Writing	Pre-Production	Pre-Production	Development (Story Outline)
Week 28	7/7/14	Annotation	Final Notes	RC Review	INTERVIEWS	INTERVIEWS	INTERVIEWS			Script Writing	Shooting Script Writing	Pre-Production	Pre-Production
Week 29	7/14/14		Annotation	Fine Cut	RECREATIONS	RECREATIONS	RECREATIONS				Script Writing	Shooting Script Writing	Pre-Production
Week 30	7/21/14			Final Notes	Transcription / Ingest			INTERVIEWS	INTERVIEWS	INTERVIEWS		Script Writing	Shooting Script Writing
Week 31	7/28/14			Annotation	Script Writing	Transcription / Ingest		RECREATIONS	RECREATIONS	RECREATIONS			Script Writing
Week 32	8/4/14	Narration	Narration	Narration	Rough Cut - Week 1	Script Writing	Transcription / Ingest				INTERVIEWS	INTERVIEWS	INTERVIEWS
Week 33	8/11/14	Audio Mix / Layback	Audio Mix / Layback	Audio Mix / Layback	Rough Cut - Week 2	Rough Cut - Week 1	Script Writing	Transcription / Ingest			RECREATIONS	RECREATIONS	RECREATIONS
Week 34	8/18/14	Delivery	Delivery	Delivery	RC Review	Rough Cut - Week 2	Rough Cut - Week 1	Script Writing	Transcription / Ingest				
Week 35	8/25/14				Fine Cut	RC Review	Rough Cut - Week 2	Rough Cut - Week 1	Script Writing	Transcription / Ingest			
Week 36	9/1/14				Final Notes	Fine Cut	RC Review	Rough Cut - Week 2	Rough Cut - Week 1	Script Writing	Transcription / Ingest		
Week 37	9/8/14				Annotation	Final Notes	Fine Cut	RC Review	Rough Cut - Week 2	Rough Cut - Week 1	Script Writing	Transcription / Ingest	
Week 38	9/15/14					Annotation	Final Notes	Fine Cut	RC Review	Rough Cut - Week 2	Rough Cut - Week 1	Script Writing	Transcription / Ingest
Week 39	9/22/14						Annotation	Final Notes	Fine Cut	RC Review	Rough Cut - Week 2	Rough Cut - Week 1	Script Writing
Week 40	9/29/14				Narration	Narration	Narration	Annotation	Final Notes	Fine Cut	RC Review	Rough Cut - Week 2	Rough Cut - Week 1
Week 41	10/6/14				Audio Mix / Layback	Audio Mix / Layback	Audio Mix / Layback		Annotation	Final Notes	Fine Cut	RC Review	Rough Cut - Week 2
Week 42	10/13/14				Delivery	Delivery	Delivery			Annotation	Final Notes	Fine Cut	RC Review

FIGURE 6.2 A Proposed Delivery Schedule for a 12-Part Series.

As surprising as it sounds, a lot of factual television budgeting is simply educated guessing. Once you have a broad overview, you can start counting days or weeks and plugging those numbers into your preliminary budget.

Budget Assumptions

When a network asks for an initial budget, they'll also tend to ask you to answer a set of broad project assumptions. This can include any of the following bits of info.

- How many episodes versus minutes?
- Total budget versus per EP budget
- Production fee (%)
- Total number of weeks budgeted (from pre-production to final delivery)
- Format the series is being filmed in/cameras being used
- Delivery format
- Staff configuration
- How many shooting days (mix of days; recreation versus interview, etc.)?
- How many offline editing weeks?
- How many online days?
- How many audio mixing days?
- What kind of audio mix? (Stereo/5.1 Surround)
- How many minutes of animation or CGI?
- How many minutes of stock footage?
- How many minutes of up-rezzed SD footage?
- Original music or library music?
- Where will the shooting take place?

The network uses the answers to these questions to gauge whether your proposed budget is realistic or not. You want to ensure that all the numbers you call out are shown in the corresponding budget and schedule. For instance, if you state that you're going to need ten weeks of assistant editing work in the budget assumptions, it's important that the numbers match your budget totals and scheduling.

Over time as you build budgets for different projects and work with the same talent, crew, or vendors repeatedly, it gets easier to produce ballpark estimates on the fly. You intuitively learn how long it takes to do certain tasks and what they will cost. At this point, we've done enough European-based shoots that I can generally plug in some rough air travel, equipment shipping, and lodging numbers right off the bat and get pretty close to the final totals.

It's worth noting that every network has their own budgetary hot button issues. Some will place a hard cap on how much you can charge for certain items. So, Nat Geo might unilaterally state that an executive producer can't draw a salary greater than 5% of the total overall budget, while Discovery might have a fixed amount that they'll spend on in-show graphics.

Some networks also have pre-negotiated deals already in place for specific repeatable vendors like music, title search, production insurance or stock footage houses. Whenever you start a new project with a broadcaster or streamer, it's a good idea to ask if they have any prearranged discounts already in place.

Building Your Budget

A factual broadcast budget contains several different elements.

The Topsheet: This is a one-pager overview of the entire production that usually includes assumptions, broad category costs, and the total funding required for your project. This is the *financial high concept* for the project. You want to ensure that you display the entire funding story in an easy-to-read manner that clearly spells out the production's fiscal requirements.

Detailed Budget Breakdown: The devil is in the details, and nowhere is that truer than a factual program or series budget. The detailed budget spells out exactly where the money goes inside of each broad category and drills down in each subcategory, or *line item*. For instance, while your top sheet might state that the field crew is going to cost $100,000 for the shoot, on the detailed budget page you'll break that spend out into its specific components with specific line items for the field producer, the director of photography, a 2nd camera person, or sound operator.

Networks Crunch Numbers Differently

Networks and streamers need content, yet they're always trying to get the best programming at the lowest cost. The less they spend per project, the greater they can stretch their budget or the more money they can spend on their tentpole programs. In a broadcaster's perfect world, they'll greenlight an inexpensive production that turns out to be a hit which allows their ad sales team to sell the commercial time at a premium. Always remember that they're spending money to *make more money*.

Even though the networks and streamers act like a business, a lot of times they'll treat your production like a nonprofit. They'll scrutinize every line item and look for ways to repeatedly squeeze a producer to take even less. Crafty producers will find elegant ways to pad their budgets to ensure that their projects maintain a healthy margin. Remember that there's no budget line for *profit*. You must build that in yourself.

If a network does object to one of your line items, instead of getting defensive you want to counter their concern with a sound rationale based in fact and logic. In the end money rules all decision-making, and your job as a producer is to try work within the broadcaster's financial framework while ensuring that you can make a profit.

Right Tool for the Right Job

At its core a budget serves as a road map for the factual-program-making process. It's a numerical way to describe how you plan on capturing the magic on screen. However, not every series or project needs a sophisticated budgeting solution.

Some producers use Quicken to manage their projects, while others utilize more industry-specific tools like Movie Magic's Budgeting program. Personally, I've never found off-the-shelf solutions a great fit for our projects.

Several years ago, out of frustration, I simply built my own budgeting template in Excel. It's bespoke to our projects, endlessly customizable, and a document whose under-hood mechanics I understand fully.

At the time I was struggling to find a budgeting tool that could help us create the initial budget for the network *and* also connect to our production's checking register. Without one document that combined these two elements, it was too easy to overspend without realizing it and hard to know where we were under budget without endless calculations. I was looking for an end-to-end solution that was always up to date.

The first page of our budget workbook features a typical line-item layout; however, all the "actuals" categories are directly connected to a basic checking register on the second page of the workbook that's categorized by a dropdown menu built from our initial budget's line items. Now, every dollar that gets spent is immediately attributed to a defined section of the budget. When we pay an employee or vendor, the total is

								1/3/19	
CHP	Cry Havoc Productions, Inc. SUPERCAR SERIES							Approved	
		Unit		Amount	Rate	TOTAL	CATEGORY TOTAL	ACTUALS	REMAINING
	Employees								
Line Item	Above The Line								
1001	Executive Producer	1	Flat	1	$ 16,000.00	$ 16,000.00		$ -	$ 16,000.00
1002	Series Producer	6	Eps	1	$ 20,000.00	$ 120,000.00		$ 80,000.00	$ 40,000.00
1003	Associate Producer	8	Months	1	$ 4,000.00	$ 32,000.00		$ 32,000.00	$ -
1004	Writer	6	Eps	1	$ 2,500.00	$ 15,000.00		$ 15,000.00	$ -
1005	Annotation	6	Eps	1	$ 1,500.00	$ 9,000.00		$ 9,000.00	$ -
							$ 192,000.00		
	Post Production								
2001	Lead Editor	14	Weeks	1	$ 1,500.00	$ 21,000.00		$ 10,415.00	
2002	Lead Editor 2	14	Weeks	1	$ 1,500.00	$ 21,000.00		$ 10,512.50	
2003	Assistant Editor 1	21	Weeks	1	$ 750.00	$ 15,750.00		$ 11,370.00	
2004	Assistant Editor 2	21	Weeks	1	$ 750.00	$ 15,750.00		$ 13,093.19	
2005	Script Annotator	6	Eps	1	$ 300.00	$ 1,800.00		$ 1,800.00	$ -
							$ 75,300.00		
	Field Crew								
4001	Camera Operator 1	6	Weeks	1	$ 3,000.00	$ 18,000.00		$ 18,000.00	$ -
4002	Camera Operator 2	6	Weeks	1	$ 2,500.00	$ 15,000.00		$ 18,000.00	
4003	Camera Operator 3	6	Weeks	1	$ 2,000.00	$ 12,000.00		$ 13,400.00	
							$ 45,000.00		
	Field Crew - Track/Action								
5002	Camera Operator 1	2	Days	1	$ 500.00	$ 1,000.00		$ 2,500.00	
5003	Camera Operator 2	2	Days	1	$ 400.00	$ 800.00		$ 1,500.00	
5004	Camera Operator 3	2	Days	1	$ 300.00	$ 600.00		$ 900.00	
5005	Extra Shooter - Track	2	Days	1	$ 200.00	$ 400.00		$ 450.00	
5006	DIT - Track	2	Days	1	$ 200.00	$ 400.00		$ 500.00	
							$ 3,200.00		
	Withholdings								
3001	Employee Tax		12%			$ 37,812.00		$ 26,976.00	$ 10,836.00
							$ 37,812.00		
	LOGISTICS								
6001	Equipment Shipping - Transatlantic	2	Moves	1	$ 4,000.00	$ 8,000.00		$ 5,645.50	
6002	Equipment Shipping - Country to Country	5	Moves	1	$ 2,000.00	$ 10,000.00		$ 7,645.00	
6002	Shipping - Carnet	1	Allow	1	$ 1,750.00	$ 1,750.00		$ 1,750.00	
6003	Airline - International	4	Flights	1	$ 1,800.00	$ 7,200.00		$ 4,096.05	
6004	Airline - Country to Country	4	Flights	3	$ 500.00	$ 6,000.00		$ 2,133.02	
6005	Hotels - Brand 1	4	Nights	7	$ 275.00	$ 7,700.00		$ 5,433.31	
6006	Hotels - Brand 2	4	Nights	7	$ 275.00	$ 7,700.00		$ 4,426.97	
6007	Hotels - Brand 3	4	Nights	7	$ 275.00	$ 7,700.00		$ 5,428.57	
6008	Hotels - Brand 4	4	Nights	7	$ 275.00	$ 7,700.00		$ 5,295.20	
6009	Hotels - Brand 5	4	Nights	7	$ 275.00	$ 7,700.00		$ 8,398.94	
6010	Hotels - Brand 6	4	Nights	7	$ 275.00	$ 7,700.00		$ 6,545.13	
6011	Per diem	4	Allow	42	$ 60.00	$ 10,080.00		$ 10,801.27	
6012	Rental Vehicles (1 x Car, 1 x Van)	6	Rental	2	$ 1,250.00	$ 15,000.00		$ 3,307.65	
6013	Gas, Parking, Misc. Travel Exp.	6	Week	2	$ 115.00	$ 1,380.00		$ 1,609.28	
6014	Expendables	6	Week	2	$ 115.00	$ 1,380.00		$ 718.55	
6015	Equipment Rentals	7	Week	2	$ 7,500.00	$ 105,000.00		$ 100,000.00	
							$ 105,610.00		

FIGURE 6.3 A Sample Budget.

automatically updated in the actual's column of the budget. The document then takes the "actuals" totals, compares them to the budgeted totals, and outputs a remaining total. The goal is to always know where every budget line item stands in real time.

The actuals column is also color coded with conditional formatting. It compares the numbers and changes their colors to represent different situations; the red represents a line item that's over budget, green is a category that's well under budget, and any number highlighted in yellow is getting close to hitting its budget cap but hasn't exceeded it yet. With a quick glance you know exactly where the budget sits.

I'm not suggesting that this workflow is the best of breed; rather, what is important is that you need to find the budgeting system that works for you. Like everything else in factual filmmaking, there's no one way to do it.

It doesn't matter what you use to budget and keep track of the spend; what does is that you understand how to manipulate it with no errors. You don't want to submit a budget and then find out months later that it didn't include one of your category subtotals. That's a recipe for financial disaster.

Put the $ Into the Show

It's not uncommon to have two different budgets on a project: the one for the network and the "real" budget that you use to make the program or series happen. There are some producers out there who take advantage of the duality. They horde the funds, cut corners, and spend as little as possible so that they can keep the majority of the budget for themselves. Personally, I'm a big proponent of doing whatever is in my power to put as much money as I can on the screen.

Philosophically, I believe that the better the show looks and sounds, and eventually turns out, the better my odds are of landing more work down the road. I'm not suggesting that you work for free – *everyone needs to make a living.* Rather I'm suggesting that within reason you always try to spend a little bit extra to make the project sing as best you can. Sometimes, this pays immediate dividends. Someone at the network sees the project and asks you to produce something else. Other times it might take a few years until the work is seen and that little bit of extra magic makes a buyer think, 'I want to work with this person!".

The quality of our work has helped. We've successfully jumped from one area or division inside of Discovery or Nat Geo to another based on the reputation of the product.

Inside the Industry With Marjolaine Souquet, National Geographic Channel

Marjolaine Souquet is Senior Director of Regional Production Management for the National Geographic Channel.

- **What advice would you give to a smart film school student entering the "real world" who wants to produce their own content for a network like Nat Geo?**

My advice to a student who wants to become a producer is to go and work on films and get experience at all stages of production, in the field, in the edit, but also in the office where projects are developed, brainstormed, and prepared to be presented to a Network. It is unlikely that a Network will entrust a special or a series to a young producer without much experience, even if s/he brings the most amazing idea, so a better option might be to associate with an already established production company. Working as a production coordinator can be the path to producing!

Once you have an idea to pitch, it is important to do your homework and know the Network you are pitching to. Watch the programs that air in the Network, get a sense of the brand, what it stands for, the type of shows it commissions. Attend markets such as Real Screen, Sheffield, Sunny Side of the Doc, or MIP or any networking event where the Network's representatives are present.

- **Tell us about production management: Is there an easy way to describe what the PM team does on a factual program or series?**

The responsibilities of a network production manager or line producer differ quite a lot from those of a Production Manager (PM) or Line Producer (LP) on a production. We don't hire crew, rent equipment, or prepare contracts.

Our job is to bring the program on time and on budget and in accordance with the Network's editorial and technical requirements. It is also to protect the Network's liability, brand, and assets by working closely with production partners to apply best in-class standards and practices at all stages of production, from development to final payment.

We work closely with all stakeholders, internally (including the programming and creative team, business affairs, legal, research, finance, and operations) and externally – that is, our production partners, to ensure that all parameters for the program are set, communicated, and implemented.

We are the interface between the production partner and the Network, tracking, filing, and distributing all the materials needed to promote, air, and exploit the program in its full capacity.

Our role is akin to risk management and comptrollership for the production, but, more importantly, we are the eyes and ears of the production and can be true advocates for the project when challenges or obstacles arise. Our production management team all have years of experience in production and will brainstorm with the production partner and the editorial team at the Network to find solutions and mitigate risks.

- **Can you help shed some light on what exactly you're looking for in a producer that's working with the network for the first time?**

Aside from a creative vision of course, what we look for in our production partners is a demonstrated experience in the production business, full collaboration, clear communication, and a certain adaptability to working with a major international Network. What we look for is a partner whom we can trust to deliver the program we commissioned, on time and on budget.

Because, in most cases, we fully commission programs for which we own the IP, we have a lot of requirements. Beyond the ability to deliver a great product, we also need the producer to deliver 60+ materials, which range from physical assets to promotional and marketing elements and related paperwork. This requires a full and well-organized team on the production side.

- **When you initially ask a producer for a budget, what are you looking for exactly? (Any "best practices" worth sharing, pet peeves, usual stumbling blocks?)**

My first task on a new project is to review, together, the treatment, budget, and schedule in the context of the parameters set forth by the Network. It is from the editorial, dates, and numbers that I will evaluate the feasibility and set-up of the project.

In terms of best practices, there are a few things that help reduce the back and forth with the Network:

- Request the Network's requirements. Each Network has a specific set of requirements related to the editorial, schedule (review time for each cut), insurance (liability limits), technical (shoot and delivery format), and so on.
- Provide budget assumptions that outline the parameters of the project and provide context to the dates and numbers.
- Transparency – I do not sit with the producer when they are doing the budget, so it needs to include clear and detailed calculations rather than allowances.
- Flexibility – a healthy budget for a factual program includes flexibility at all stages of the production, room for the unexpected.

My main pet peeve are budgets that are prepared too fast and before a treatment has been approved. They typically only include allowances rather than detailed calculations, are often unrealistic, and end up delaying the review process.

- **When you were initially starting out, what was the best piece of advice that one of your mentors shared that has had the greatest impact on you and/or your career?**

I have received a lot a great advice throughout my career, and, despite having been in this line of work for over 25 years, I am always opened to learning more, not just from the people who have more experience, but, as importantly, from the ones who are coming up and may have a different, a new way to look at things.

When I started, I was lucky to work with people who didn't think "impossible" was a word in the dictionary. They pushed me beyond what I thought I could do, they taught me that there is always another way to look at a problem, that there is always a solution. They also taught me that nothing should be done in a vacuum and that, sometimes, you have to step back to look at the cards in front of you to rearrange them to find a way through.

The other piece of advice I received which is constantly with me is "it's only TV!". This is an entertainment business, and our job is to produce good and interesting programs to allow our audience to explore the world and its people from their couch. We are not changing or saving the world, only helping people to know more about it. It's important to remember when dealing with people in general, in the office, on the phone, or in the field.

- **What is the best investment in yourself that you've ever made?**

Learning to trust my instinct, find and listen to my inner voice, and keep a cool head! To survive in this business, it is important to have perspective. It's only television after all!

Accepting that not everything can or should be solved right away. Most production managers have type A personalities and want to solve and control the situation. Working as I do with different cultures and with people who do most of their business in a language that is not their native language – as is my case since English is my second language – you learn to accept a certain amount of chaos, to respect the fact that there are different ways of working, and to listen to people with the intent of understanding the meaning behind the words.

Maybe more importantly, I have learned to surround myself with people who are not only good at their jobs but who also care about working together, sharing, learning, supporting each other.

Negotiating the Deal

Once a network or streamer decides to move ahead with your project, or *greenlight* the project, it's time to roll up your sleeves and start working out the deal terms.

The key is to remember that everything is negotiable.

Up until now you've only interfaced with the development team. However, once the decision is made to go ahead with the project, you'll be handed off to a network lawyer.

Generally, lawyers act like their deal terms are iron-clad and inviolable, but that's not entirely true. It's the network's lawyer's job to get the best deal for their client (i.e., the network); however, *their first offer is seldom their best offer.* They know that there's give and take involved in the process.

During the initial development conversations, most network development exes will ask about the project's CPH because it directly impacts their operational budget. After you've sent in your initial budget, the broad strokes of the deal start to set in place. So, by the time you start talking with the legal team, the general fiscal parameters have already been sorted out; however, there are several ways to extract *more value* that doesn't "cost" a network today. Usually, the current network team is much less sensitive to deal points that don't directly affect them or their immediate budget constraints. It makes great sense given that the current network team is being judged on the ratings for the programs that they commission, not what happens five or ten years out.

There have only been a few network teams that I've worked for that have the foresight to not only think about current ratings needs but also future potential content requirements. So, while I might not ask for the moon financially with regard to the CPH, I often try to make alternative asks that can be easier for the network team to agree to instead. This can run the gamut from who owns the original field material and source footage to reduced insurance requirements or a reduced deal term length.

Repeat after me, *everything is negotiable.*

Price and Terms

Every deal has two key aspects – the price and the terms.

Price: The price is the total CPH or full budget divided by the number of episodes if it's a series. This is the hard money that the network is going to send out the door that allows you to turn the project into reality.

Terms: The terms are all the deal points involved in the contract besides cost.

Most producers only focus on what the overall deal is worth in terms of dollar signs, yet the deal structure and clauses can often be equally or more rewarding.

As the expression goes, "you can have your price and the network's terms or the network's price and your terms, but you can't have both".

Project cash flow is one of the most important deal points. Great cash flow is a producer's best friend and makes nearly anything possible. Bad cash flow on the other hand can completely hamstring you and potentially even doom your project to failure.

A typical network budget will include a payment schedule based on *project milestones* or events that trigger payments. This usually includes the contract's execution (signature payment), the start of principal photography, the delivery of a rough cut, the delivery of a fine cut, and final delivery. When you hit each milestone, more funds are released to you. Where cash flow can really trip you up is when you're on a fast turnaround project for a notoriously slow-paying network. Often in this situation, you're completing milestones quicker than payments are being made, which often puts a production in a cash flow bind. So, it generally behooves a producer to front load the payment terms as much as they can to ensure that they're always staying cash flow positive.

Here is a sample project milestone payment schedule.

Payment Schedule Budget		
Total Amount of Budget to Cash Flowed for Fast Factories ***$278,757.40*** *on a five (5) payment schedule:*		
1)	*$89,202.37 (32%)*	*Upon execution of the Agreement, proof of Insurance Certificates, approved Budget, approved Shooting Outline, proof of Segregated Bank Account and receipt of original invoice.*
2)	*$55,751.48 (20%)*	*Upon commencement of principal photography, receipt of monthly cost report and receipt of original invoice.*
3)	*$78,052.07 (28%)*	*Upon networks' acceptance of the Rough Cut, receipt of monthly cost report and receipt of original invoice.*
4)	*$27,875.74 (10%)*	*Upon networks' acceptance of the Fine Cut, upon networks' acceptance of the Picture Lock, receipt of monthly cost report, receipt of original invoice.*
5)	*$27,875.47 (10%)*	*Upon networks' acceptance of the final, technically acceptable Program conforming to the Technical Specifications as outlined in Exhibit C plus all program Deliverables as outlined in Exhibit C, receipt of monthly cost report and receipt of original invoice, and upon networks' acceptance of all final paper deliverables including all completed Legal Rights and Clearance information as specified in the Binder and final cost report.*

Nets will try to move as much money as they can to the end of the project. This mitigates the network's risk and ensures that enterprising hustlers can't go to Vegas the production funds and bet it all on black.

Producers who have cash on hand can get their hustle on and try to negotiate better deals with vendors or crew. The faster you can pay people, the better rate you can usually secure. Paying Net-10 or Net-15 or day off can save you 10–20%. It might sound like a small savings, but *little bits of money add up fast.*

An additional positive benefit of paying people quickly is the boon to your production company reputation. A lot of production companies are notorious for paying Net-45 or even Net-90, and crews usually *hate* working for them. Do the opposite, and you'll reap the rewards well into the future.

Other deal terms worth thinking about during your negotiation.

Territory Rights: Generally, in the United States on a fully commissioned project the network or service takes all territorial rights. Typical stateside deals are essentially a full buy out of your intellectual property, or IP.

In other countries this can vary greatly due to their country-specific IP laws. In particular in the UK and former British territories, production companies usually keep their IP.

One of the most powerful asks that you can make as a producer is to seek the right to keep outside territories and monetize those regions in the future. Using this model, you sell the project to a funding network in one specific region and keep the territorial rights to the rest of the world, where you resell the finished film or series later on for additional monies. For decades a lot of factual industry deals were done this way; however, as the world becomes increasingly global thanks to the advent of streaming services, a lot of global or pan-regional nets are now insisting that they keep as many rights and territories as possible for their future streaming platforms.

However, never forget that *it's all negotiable, all the time.*

While trying to keep broadcast rights beyond the region, initially funding your project sounds simple; it's actually a very tricky proposition. It's a big world with a lot of tricky territorial lines drawn on the map, and it takes time to learn the game. For example, French rights usually require Northern African broadcasting rights too, while some U.S. nets need the Caribbean carriage rights because their broadcast feed spills into the U.S. Virgin Islands. I'd strongly encourage anyone who wants to go down this road to connect with a factual program distributor. They'll help you sort out the intricacies of territory sales and how best to unlock future profit.

Deal Length: Generally, in a full-commission project the network buys out your rights to the project *in perpetuity*. However, in a co-production model, where different networks come together to fund a project you can often not only retain your IP but also *license* the project to each participating network for a set term. This means that the initial distribution window, or *1st window*, gets structured based on a specific number of years. At the end of that term, the project rights will revert to the producer. When that happens, you can then re-license the project to the original broadcaster *or* sell it to a different network in the same region for a second run, or *2nd window*.

Showings: Some producers can negotiate a specific number of showings for each finished program. For instance, a broadcaster might only be able to air a factual film ten times over a four-year period. Capping the amount of viewings can help make it easier to sell the finished project in its 2nd window run because a new network might feel it's still relatively unknown or unseen. A decade ago, pre-streaming, this was a powerful ask. Today, it's a bit less relevant given the nature of always-available content on streaming platforms.

Platforms: Today, nearly every network is attempting to jump into the streaming service fray; however, not every linear network's financial future is tied to online or streaming viewership. If you're dealing with a linear network that has no online or streaming component, you might well be able to carve out Video-on-Demand (VOD), SVOD, or AVOD rights for future sale.

Merchandising: Not every factual TV show or series lends itself to merchandising, but some certainly do. The rights to sell swag can add up quickly if you're able to keep those rights. Think about how many T-shirts *Orange County Choppers* sold thanks to their hit series *American Chopper*. It's been said that the Tuttle family made more from T-shirts than motorcycles or TV!

Home Entertainment Rights: Home entertainment rights aren't as valuable as they once were; however, some producers still make a good living off discount DVD box set sales at big box retainers. This tends to work best for producers with extremely high-volume projects.

Inflight Rights: Another potential profit center is the right to sell your finished production directly to commercial airlines for their inflight entertainment services. As the travel industry grows, the need for fresh content continues to increase. When airline customers are flying halfway around the world, they need fresh content to watch to keep them entertained. Why not profit from this continually expanding content opportunity?

Non-theatrical Showings: Non-theatrical showings are a grab bag of different monetization opportunities, such as licensing a film to an education organization for in-class showings. This is a sweet spot for factual films if they're slanted toward knowledge-based entertainment and have a high level of take-away information.

The Raw Footage: Perhaps one of the most interesting deal terms these days is ownership of the raw field production footage. With the advent of YouTube and other online distribution platforms, there's an increasing ability for producers to monetize their content in new ways by cutting together reel ends, leftover footage, or segments that don't make the final cut.

A Fair Price for a Fair Project

Right or wrong, I've always taken the approach that a fairly budgeted project leads to a better network relationship and more work later on down the road. I'm a big believer that being equitable in a financial negotiation pays off in hidden ways in the future. Perhaps you get known within a network for striking a fair and easy deal or maybe less haggling encourages the legal department to give you better terms. I've never wanted to be known as a price gouger or pain in the ass haggler who's only in it for the money. After all, I got into this game first and foremost to make great content.

Other producers might very well disagree, since nets monetize your work in any number of ways. However, I try to take the long view. It's not a zero-sum game in my book. I want the buyer to think to themselves, "This is an outstanding project at a reasonable price point that I can show to my bosses as an example of stretching our bottom line".

This makes them look good to their superior and hopefully reinforces your cost-conscious abilities while planting a seed for the next project or negotiation. A fairly budgeted project is just the first step, however. You also need to decide what kind of deal structure makes the most sense for both parties, and there are some very different ways to do that.

Types of Deals

Being a successful producer doesn't always come down to having the best ideas or best programs – it comes down to landing the most deals. . . . And there are a number of different ways to structure a deal in the factual industry.

Full Commission

This is the most common and biggest financial type of deal in the United States. A **Full Commission** is when a network pays the entire production budget for a project or series and in exchange typically takes ownership of all rights, including intellectual property (IP) rights. Fully commissioned projects tend to take the longest to get off the ground and almost always are shepherded through the development process by the commissioning team.

- **Pros**
  - Most lucrative initial financial path
  - Larger budgets, more promotion, greater potential for additional seasons because the network is *invested* in the project
  - You can afford larger crews, better kit, and have more resources at your disposal
- **Cons**
  - More pressure
  - More network oversight
  - Network takes all rights
  - No IP ownership

Co-production

The easiest path forward for many productions is a **Co-production**. This is a type of deal where more than one network or parties agree to support and fund a project together. A co-pro can take place between multiple networks, a network and a distributor, or a network and a production company. While the players might change, the result is the same; two or more entities agree to mutually invest in a project and share the rights to it.

Typically, in a co-pro, one network will take the editorial lead when it comes to notes, suggestions, and creative choices. Usually, this is the network or entity that puts in the highest contribution to the overall budget. As strange as it sounds there are some networks that don't want to take an editorial lead. They've built their business model on partnering with bigger nets and leveraging the other channel's ability to develop content.

One of the dangers of a co-pro is that each relevant party might want a different version of the same project. This can be as easy as mastering two different program masters with two different narrators, or as complex as requiring the delivery of a 44-minute cut for one market and 50-minute cut for another.

Historically, American networks have been loath to co-pro. They want to fully commission their projects in order to own all the rights and IP so that they can build a massive content library and monetize it long into the future. When you hear people say that *content is king*, this is what they mean. The more content you own, the more you can leverage it globally over the long tail of time. However, as streaming services have gained market share and advertising revenue has declined, more U.S. nets have looked to the co-pro market to maximize their content spend. It's an easy way to maintain the same number of debut hours at half the cost. Often, they'll relinquish all editorial control and agree to limited term deals in exchange for a steady supply of acquired content.

- **Pros**
  - Since the funding is split, there's a good chance for you to retain ownership of the IP rights (or IP)
  - Potential to have the program's rights revert to you after the initial licensing term expires, potentially allowing you to relicense or resell your old programs or series in 2nd window
- **Cons**
  - Less up-front funding monies
  - Potential for multiple final deliveries
  - Owning the IP and relicensing the production works best for timeless or *evergreen* content. Anything that's too topical will lose its value by the time that you gain your rights back.

Co-production Confusion: The term "co-production" holds multiple meanings. It's primarily a funding model; however, it's also a way to describe when two or more production entities join forces to pitch and produce a project. When that happens, it's often a small indie producer who originates an idea and then takes it to a larger production company, which has more muscle in the marketplace. The larger production company will run the production and typically handle all monies. The indie producer will usually receive a split of the production fee and a line item in the budget for creating the series (aka the created by credit). If the producer from the smaller production company does any real work on the project, they'll also earn a second budgetary line item as a producer on the project. There are plenty of producers who make a solid living coming up with ideas but never actually make the finished content themselves. Their entire business model revolves around partnering with larger production companies and effectively selling them ideas that they then in turn go sell to networks.

Acquisitions and Pre-sales

Generally, most co-productions don't go through the main development team but rather are submitted and negotiated with the **Acquisitions Department**. They're an offshoot of the commissioning team that aims to buy content that can support the commissioning team's fully funded original projects. Typically, an acquisition team's goal is to fill the voids between major tentpole projects with cost-effective higher-volume programs or series. Acquisition buyers look for both finished content and *pre-sales*, which are budget-friendly projects looking for seed money investments to get off the ground. In a pre-sale scenario, a producer or producer with a distributor's help will aim to get just enough networks engaged in an idea so that they can raise the capital to get the project into production while retaining as many rights as possible for future sales. If a fully commissioned project is a producer's holy grail (and top dollar funding option!), then the acquisition route is the hidden way to salvation.

Top-Off Funding

An offshoot of the co-pro model is **Top-Off Funding**. This describes a last-minute additional co-production partner who jumps in at the very last moment to provide the final bit of financing required to get a project into production. Typically, the networks that do this are looking for a deal. They know the other channels involved want to see the project move forward, and they certainly know that the production company is ready to go, so their aim is to leverage the group's committed enthusiasm into a better deal for themselves. Usually it's a very small spend, which lets the last network maximize their cost relative to the resulting end product.

Deficit Financing

Deficiting a project is when a producer, distributor, or production company puts their own money into the program or series to get it off the ground.

One of the best pieces of advice I ever received was back in film school when one of my professors made us swear never to put our own money into a project. As passionate filmmakers and producers we often fall in love with our ideas, and it can be hard to see the downside risk attached to our dreams. However, these days, as new funding models emerge and the costs of production go down thanks to the democratization of the tools, it's critical to keep an open mind. No two deals are the same, and no two opportunities are identical. Sometimes you have to do what you have to do to get the next project going. The key is mitigating the risk as best as you can so that you can go into the venture with your *eyes wide open.*

- **Pros**
  - More Ownership: You keep the majority of the rights and own the entirety of the project because you've got the most skin in the game.
  - More Control: The higher your ownership and financial stake is, the more likely you'll be the only one calling the shots on creative and editorial decisions.
- **Cons**
  - The $$$! There's no guarantee that you'll make your money back.

Many years ago, I flew up to Vancouver, Canada, to meet with a Canadian production company to discuss a potential co-pro deal. During the discussion, the company's founder candidly mentioned that he took out a 2nd mortgage on his house to fund the initial season of their reality-based series. It was a huge personal gamble, yet it ended up paying off handsomely as the series became a global juggernaut, selling worldwide, and eventually was renewed for multiple additional seasons. Without this initial contribution the series never would have happened. Yet had it not been successful, that same producer would owe the bank hundreds of thousands of dollars with potentially only limited ways to pay it back. Deficiting your own projects comes down to your own personal risk tolerance and willingness to roll the financial dice. It's not for everyone but for those who can harness its power; it can literally be life changing.

Sponsored Programs

Another way to find funding for your project is through sponsorship. Sadly, for many years *ad-funded* programming was greatly looked down upon by large swathes of the factual community. Visions of cheap-as-chips late-night infomercials no doubt roamed through their minds. Today, sponsored programming is becoming an omnipresent staple throughout the over-the-air, cable and streaming universe.

Typically, the route to a successful sponsored project initially requires you to work out a deal with a broadcaster for distribution. All networks will have some kind of *rate card* that states how much they value a slot in their programming line-up. The rate card is a good starting point for a negotiation, but several different factors determine the final price for the programming time, including the number of repeat (or encore) presentations, the amount of network on-air promotion, and who controls the commercial ad inventory throughout the program.

Once you have a rough deal in place with the network, it's time to take the combined cost of airing the project and producing it to a potential sponsor. Your goal is to have them write a check to cover all the costs. Deals like this are usually brokered through **Marketing Agencies**. They tend to be the best conduit for binding networks, production companies, and client companies together.

- **Pros**
  - $$$ Talks: This can be another way to get a project off the ground. If the sponsor is willing to write a big enough check, the network machinery can move fast!
  - Bigger Budgets: Sponsored programming almost always pays full freight because there are a lot of mouths to feed financially.
- **Cons**
  - No Ownership: Sponsored programs are almost entirely work-for-hire arrangements.
  - Two Clients: On ad-funded projects you'll effectively have two bosses: the network and the sponsor. Expect two sets of notes and multiple rounds of revision.

Other Types of Funding

While the bulk of factual television funding comes from commissioners, networks, and channels, every production is born from different circumstances. This often necessitates needing to find a unique funding model that often lies outside of traditional financing sources. Like many things in television, there's never just one way to do anything – and that includes finding the money to make your project happen!

Here are a few examples of non-traditional funding sources.

Private Money: Like a Silicon Valley start-up, driven factual producers can try to get their hustle on and find individuals or companies willing to invest in their factual ideas. These investments will trade up-front cash for a share of ownership in the project and a percentage of the revenues.

Generally, if you bring in an outside investor of any kind and they put money into your project, then they'll expect to be the first entity paid back when you complete a sale to a channel, network, or streamer. This is often referred to as *recouping in the first position.*

Soft Money: Sometimes called *free money*, soft money is a very broad term that encompasses a wide variety of additional funding solutions. It differs from top-off funding, deficit financing, or a distribution advance (DA) for one very important reason. Soft money doesn't need to be paid back.

- **Tax Incentives and Rebates**: In order to qualify for a tax incentive or rebate, your production needs to spend a certain amount of money (or a certain percentage of the total budget) in a specific city, state, or country. Most tax incentives are focused on theatrical film productions given the large size of their crews; however, there are certain jurisdictions that also cater to factual programs and series. Your best bet will be to check out an area's local film commission to see if they have current incentive offers.
- **Grants**: There are a wide range of film and television grants available through government organizations, companies, nonprofits, film festivals, and film institutions. While they don't have to be paid back, they do often come with strings attached. These can take the form of specific requirements, restrictions, and even editorial controls.

Streaming Services

Producing content for a streamer is fundamentally no different than producing content for a linear broadcaster. The main differences lie in the project's budget, territorial rights, and exclusivity.

Budget: When streaming services first emerged on the scene, they held little cache for the creative community and therefore often had to *overpay* content creators in order to acquire or commission programming for their services. Today, that's no longer the case as the scales have tipped in the streamer's favor. Amazon, Apple, and Netflix in particular now hold tremendous sway in the marketplace. They're seen as creative-friendly outlets and signifiers of high-quality productions. Nearly every major producer wants to find a way to work with them. It also helps that their vast tech-built financial resources allow these services to spend incredible sums of money to secure the rights to whatever their detailed viewer data suggests will generate the most views. On the other end of the spectrum sit AVOD streaming platforms like Pluto or Crackle, which tend to have less up-front money to spend on content but can offer producers the potential for a revenue share on the advertising dollars generated by a project.

Territorial Rights: Generally, the major high-end streamers want to own all the IP and be able to monetize a program or series across as many territories as possible. They typically only co-produce with production partners that have highly segregated distribution feeds. The smaller streamers are more likely to consider *territorial carve outs*, which is when you negotiate cutting out specific regions from a master distribution agreement. This allows a producer to monetize additional territories through other distribution deals.

Exclusivity: The major SVOD streaming platforms historically require total exclusivity; however, the smaller AVOD players often work on a *non-exclusive basis*. This allows a producer or distributor to license the same program or series to multiple streamers in the same territory and generate revenue from all of them at the same time.

Intellectual Property

For the majority of my production company's first decade in business, we almost exclusively sold fully commissioned projects. As we proved our stripes as a network provider, it was powerful to see the budgets go higher and higher. However, when a project wrapped and the funding ceased, it was a constant hustle with some real moments of concern to get the next gig going just to keep the lights on. Nobody should feel that sort of stress. What I had to learn the hard way was that there is a better business model.

On a flight back to the United States after one of our European shoots, I had an epiphany. This was prior to our current era of travel when you can find ubiquitous individual screens on the back of every headrest. Back then jumbo jets used to have one main screen per cabin. On this particular flight, right after the Hollywood movie wrapped up, one of our programs came on the screen. At first it was mesmerizing. Here I was sitting on a major airline carrier crossing the Atlantic and one of my projects was playing – I remember thinking *how insanely cool is this!?!* It was like an out-of-body experience. However, as I looked around the cabin and saw people enjoying the production, I started wondering *how exactly did this happen? How did my program end up here? This isn't the network we sold it to.* Slowly it dawned that the network had sold the rights to display our program to the airline. *Someone had been paid* for our work, yet we never saw a dime of the transaction.

While it was a frustrating moment to live through, I'm grateful for the lesson – that was the day that I swore off fully commissioned projects. Since then, I've been on a quest to retain as many rights to as many projects as I can.

Networks love to talk about the *long tail* of content, the ability to monetize the same product over and over again. Retaining IP works the same way; however, as an indie production company, it's also a bit of a gamble. Sometimes, the territorial rights that you hold on to sell before the series you're working on is even completed. Other times the rights that you think will sell never actually find a buyer and seem impossible to monetize. No matter how many forecasts you do, you never really know what will happen because every deal is different. The way that I look at it, right or wrong, is that if I'm going to bet on anyone it might as well be myself. On the other hand, I've spoken to countless other producers who absolutely refuse to sign any deal that isn't fully commissioned. They'd rather take the largest check up front that they can and don't want to be bothered with distribution deals or foreign rights. There are pluses and minuses for both cases. You simply have to find your own comfort level as you move forward in your career.

Inside the Industry With Adam Jacobs, Quintus Studios

Adam Jacobs is Creative Director at Quintus Studios, a next-generation broadcaster and distributor. Formerly, he was an executive producer at Woodcut Media and spent a decade at Discovery Channel as a buyer and commissioner.

- **What advice would you give to a smart film school student entering the "real world" who wants to produce their own content for a network like Discovery or Nat Geo? How would you suggest they start their career?**

For me it's two things – first, it's relationships. Identify the correct people to approach at the network (maybe not the CEO or MD just yet though!) with your ideas and try to connect with them in the first instance. Get them on side first, and it then makes life easier when pitching. In the first instance, it might be worth connecting with an indie who has produced for the network already. It might be that you work with them on your idea as a first "in" – that way it's less of a cold call approach. Second, if there are certain networks that you've pinpointed as your targets, watch the channels and really get to know them; try and find out what has been working well and hone your ideas and pitches, so they feel more bespoke. That way, you give yourself the best chance of finding something they'll find it hard to turn down.

- **You spent many years on the acquisition side at Discovery UK. How would you describe the international pre-sale and acquisitions market versus the full-commission programming pipeline?**

It's generally a lot quicker. At Discovery I was empowered to make decisions on the programming I acquired, so if I liked a series, I could greenlight it myself and we'd go to contract. Generally, with commissions it's not just one person that makes the decision (although there are exceptions) but a committee. There is the person who speaks with the indie and champions the project internally with the wider editorial team. Ultimately, with a full commission, you are asking for a lot more money, and hence the decision takes longer. What can be frustrating is waiting a long time for an answer (weeks and months!) with your project then being passed on.

- **In your mind, what are some of the advantages or disadvantages of pre-sales and acquisitions versus full-commissioned projects?**

A big advantage with a commission is that the whole thing is paid for by the network and you should have a nice production fee to go with it. The downside is that there are no international rights to exploit as the channel usually takes a lot. Your project can take a long time to fund via pre-sales – it can be very piecemeal finding several broadcasters to come on board and complete the project. Plus, feedback and interest are occasionally slow . . . you may have one broadcaster on board, but by the time others say yes to it, the first has dropped out! One other route is that if you can get a decent pre-sale from the United Kingdom, or even better the United States, it might be enough to then go to a distributor with who can deficit finance with an advance and then you're covered and ready to go.

- **Is the pre-sale/acquisitions route a better or worse avenue for a young producer to explore compared to the fully commissioned route?**

It depends on the project really and what the budget is. If it's an expensive show, then best to try and get it fully commissioned first as the network might cover the whole lot. If you went via the pre-sale route for something that costs a lot, it would leave you with too big a deficit to then find as these teams have less money to spend. Also, I'd only look at a full commission if the project really has something about it – be it talent, access, exclusive story that someone would find it difficult to say no to.

- **How would you suggest a young filmmaker grab a network's attention if they have no previous track record?**

This may sound obvious . . . but they need a killer idea or access to talent. If you bring something that no-one else has or could perhaps get access to but only you, it puts you in a very strong position!

- **Some programs get greenlight across all the global regions, while others sometimes only secure funding from specific territories – can you explain how that process works?**

It's really to do with local and regional similarities – taking Discovery as an example, there are some regions and countries with channels that are similar in demographic, audience, and what they like to watch. So, we'd therefore pick up a show for multiple territories. At other times however, due to cultural differences, there may be something that only works for one or two regions only.

- **When you worked at Discovery, how important were cost-effective projects versus bigger budget projects?**

Extremely important! At Discovery, there was and still is the audience expectation for the big, the bold, and the channel defining. But you can't just have a schedule full of those. We needed the repeatable and returning lower cost/high-volume series that essentially made up the bulk of the schedule. The ROI on these projects was generally favorable as opposed to an expensive tentpole piece that looked great in the schedule but would perhaps not make its money back.

- **I imagine you've sat through a lot of pitch meetings in your career – what are some 'best practices' for pitching? Any tricks of the trade that you might be able to share?**

Keep it short and to the point, say what you need to without waffling too much. If the commissioner wants to hear more, they'll ask! Always come as prepared as possible though – know the pitch inside and out, know what the topline budget and schedule are. Tailor your pitch or pitches to the channel you're presenting to and make them feel that this is just and only for them – know their channel and why your content is a great fit for it. If an idea is passed on, don't dwell on it or try to convince them, just move onto the next one – it will be obvious once you hit upon the one that does work.

- **As a producer it's always a great sign when the development team asks for a budget and schedule – what exactly are you looking for in those documents?**

With regard to the budget, it's to see the breakdown of cost, not because I don't believe them of course but to see where the money is going and if between us, we can see if there are any potential savings to be made or areas that may need a boost such as archive.

The schedule side is more important for a linear network than a streamer or AVOD channel. For the former, the premiere schedule (often called a "TX schedule" in the international market) is planned months in advance, and there are specific gaps that need to be filled. So, it's crucial to know when something will be delivered. For the latter, it's less of an issue as the content can be placed on the platform at any time.

- **When you were initially starting out, what was the best piece of advice that one of your mentors shared that has had the greatest impact on you and/or your career?**

Be responsive! I've prided myself on always going back to people as quickly as possible, even if it's just to acknowledge their note and that I'll get back to them when it's more convenient. It sounds like a simple courtesy, but personally, I think it makes a huge difference, especially when indies are waiting on a response that could make a huge difference to their bottom line.

- **Is there anything fundamentally different about greenlighting programming for a streamer versus a linear network?**

Well for a start, the process is a lot quicker! At a linear broadcaster, you make your decisions based on audience and channel data. But for a streamer or AVOD player, you can drill down into the most minute of detail to help make the process quicker. We know what really works, and we aim to super-serve the existing audience, so there is less sitting on ideas and making the producer wait; rather, we need a short period of time to determine if the content will work on the channel and if we think we can sell it, and if both are yes, then we move ahead.

- **When you're making a greenlight decision, how do you determine whether to move ahead with a project or not?**

Essentially, whether the indie can deliver on what is promised, have done their homework on what is realistic in terms of budget and schedule and in all honesty, I'm still a gut feeling person too, if the relationship is there and I feel they are the best partner to produce this project, then I'll say yes to it. I'm therefore open to all approaches regardless of the size or age of the company. I always think of it as a Dragon's Den/Shark Tank pitch in that you have my attention and you've piqued my interest – now sell it to me the best you can with all the necessary information that I'd ask and need to know nailed down. Then if it goes well, you may just have yourself a commission!

- **How has failure, or apparent failure, helped shape your career?**

I have been made redundant, and at the time it felt my world had fallen apart. But once I pulled myself together, it made me more determined than ever to not only succeed but be more adventurous in where I went next, who I spoke to, and how I positioned myself to the market. It allowed me to consider who I was, what I was good at, and what I could offer my next employer.

- **What is the worst advice that you continually hear people giving new or young producers?**

That TV is dead! Based on the quality of shows that have emerged in the past year, it really isn't the case. Yes, there are more streamers and more AVOD players. But they can coexist together, and there is still an appetite for appointment to view to sit alongside binge watching. As someone who works for an AVOD broadcaster/distributor business, I know that linear and digital can coexist and work together.

- **Figuring out what the market will bear versus what a producer thinks a project is worth is often tricky the first few times you negotiate with a network. Do you have any advice or best practices for how a producer should correctly determine what a project or series is worth and/or how to barter with a network about the final budget?**

I think it depends on who you are pitching to. If it is a smaller network which you know has lower tariffs, then you'd likely not approach them with a high budget, or to be the lead broadcaster. But if it was say a larger network such as Discovery, Nat Geo, or one of the streamers, then a higher price point is OK, and it can even put them off if the rate is too low. In terms of bartering, there is obviously a point of no return if you're looking to bring the tariff down – that is, the absolute minimum an idea can be produced for. But this is risky and not advisable as you then run the risk of potentially not being able to deliver on the promise of the pitch.

- **How would you describe the industry's use of the term *specialist factual* versus the traditional factual entertainment that we've come to know and love on the television?**

Specialist factual is a genre that hones in on a particular area of unscripted and, I'd say, usually but not always consists of a show that's made up of archive, experts, and perhaps a presenter and some CGI that goes into great detail on a topic. Factual entertainment is broader, and character driven, sometimes lightly formatted that can still include a specific topic but is more lighthearted in tone, pacier, still with take-out facts but with more of an emphasis on the talent or characters doing something fun rather than showing things to the viewer. Top Gear for example is a motoring show but also a factual entertainment one. Whereas a series on the history of cars would be classed as specialist factual. (It's actually quite a tough question!)

Distributors

If you decide to retain your own IP or territorial rights, eventually you're going to need an international distributor. Finding one is paramount to your future success. They're the multipurpose tools of the factual industry and help a producer unlock hidden tranches of funding, secure sales after a project is completed, and help in a myriad of other ways.

Historically, the role of a distributor was very simple – a producer could engage a distributor to help sell their completed programs in foreign territories. This was particularly effective for production companies back in the 1980s and 1990s when networks didn't view factual television series as a global commodity.

These days distributors do a whole lot more! They can help a producer *pre-sell* their idea to a network or streamer, they can help fill a budget deficit either before or during production, some distributors even have their own in-house production assets that can help source footage and materials, and then once the project is finally completed, they can help a producer monetize the content across multiple outlets and platforms throughout the world. This includes linear television, streaming platforms, home video, in-flight and a host of other potential sales opportunities.

A factual programming distributor is not to be confused with a theatrical distributor. They sound similar but are vastly different entities that live on opposite ends of the broad creative content community. In the independent film arena, a distributor secures theatrical exploitation of the work. However, in the factual industry the term "distributor" refers to someone who helps you sell your content throughout the world. Often, they take on a role that at least on a surface level feels quite similar to an agent.

Here are a few of the ways that a distributor can help a producer.

Pre-sales: As network budgets have tightened, many distributors have jumped into the fray and begun acting as de facto agents that can help a producer pitch and sell their ideas to buyers in foreign countries *before the project has been made.* Generally, pre-sales differ from fully commissioned projects in two crucial aspects: the size of the financial commitment and the scope of the territorial rights. Instead of asking a single network entity to front *the entire* production budget in exchange for global rights, a distributor will strategically target a specific regional network or platform and aim to sell them rights just for their regional broadcast feed. Because the broadcast rights are restricted, the budget contribution is usually smaller. Typically, this means that a distributor will have to piece together multiple networks in different regions to find the necessary funding to get the project or series into production. The upshot however is that if they can secure a producer the required budget to get the project made, then they can sell the remaining territories for nothing but profit.

Pre-sale Fees: The general industry standard for a distributor's pre-sale transaction fee is typically 10%. They'll take this on any sale that they help land *or negotiate*. This means that if you get a network on the hook, but the distributor's legal team seals the deal, they'll expect a fee for their help. When that fee is paid is just as negotiable as any other part of the deal. Oftentimes it's possible to arrange for the distribution pre-sale fee to be paid out from the remaining back-end territory sales after the program or series is completed.

Catalogue Sales: Completed programs or series go into a distributor's catalogue, and their sales agents then try to place the projects on networks or platforms in various territories where rights are available.

Completed Program/Series Sales Percentages: Generally, distributors charge anywhere from 20% to 30% for every sale plus up to 5% marketing costs.

Commissioning: Some distributors fund their own series outright as if they were their own mini network. Initially, the goal was to fill their own content pipeline before selling the finished programs to networks across the world. However, with the advent of *FAST streaming channels*, or Free Advertising Supported TV, some industrious distributors have begun curating their own content and placing it on their own streaming services.

Distribution Advances: Since distributors are squarely in the content game, they need to ensure a steady flow of new programming for their content catalogues. Without fresh content there's no reason to meet with hundreds of networks in different parts of the world because they have nothing to sell. To hedge their bets and ensure they have plenty of content, some distributors will offer money up front in the form of a *distribution advance* (DA) in exchange for the right to sell a producer's content. The larger the advance, the more faith a distributor has in the finished program or special. The distributor will recoup their "advance", or investment, from the initial sales their team makes before a producer sees any royalties. It is effectively a *first-in, first-out* *financial* scenario, where the producer is always the last entity to be paid. Distributors will offer DAs on both new content that they're actively trying to secure and entire library catalogues of a producer's previous work.

Alternative Revenue Streams: Most producers tend to think about content sales in very linear terms. They're producing content in order to get paid by a broadcaster or streaming platform. However, there are other revenue streams that range from home video and education sales to in-flight opportunities or merchandising rights. These can all be powerful financial levers depending on the type of project, and a distributor can help both navigate and monetize these opportunities.

A distributor not only can help find these additional alternative revenue streams for a producer, but they can also *project* how those sales will unfold over any number of set terms such as a 12–18 month, three-year or five-year outlook. This sort of projection is often described as a *revenue waterfall*, and it represents your entire potential earnings over a set period of time.

Reporting: Once you have a completed show or series ready for a distributor to sell in the marketplace, you'll want to know how the project is doing and where it stands financially.

Every distributor has their unique reporting system; however, generally each quarter they will supply a producer with two distinct documents: a **prospects report** and a **royalty report**.

The prospects report details *the future* of your project. It tells you where the project has been pitched, which networks have passed on it, and which nets are still considering it. Typically, this document will also show pending sales – deals that have been verbally agreed to but have not yet been financially transacted.

The royalty report records your project's *past*. It shows which territories have agreed to buy your programming and highlights the licensing terms and fees involved. For example, one region might license your project for two years, while another might want to broadcast it for five. Each quarter, at the bottom of the royalty report you'll see how much revenue your project generated and the royalties you're owed.

Finding a Distributor

Meeting the right distributor utilizes a similar process as working your way into a network or streaming service, only now you potentially arrive with an asset in hand in the form of your idea or completed project.

Often, it's best to keep your eyes and ears open to see which distributors are crushing it in the marketplace and then finding a way to connect with them. This can be done through cold calls, trade show or marketplace introductions, or a host of other routes.

In my case serendipity ultimately helped connect me with our first rockstar distributor. I was sitting inside of Nat Geo's Washington, D.C., headquarters having a pitch meeting when the gent on the other side offhandedly mentioned that I should connect with a British chap named Paul Heaney who was starting his own boutique distribution company. Even though the pitch meeting wasn't an amazing success, I'm grateful for the connection that it helped forge because Paul ended up being my entree into the world of distribution and ultimately helped land us a deal for our *Supercar Superbuild* series at Discovery International.

What to Look for in a Distributor

Personal connections are always great; however, when you're hunting for a potential distributor, the very first trait to seek is a trustworthy soul. Distributors can hold a ton of sway in the marketplace, yet they're not all created equally. In pre-sale situations they are typically the ones who speak to the broadcasters first about a new idea, so you want to make sure that you're in good hands. Additionally, it's worth pointing out that any deal a distributor helps negotiate often falls under their master network agreement, not yours. That means the money flows through *them*.

Once you've made contact, I would strongly encourage you to reach out to other producers whose finished content lies in the distributor's catalogue and ask about their experience. They may not tell you how their deals are structured; however, they almost certainly will tell you if they regret working with a particular distributor.

Retaining the rights to your projects sounds glamorous; however, there is a downside. There are no guarantees that you'll eventually be able to monetize the project on the backend. As a factual filmmaker, you might think there's no way that your project won't be picked up in other markets, but as they say in real estate, *the house isn't yours until you've got the keys*. Until a project sells, you have no reasonable way to predict where the market will like it or how they'll assign a price to it.

Another downside is that distributor sales agents are paid on commission. Many of them look for the easiest sales possible, regardless of whether it's a pre-sale, a commission, or a finished program, and you never know exactly how hard they're advocating for your projects versus looking out for their own interests. Some distributors are even part of mini conglomerates that also happen *to own other production companies*. A healthy bit of their attention is spent hustling for their sibling companies' ideas.

Inside the Industry With Roger Vanderspikken, Fred Distribution

Roger Vanderspikken is Chief Operating Officer and General Manager at Fred Distribution. He manages the daily operations and the work of its staff, including sales, acquisitions, development, legal, human resources, marketing, finance, and operations.

- **What advice would you give to a smart film school student entering the "real world" who wants to produce their own content for a network like Discovery or the National Geographic Channel? How would you suggest they start their career?**

On-the-job experience and networking is the best way to make the most of a career. I would suggest mixing experience between major production houses and very small independent companies. Very large entities might be better organized and offer training, induction programs, and some market standard. They might have access to better tools, software, and perks. Now the experience gained from a much smaller entity is invaluable. In small or midsize businesses everyone is doing a bit or sometimes a lot more than their job descriptions.

If little to no experience starts somewhere with transcribing, research jobs, assistant positions with access to "on-the-field" situations. Accept your newbie status and embrace the work that comes with it. Have a strong work ethic and positive attitude. Menial tasks will eventually lead to more. You need to build trust with people around you and show you can perform with simple things first.

Not everyone is an extrovert or can be "people person", but it is a huge advantage to build a network early on. A way to work around this is to have a mentor to show you the ropes and share his/her network.

Networks like Discovery or Nat Geo are the top of the pyramid for factual producers and distributors. They are the most curated networks with the highest expectation, so it is realistically not easy to tick all the boxes from production value to expected deliverables to legal, insurances, and so on. If some production tools are cheaper and more accessible, the barriers to entry have moved and new producers compete against other producers but also these vertically fully integrated global media companies (Discovery–Warner, Nat Geo–Disney, etc.).

- **I was hoping that you could clarify what exactly a distributor does in today's factual universe? What is their purpose, and perhaps how has that changed over the past decade?**

A distributor is a business generating revenue from the distribution of a catalogue. The catalogue is of finished content (also called tapes or ready made), format, or content in development (from a tag line to a full development project with a sizzle video and deck describing the project in detail).

Distributors are meeting and negotiating television rights with networks, agents, local distributors (sub-licensing rights) and anyone using content on a screen. The distribution is region or country based, and sales managers are often multilingual with a deep understanding of the local TV markets and culture (English is the sole language of business).

There are over 25 types of rights from inflight to ancillary or home entertainment. A fast-growing medium are FAST Channels – Free Ad-Supported Streaming TV Services (streaming live TV without the subscriptions).

A decade ago, most distributors were independents and focused on finished content. The role and position have changed with distributors now involved in all stages from creating, developing, funding, and selling TV. To remain competitive but also independent, distributors help producers to make great content and complete the funding puzzle. Distributors are involved early in the development process and in gap financing, and they are pre-selling bigger projects with multiple networks. They are becoming experts in tax and public funding but also in finding ways to monetize the content. Distributors are now starting FAST and VOD channels to monetize their content directly to viewers, competing directly with some of their clients.

- **For a producer who's just starting out, what is the best way to connect with a distributor and/or leverage their unique skill set to help level up their own content?**

It is important for all producers to understand the specificity of each key distributor. In the unscripted space 90% of the content is probably sitting in the top 5–15 distributors; the rest are boutique size companies from a single person with multiple hats to larger business with multiple commissioners, acquisitions, and development managers. A new producer will need more support, and some distributors are happy to help and backup some projects. It helps to work with a distributor who has a specific but similar niche or genre (e.g., Lifestyle, Reality, Nature Documentary, Crime). The sales and acquisitions teams not only can provide feedback but can also provide trends and market pulse. Working as a "POD" (Producer Overhead Deal) is a great way for a newbie to beat the development odds by striking a production and development arrangement.

- **What should a producer look for in a distributor? (If it is helpful, how should they vet them, how should they appraise their catalogue, how do they determine if the distributor is reputable or an honest broker?)**

A good distributor will renew content with existing producers and distribute newly available products. I would suggest reading specialized press (i.e., TBS, C21Media, Variety) and follow distributors on social media (LinkedIn). Once they achieve a certain size distribution, companies will tend to do more media releases to advertise their deals, success, and key activities. Now some companies might look successful, but they are part of one of these vertically and horizontally integrated public or private media conglomerates only selling "internal content". A reputable distributor will work "with the end in mind" and will try to build a relationship that goes further than the next deal.

- **How would you describe a documentary versus a factual program? What makes them similar or different in your eyes?**

In the distribution business there is a distinction between documentary, factual, and factual entertainment. It seems very clear in the UK (London is the center of the distribution world) but a bit less in other regions. Documentaries deal with real-life events and facts, with the main purpose being to inform or educate. The factual genres include current affairs, news, documentaries, observational documentaries, and all genres where the purpose is to be entertained as much as informed. Factual entertainment goes further in the entertainment side and includes reality TV and docudrama.

- **Are there any tricks of the trade or best practices that a producer should follow when it comes to distribution?**

Make sure to understand the expected deliverables from publicity and promotion images to E&O insurances. Don't hesitate to ask for projections from the sales team on a given project or initial feedback. The contract needs to be manageable for both sides (i.e., not requesting approval for every discussion), and there are various ways to work with a distributor: traditional distribution agreement, first-look agreement, co-production agreement, POD deal, etc.

- **Talk to us about finding funding. The world is changing quickly these days and new players are entering the content market. How has that changed how documentaries are made and paid for?**

Less and less titles are fully commissioned or fully funded. Funding is now often the result of multiple pre-sales deals, finance gap funding by the distributor, investor(s), or a network. These days a full commission can be the holy grail for a new producer but not for an established company. A full commission would generally mean a share or loss of IP, maybe even a share or loss of the creative/direction and little to no secondary source to monetize the content (i.e., second life online).

- **What do you look for in a producer when you decide to take them on as a client? (Quality of work? Industry reputation? Something else?)**

In a company our size it is all about the ideas and projects. We rather have a couple of great projects than volume. It really helps if a producer already delivered content to major networks.

- **What do you consider the important festivals or markets when it comes to factual distribution, and how crucial is it for a young producer to attend?**

This is critical for companies that are not established with good relationships and clients. MIPCOM and MIPTV as global markets and then NATPE Miami/Budapest, Realscreen, ATF Singapore, Discop Africa, Content London, and so on as regional markets. Some are even more niche like Sunny Side, World Content Market, Busan markets, and so on.

- **Can you explain IP and how a distributor can help a producer leverage it across multiple territories?**

The central job of a distributor is to protect and monetize the IP rights of a producer or rights owner. A producer signs a distribution agreement with an agent or a distributor and gives the distributor the rights during a specific term (3–7 years) to market the content. The same content can be distributed by multiple distributors in various regions, limited to some rights or have special conditions attached to them. The producer should always make his content as future proof as financially possible (from format, promotion and publicity, and deliverables).

- **What exactly is a format versus a factual series?**

A format for a television series includes but is not limited to themes, situations, concepts, incidents, titles, principal characters, music, or any other distinctive features. When creating a new factual series, it is very important to consider what makes or can make the concept unique and what are the distinctive features (i.e., the Stig character from the British motoring television show Top Gear). A client can broadcast or adapt (dubbing, etc.) a foreign program but can decide to "option" a format to create a local version. The format right owner can negotiate what distinctive features need to remain or can be modified. Some concepts are "format papers" only, but the most successful format started by a network backing up an original idea.

- **Is it better to be a high-end producer or a high-volume producer?**

Without any doubt high-end producers. Good-quality productions are more likely to be renewed and become a high-volume series. With all the new platforms and ways to consume content, high-end productions will always have an edge.

- **How has failure, or apparent failure, helped shape your career?**

Failures and mistakes are the stepping-stones to learn and improve. It helps to understand value and self-esteem, to become more resilient and learn skills.

- **What is the best investment in yourself that you've ever made?**

I have always done my best to not cut corners. I really believe that doing the little things help sharpen the saw. If you commit to working eight hours, do it and do the most of it. The results might not be obvious in a day, a week, or a month, but it will be a striking difference over a few years or a career. I consume a lot of media and have always read extensively (newspapers; daily, several in several languages), news, books, and in all sorts of subjects. I searched and worked with mentors who gave me the best insight into various phases of my life.

- **What is the worst advice that you continually hear people giving new producers?**

I actually don't know as I don't continually hear people giving bad advice. I don't hear bad advice, but I would mention that a difficult part in the producer–distribution relationship is to manage expectations from both sides. Being transparent without hiding the truth or sugar coating a situation is the best policy.

Inside the Industry With Ludo Dofour, Blue Ant International

Ludo Dufour is Senior Vice President of International Co-Productions and Sales at Blue Ant International. The company's distribution division offers a catalog of over 4,000 hours of content, including one of the world's largest 4K natural history offerings.

- **How would you describe the role that a distributor plays in today's factual universe?**

A distributor plays a multitude of roles:

- Advisor: They help guide a producer through various distribution strategies and windowing scenarios, based on the producers' goals.
- Promotor: They attend dozens of industry events throughout the year and leverage them as platforms to promote projects.
- Connector: They have a wide network of relationships in the industry and can connect the right projects to the right clients.
- One-Stop-Shop: Their volume of content offered, reputation, and expertise make it easier for distributors to access clients, package content, and receive feedback on projects from clients who simply can't speak to every producer.
- Negotiator: Once an offer is made, and based on trading experience, distributors are well placed to negotiate the best terms on behalf of a producer.
- Content financier: Increasingly, distributors also help experienced producers secure financing for their projects in the form of pre-sales and co-productions.

- **For a producer just starting out, what is the best way to connect with a distributor and/or leverage their skill set to help level up their own content?**

  - Ideally, a producer would attend one of the key industry events on the TV calendar to meet distributors in person, receive advice, discuss strategies, and understand better what each distributor is able to offer. The most productive event in the calendar is arguably the Realscreen Summit, but other very valuable events for the factual business include the World Congress of Science and Factual Producers, Sunnyside of the Doc, and Mipdoc/MipTV. These events can be costly once travel, accommodation, and accreditation are factored in, but most distributors have an acquisition executive, who would be happy outside of markets to schedule a call to discuss projects, what services they offer, and whether the project and business would be good fits.

- **What should a producer look for in a distributor? (If it is helpful, how should they vet them, how should they appraise their catalog, how do they determine if the distributor is a reputable or an honest broker?)**

All distributors have a website and screening portal where they list which producers they work with, the deals they have secured, the team they work with, and so on. These websites will give producers a good idea of what the distributor can offer, how long they have been in the market, what genre they specialize in, what titles might complement the producer's content, and what clients they work with. Trade publications are also informative, and a quick search in Realscreen, TBI, C21 Media, Variety, Deadline Hollywood or the Hollywood Reporter will provide additional details. Producers can also reach out to fellow producers who are represented by the distributor to ask them about their experience and whether they would recommend them. Some producers have output deals with distributors who they trust with their entire output, but most like to work with various distributors.

- **A lot of the producers I know in the United States don't know very much about international distribution. Are there any tricks of the trade when it comes to distribution?**

The international business represents about 50% of the revenue of a production, but this portion is generated over time by a myriad of mid-size (Western Europe) to small deals (Rest of the world). These deals are resource-intensive, require foreign language skills, and can take a lot of time, so working with a European-based distributor is a smart way to facilitate that process as they tend to be more international.

- **What do you look for in a producer when you decide to take them on as a client? (Quality of work? Industry reputation? Something else?)**

A track record: what projects were produced in the past, who for, how did they rate (TV) or fare on platforms like IMDB or Rotten Tomatoes, have they won any significant awards? And so on. A project which is either unique (unseen archive, unique access, an extraordinary story told for the first time, A-list talent attached, etc.) or very suitable to the needs of the market and expertly produced. A personal connection: The TV business is a people's business, and working collaboratively with a producer with whom a relationship based on mutual trust and respect can be established is paramount.

- **What do you consider the important festivals or markets when it comes to factual distribution, and how crucial is it for a young producer to attend?**

Markets: Realscreen Summit/World Congress of Science and Factual Producers/Sunnyside of the Doc/Mipdoc & MipTV/NATPE (more info above). Festivals: Cannes Film Festival/CPH:DOX/DOC NYC/Hot Docs/IDFA/Sheffield Doc fest/Sundance Film Festival/SXSW Film Festival/Telluride/TIFF/Tribeca. These are the most prestigious festivals that can transform the potential of a project. Accolades at other festivals will be considered a stamp of approval and will help promote the film so they are meaningful, and I would recommend entering projects at festivals, resources-permitting.

- **Is it better to be a high-end producer or a high-volume producer?**

Historically, it is better to be both in order to mitigate risks and cater to different segments of a constantly changing market impacted by business, cultural, and technological forces. That said, currently, with the rise of the streamers who are keen to drive new subscribers to their platforms, high-end projects are the most sought after.

- **How has failure, or apparent failure, helped shape your career?**

Failure is a key component of any business and a great way to grow as an executive. It can be self-inflicted or for reasons completely outside of one's responsibilities. The most important part is how to react to failure. A deal can fall through – the key is to know how far to push to try and save it, and when to stop because failure is inevitable. How to graciously and respectfully leave the negotiating table to ensure that the client will want to re-engage with you on another project will have a lasting impact on one's career. The TV industry is a very small one; reputation is everything, and good deals are not the ones where one of the parties feels taken advantage of.

- **What is the best investment in yourself that you've ever made?**

Taking the time to give back and help others by sharing what you know will always pay off eventually. Half of your career will be spent trying to achieve the success that a young producer deserves in a new industry, while the other half will be spent trying to keep up with the talent of the fresh newcomers who have just entered the game. The mentor–mentee relationship is a two-way street where both parties win in, and an investment in others is often an investment in oneself, so I would recommend sharing ideas, knowledge, contacts, and experiences for the industry as a whole to grow.

- **What is the worst advice that you continually hear people giving new producers?**

First-time producers can self-finance their project and recoup their investment once it is finished and ready to sell. I am sure some have, but the overwhelming majority will not, and I would always recommend getting partners on board at the development stage to help with the financing, editorial steer, and additional resources a network or streamer can offer.

Closing the Deal

Ultimately, there comes a point in every negotiation where each side has gone as far as they're willing to go. The only question left is whether the deal is equitable enough for both parties to agree to jointly move forward.

Generally, if the network agrees to most of my asks, then I'm happy to agree to go ahead. You're never going to get everything on your wish list, so you need to decide what terms are the most critical to you. For some it might be territorial rights, while for others it might be the up-front compensation. In the end neither is right nor wrong; rather, it's up to each producer to define what matters to them in that moment. For example, documentary filmmaker Ken Burns decided early in his career that he wanted to retain ownership over his films. That single commitment forced him to make dozens if not hundreds of other resulting choices, yet he drew a very clear line over his IP. Today, his library is worth millions. A perfect case of someone deciding what matters the most to them and fighting for it.

While negotiating a network deal is an inherently adversarial process, you want to make sure that everyone feels like they win in the end. Production companies come and go and network execs move on; however, lawyers tend to stick around forever. It's worth your while to build as strong of a relationship with the network council as you can. While discussing the first deal might be exhausting, it often helps set the table for the deals that follow. If the network's lawyer believes that you're an upstanding producer, then they'll be more likely to grant additional concessions the next time around. If you leave them with the impression that you're a jerk, then the next time around be prepared to battle for everything.

Tenacity

Getting the other side to say "yes" isn't easy. In fact, it's the hardest part of any creative venture. If you want to survive as a professional factual producer, then you must learn to be incredibly tenacious.

It's important to constantly find a way to keep your project at the top of the pile. This means you need to consistently feed the network positive progress updates, new opportunities, new solutions, and ultimately new reasons to say, "let's do it".

Momentum rarely happens on its own. It's up to you as the producer to create inertia. Every single day is a new opportunity to move the project forward in a meaningful way.

You have to be willing to scratch and claw your way to a successful outcome. *No matter what happens, whether it's good or bad, just keep pushing – you never know what turn of events will unfold next.*

In the end producing is a war of attrition that rewards those with the strongest belief in themselves and their project. You need to be resilient in the face of adversity.

True tenacity is an underrated skill set – the longer you scratch your way toward success, the sharper your claws will become.

Ethics

Producing factual content is *all about the hustle*. Yet when you're gaming situations to your advantage, sometimes you have to work in the gray. Some producers take it a step too far and conveniently lie to gain an upper hand.

That might work for a time, but all too often it's a quick way to destroy your career. Bending the truth eventually catches up with everyone, and karma *in this business* has an interesting way of coming back around to bite you when you least expect it.

Being forthright will ultimately get you further. Networks want to be in business with honest brokers, not cheap salespeople jumping from deal to deal. This is a relationship business, and once you violate a network's trust, then it's nearly impossible to regain it.

Factual producing success is all about being truthful, honest, and actionable.

The more repeatedly truthful you are, the more your trustworthiness grows in the eyes of others. When trouble finds you, *and it almost certainly will at some point*, the years spent cultivating an honorable reputation will ultimately prove your path forward.

Here are a few suggestions to ensure that the network's legal team looks upon you favorably.

Be Clear and Constructive

When you're negotiating with the network, be crystal clear about your major deal points. Don't bury the lede and hide your true feelings. Long-winded emails with never-ending paragraphs are a death knell. Instead, try to summarize your specific items with bullet points and clear thinking.

It also often helps to have a well-thought out rationale underlying your needs or wants.

For example, on a recent project the budget went up by 65% from Season 1 to Season 2. Normally that would be a major sticking point and point of contention with a network's legal team; however, when I presented my case for why we needed the additional funding, I presented four key reasons as my rationale: inflation, Brexit, the pandemic, and an inability to be as efficient as we were pre-pandemic due to specific timing circumstances. Everyone immediately understood that our asks weren't a negotiating tactic or ploy but rather systemic issues at a global level that were outside of our control.

LIES ABOUT THE BOTTOM LINE

Just as you must take a network's discussion about what they're willing to spend with a grain of salt, you equally have to find your absolute bottom line when it comes to an overall price. What is the lowest you're willing to accept that ensures after all the negotiation you're still making a livable wage and a profit?

LACK OF RECIPROCITY

Generally, in an honorable negotiation, when one side makes a concession, then the other side will return the favor and concede on a different point of equal value. This one-for-one trade assigns a level of fairness to the discussion. However, if the other side refuses to match your level of concession, then it's time to walk away. We tend to use facts and figures in contract negotiations, but at its core a negotiation is really about mutual respect. When one side takes advantage of that respect, it's not a fair or level playing field, nor a good partnership.

LAST-MINUTE CHANGES

Once both sides come to a general agreement, don't try to make changes at the last minute. It's both a bad look and counterproductive. It preys upon the other side's desire to close the deal, yet it always leaves the other party with a bad taste. People remember these kinds of late in the dance shenanigans, and it'll come back to haunt you later.

Etiquette

While a negotiation might be the most important thing to you personally, it's worth remembering that it's just one of many deals that your network counterpart is working on at any given time. Be conscious of their time, their feelings and their motivation.

When you finally receive a final contract for signature for your project it's time to be thankful, humble and helpful.

No matter how combative the negotiation process might have been to this point, now that you have an actionable contract, it's time to put all of that past. It's worth taking a quiet victory lap and then focusing on the journey that lies ahead.

Because the race has just begun.

Chapter Seven

Pre-Production

Once you've landed the sale, it's time to dive deeply into the pre-production phase of your project. You're ready to turn an idea into reality, roll up your sleeves and prep for the field production of your project. Every positive step taken during pre-pro has a direct doubling effect – the more efficient you are now, the easier you'll make your life later.

DOI: 10.4324/9781003292289-7

Every Minute Counts

You either get better or worse every single day. You never stay the same. And procrastination is the enemy of every factual project. Every moment counts and the clock is always ticking. When you first begin discussing your project's final delivery dates with a network or streamer they can feel far off in the future. Trust me they're not. They're just around the corner, and the more that you get done now, the closer you'll be toward wrapping things up successfully tomorrow.

A lot of creatives find it difficult to get things done when they're not *in the zone* or *feeling it*. That might work just fine for traditional artists like sculptors or fine art painters, but it doesn't survive the real-life litmus test when you're producing visual content for a global audience. In the factual arena creativity goes hand in hand with commerce and you reach maturity when you learn how to get going when you feel like taking the day off. Just as fortune favors the bold, constantly chipping away at your project and its deliverables ensures victory. Every action that you take now is a vote in favor of the project's eventual success. Learn to wring as many moments out of every single workday as possible because problems with simple solutions become hard to unwind later if too much time goes by before you tackle them. There are endless opportunities to find speed and efficiency along the way if you're willing to push to get just a little bit more done in the here and now. So don't wait for the opportunity, seize the day today.

Engaging With the Network

Once you sell your factual project to a network or streaming service, it's time to meet some fresh new faces on the *network production team*. These are the three key roles on the network or streaming side that will determine the success of your project moving forward.

The Executive Producer

The EP is your main point of contact on the production side at a network or streamer. They're the creative link between you and the broadcaster, and their role is to help make the project the best it can be while also adhering to the platform's brand promise. They're usually the highest-level decision-maker that you'll interface with and the person who will shepherd your project through the various phases, review edits, and deliver guidance. Their main job is to make sure that your project adheres to the service's current programming vision, standards, and legal requirements. If you cultivate this relationship correctly, it can become your greatest advocate inside of the building.

The Production Manager

A production manager is the network or streaming service's internal banker. During the development and selling phase of the project, the production manager reviews initial budgets and gives notes on where to add or subtract funds. They'll also double check your assumptions and fill you in on any network-specific deals that are already in place, such as title search costs, narrator fees (for long-running anthology series), and/or network budget rules.

After the project gets the go-ahead and is greenlit, the production manager's role switches from advice to oversight. They're responsible for ensuring that the field and post-production phases stay on budget, and they release all milestone payments. You want to kill the PM with kindness and befriend them as quickly as possible. Having a great relationship with them will make your life much easier throughout the process.

The Unit Manager

The unit manager is the network's air traffic controller. Their job is to ensure that the producer or production company is hitting all their milestones. You'll funnel all deliverables through them, including any pre-shooting outlines and scripts, cuts for review, promotional photos, logs, legal docs, and final binders. The unit manager's job is to keep your production on track, and the easier you make their lives, the less invasive they'll be in your production.

It's also not uncommon for unit managers to work their way up within the network system to eventually become production managers, producers, or even executive producers. So, it behooves you to forge a strong bond with them. You simply never know where they might end up down the road.

The Good, the Bad, and the Ugly

Every project starts with a tremendous amount of optimism and nearly unlimited promise. The dream is for your program or series to be a shining success from start and to final delivery. At the core of that potential success lies the producer–network EP relationship. This is the most sacrosanct part of the producer–broadcaster collaboration and the key to having a great experience working on a factual program or series.

Great Network EPs: When the producer–network EP relationship is going well, your network EP will become a creative collaborator, a *comrade-in-arms*, and your fiercest advocate internally at the channel. They view your success as their own success and act as an active participant in the creative process. The best EPs don't demand wild alterations or speak in vagueries but rather ask for meaningful changes and are willing to roll up their sleeves, open the script, and add suggested *solutions*. Great network EPs know exactly what they want, often have impeccable standards, and continually push you to be the best version of yourself. They will look at a cut and slice it and dice it until it barely resembles your original brief and push you and your team to greatness. Working for them isn't always easy, but the *great EPs* often unleash a torrent of creative talent that you never knew you had inside. It might be painful at the time and require numerous reshoots or recuts, but when you finish what you once felt was the upper limit of your skill set will now be your new floor. When you find a *great EP* take them for all they're worth; constantly pick their brain, ask questions, dig deep into their psyche, and try to unearth what makes them tick. The lessons you'll learn from them will help you repeatedly down the road.

Bad Network EPs: The vast majority of EP relationships are fantastic. You work so closely that many will become cherished and valued industry colleagues, and some will transform into great personal friends. Unfortunately, you won't hit it off with every single EP. When that happens, trouble often follows. When I look back at the most challenging projects that I've worked on, it's almost always the lack of a great producer–EP relationship that sank the endeavor. The absence of an open and honest line of communication and any mutual respect adversely affected the end product and doomed the entire enterprise. These EPs tend to be the folks who talk but never listen and usually feel a limited investment in your project. They will offer vague generalizations, but no concrete constructive criticism. Worse yet they almost certainly don't view helping find solutions as part of their job description.

When you're paired with a substandard network EP, you need to stick to your guns and make the program or series that you wanted to make in the first place. After that all you can do is let the chips fall where they may, but at least you've provided your team with direction, aimed for a target, and hit it. Each time I've dealt with a challenging EP has been difficult; however, I'm extremely thankful for those experiences because they taught me how crucial great communication is and the importance of forging a lasting bond with the network team.

The Kickoff Call

Once you sell your factual project, the first real order of business that takes place is the **Kickoff Call**. This can be a one-on-one chat with just you and the network EP, or it can be a conference call with dozens of stakeholders from inside the network. Regardless of how many people join the conversation, the goal is to get the ball rolling and introduce you to the network's way of doing business.

Every network operates a bit differently, and no two channels do things the same way – oddly even if they're part of the same media conglomerate. They all have their own institutional knowledge and unique culture. Your job on the kickoff call is to suss out as much of this unique business ideology as possible.

Generally, at this stage the project is running on pure enthusiasm. Everyone at the network has just bought a new shiny toy (your project), and their dreams for it are grand.

By now the network's production team has held multiple meetings about your project, and they have their own ideas for how it might turn out – only you don't know anything about their thinking, so in many respects you're flying blind and need to *uncover what they love about your idea*. Suffice to say at this stage it's not uncommon for each network or platform stakeholder to have a slightly different vision for the project as well. Navigating all these various versions of your own idea is a tricky bit of business of balancing confidence in *your* project while also listening to *their* ideas for it.

Often new ideas or concerns will also emerge during a kickoff call. Expect to have some out-of-left field questions lobbed your way. There's nothing wrong with being humble enough to say, "I don't know the answer to that, but I'll investigate and get back to you shortly", should anyone pose a query you don't readily know. Ultimately, you want to leave the call with the network feeling like the project is in great hands and that you're adapting to *their way* of doing business.

Protect Your EP's Interest

As a producer running your own productions, and maybe even your own production company, it might feel like you're your own boss. However, the truth is that everyone in this business has someone above them. On each creative project you need to figure out who that person is and *how best to protect their interests*. Usually on a factual project this will be your network or streamer EP. They're the eyes and ears of the channel or service and the person held most accountable for the end product. The better you make this person look, the better your chances are of landing another commission or sale.

Ultimately protecting your boss' interest comes down to just one thing – *never surprise them*. I've heard horror stories where production companies go off and hire unapproved bits of kit for half a million dollars and then shock the network with the bill. That's bad business and a quick way to permanently sever your EP relationship.

Whenever I'm presented with a major issue I immediately get in touch with my EP via phone or email. I want to inform them of the problem while also being considerate of their time and come to the table with a suggested solution that offers them the chance to quickly agree or allows them to offer their own opinion instead. If it's a phone call, I always follow up with an email. This is of paramount importance since we live in a litigious world. You want to create a proactive and positive paper trail about the issue. This way, later on, no one at the network can claim they weren't properly informed of a situation or that you acted unilaterally without their consent.

The Big Boss

While all your interactions will be with the EP, there's one other person you must keep in mind – the *Big Boss*.

Most likely you'll never meet them; however, their directives will shape your factual program, mini-series or series. The *Big Boss* can be a network president or general manager, the head of production, or sometimes the head of development. Your EP will pass along the Big Boss' thoughts and visions in their notes and on your phone calls, often under the guise of their own voice. Sometimes this will run in sync with their own words, while at other times it'll throw you for a loop.

Many years ago, we were producing a one-hour special on a new Mercedes-Benz model for the National Geographic Channel in the United States. The prior year we had produced a similar project on a different brand, and it was praised internally for the great action photography. Since the fast "zoom-zoom" scenes had done well in the previous project, we decided to film a number of action sequences in the new Mercedes program. However, when our EP saw the rough cut, he asked for all the fast action scenes to be deleted. At the time it made no sense, and I remember articulating that to our EP. It was only later on that I found out that in an earlier meeting our EP *had been told by his boss* that all car shows now needed to focus exclusively on engineering not visual entertainment. The Big Boss felt the programs had strayed too far away from the manufacturing elements that he thought their core audience appreciated the most. To this day I think it was a bad call, but even though it was voiced by our network EP, it wasn't really his call. The Big Boss had spoken, and now everyone below them had to listen.

Inside the Industry With Dan Korn, A+E Networks UK

Dan Korn is Vice President of Programming for A+E Networks UK and heads up a team responsible for sourcing, acquiring, and commissioning between 2,000 and 3,000 hours of content a year, for the broadcasters' four-pay TV brands – SKY History, Crime+Investigation, SKY History2 and Lifetime, as well as its free-to-air channel, Blaze.

Prior to joining A+E Networks, Dan spent ten years as Senior Vice President and Head of Programming for Discovery Channel UK and EMEA, which he joined, in 2005, from leading independent production company, 3BM Television Ltd. At 3BM, Korn was Managing Director and Executive Producer, winning a BAFTA for the film *Nuremberg: Goering's Last Stand* in 2006, a Broadcast Award for the series Age of Terror for Discovery, as well as producing the Emmy award–nominated *Holocaust on Trial* and RTS-nominated *Boy With a Tumour* for a Face.

- **What advice would you give to a smart and hungry film school student entering the "real world"?**

I think to be open to sheer breadth and range of content being produced across all platforms. Never has there been such an exciting and diverse ecosystem of content forms and opportunities. You don't need to fixate on creating your Bernardo Bertolucci masterpiece from the get-go. You can start with creating short-form, promos, and little bits of metadata/celluloid magic, before graduating onto the big stuff (much as directors like Paul Greengrass or Yann Demange did).

- **How would you suggest a young filmmaker approach their producing career, and what is the best way to grab a network's attention if you have no previous track record producing content?**

Grabbing a network's attention is really all about aligning yourself with the right production house. There used to be a "rite of passage" in production, whereby you started (as I did) on the lowest rung of the ladder, as a runner or researcher and then worked your way up, via assistant producer or production manager to producer/line producer, producer/director and then Series Producer/Showrunner and Exec Producer. The great thing about the plurality and diversity of media now is that you can attract the attention of leading production companies with your ingenuity and versatility via the brilliant bits of tape you put together yourself and then, from that, you can work with them to attract the attention of the networks.

- **You commission hundreds of hours of programming each year. When you're making greenlight decisions, how do you determine whether to move ahead with a project or not? (If helpful, it could be best practices for pitching or drafting treatments, any places that people usually trip up, or any advice you'd have loved to hear when you started, etc.)**

There are a number of factors which play into this decision-making process – logistical, commercial, budgetary, and so on – but by far the most important is that spark of creative/editorial inspiration and originality which compels you about a particular project. That is usually conveyed through tape and treatment and then a pitching session. If it makes the hairs on the back of your neck stand up, you (or certainly I) will move heaven and earth to try and find the resources to get it made.

- **When it comes to the programming itself, do you have any core documentary filmmaking tenets or beliefs that you think young producers should focus their energies on learning or honing? (Style or techniques that you think are missing in today's creative community?)**

For me personally, one of the key tenets is to have a layered/multifaceted storytelling approach. Audiences love the twist-and-turn and gear changes within a narrative. If it's too linear or too "steady state", it won't engage viewers in the way that you want. Also, it needs to have an emotional intelligence, as well as an editorial/journalistic one, so that people feel it as well as see and hear it.

- **What in your estimation helps win ratings wars and/or makes programming "sticky" for viewers who have so many content choices in today's world?**

Distinctiveness and originality – a different way to tell a story. Look at the impact, say, of *Don't F**k With Cats* or *Once Upon a Time in Iraq* or *My Octopus Teacher*. Not exactly original precincts for documentary storytelling but brilliantly and beautifully executed documentary storytelling which gripped you from first to last.

- **How has failure, or apparent failure, helped shape your own career?**

I think in any creative endeavor, you have to be able to take risks and give yourself permission to fail. I have failed and had setbacks on several occasions in my career and each time, have tried to learn the lessons from it. I always try to remember a piece of advice which my mother gave me, "if you don't want to make mistakes, don't bother getting out of bed in the morning".

- **Once you decide to move ahead with a project, how do you think a young or first-time producer should approach storytelling and structure? Do you have any core beliefs about factual filmmaking? (For example, a reliance on Nat Sound or a certain kind of editing style?)**

I think with great care and attention to detail. The more thought and consideration you give it up front, so you're entirely confident of the robustness of the narrative and sub-narratives, the better. If, as Dostoyevsky said, "genius is the infinite capacity for taking pains", then that's doubly the case when it comes to filmmaking, particularly for your first film.

- **Is there any advice that you gleaned from your mentors that you feel has been particularly helpful to your career and perhaps might be helpful to the next generation?**

Grab opportunities that come your way with both hands – they may not come again.

- **What is the best investment in yourself that you've ever made?**

I'm not sure it necessarily qualifies as an investment in myself, but what I would say is that I took advantage of the opportunity which was kindly given to invest in the production company I was a part of earlier in my career and having an equity stake in that company gave me a stronger sense of affinity and pride in its endeavors than I suspect I might otherwise have had. I was always grateful to the enlightened owners of that company that they gave me that opportunity.

- **What is the worst advice that you continually hear people giving new or young producers that you think should be avoided or disregarded?**

I generally hear people giving very sound advice to new or young producers. One thing that frustrates me is when I hear people say, "it's only telly". It may be "only telly", but we do have a responsibility to educate, inform, and entertain. I think the things to remember are to not be afraid to take risks, to throw yourself into it, and above all to enjoy it. It's a wonderful privilege to have a chance to be involved in such a creative process, and in any case, to finish with another quote from my long-suffering mother, "life's too short to be anything but happy".

Turning Pitches Into Reality

Great pre-production is about forming a bullet-proof battle plan. The good news is that you already have a leg up on the process thanks to the brilliantly written treatment that helped you sell your idea to the network. You may not realize it right away, but your treatment is a coded outline that allows you to build the perfect *shooting plan.* All you have to do is break down the key themes and subjects that you've already spelled out in your deck.

Surviving The Inevitable Shooting Outline

Teaser

Sportbikes – They're fast, wickedly powerful machines and for years considered extremely dangerous by most of the public – yet they're not any more!

Thanks in large part to some incredible advancement in technology over the past five to ten years, today motorcycles are not only faster then they've ever been before but also considerably safer too!

Act 1 - ALPINESTARS

Intro to Motorcycles – Motorcycles; Today you see them everywhere, parked outside the grocery store or the café, sitting in the parking lot of your local gas station and of course out on the open road. They've managed to infiltrate every walk of life, spanning from the hardcore riders to legions of weekend warriors looking for an escape from their normal lives.

> **What we learn:** Amongst this incredibly diverse group of riders there's a well-worn saying which highlights the inherent danger involved in riding… "There are two kinds of motorcycle riders, those who've crashed and those who will".

How The Times Are Changing – While the danger of crashing still exists for everyday riders, the results of what happens after a crash are dramatically changing thanks to some incredible technological advancements that are happening not on the street but on the track!

Let's Go Racing! – Racing has always been the technological providing ground for motorcycles, starting with early Speed Runs on the Autobahn and continuing today at the highest level of American road racing, the American Motorcycle Association's (AMA) Superbike series.

> **What we learn:** The Pros are always pushing it because that's what they have to do in order to win a race! But sometimes in the hopes of winning racers push it to far, and often when that happens, they crash…

Racers Talking About Crashes – Our collection of AMA or WSBK racers explain what happens when they crash and why they crash.

What Causes A Crash? – There are two basic types of motorcycle crashes, **high-sides** and **low-sides**. Ten years ago both were considered horrific events to go through as a rider and you were lucky if you could walk away from either kind of crash with just minor injuries. Of the two, high-side crashes have always

FIGURE 7.1 A Shooting Outline for a Motorcycle Documentary We Produced for Nat Geo.

Chances are that the treatment or pitch deck is the only document that your network EP has seen about your project. Often in the early stages it's really all that they know about the idea. So, use it to your advantage and craft your shooting treatment by liberally lifting the same verbiage and structure the deck already contains.

There are several different types of shooting treatment, and every network asks for a slightly different variant. Some nets will request a lengthy document that spells out exactly what the viewer will see, hear, and learn in each act of the project. These tend to be verbose, verbiage heavy documents that expand your treatment into a factual novella of sorts. Crafting these documents can be time-consuming; however, they can help clarify your thinking while also creating an easily shareable vision for the project.

Building a Shooting Outline

A well-written shooting treatment does a great job of giving a 360° holistic view of a factual program; however, they're often too text dense to use quickly in the field. So, it often helps to go one step further and break your shooting treatment down in a *shooting outline*. The shooting outline is a simplified document that distills the beats and themes discussed in the shooting treatment into an actionable bullet point-like roadmap for the episode's structure.

Once you have a broad stroke structure, you can start game planning how much total running time, or *TRT*, each topic, or *beat*, needs. Try to sit back and envision how long you can narratively hang on a subject before it becomes tired or boring. Some of the estimated screen time you're willing to dedicate to a subject will be a pure guess;

INSIDE THE RING BEAT SHEET v2

BEAT	BRAND	LOCATION	SUBJECT	TOPIC	ESTIMATED TRT	INT. SUBJECT	ARRANGED	NOTES
	ACT 1 (Estimated TRT : 10 Minutes)							
1.1	Multiple	N/A	Opening	Teaser	1			Archive: WIGE Group
	Local	Nürburgring				Ron Simons, RSR Nürburgring	Yes	
	Local	Nürburgring				Ossi Kragl, Ok-Speed	Yes	
	Local	Nürburgring				Mike Frison, Nürburgring Blogger	Yes	
	Journalist	TBD				Jens Meiners	NO	
1.2	Multiple	N/A	Set-Up	What Makes it Special?	2			Archive: WIGE Group
	Local	Nürburgring				Ron Simons, RSR Nürburgring	Yes	
	Local	Nürburgring				Ossi Kragl, Ok-Speed	Yes	
	Local	Nürburgring				Mike Frison, Nürburgring Blogger	Yes	
	Journalist	TBD				Jens Meiners	NO	
1.3	Multiple	N/A	Set-Up	A Cathedral to Speed	2			Archive: WIGE Group, Mercedes, Porsche, BMW
	Local	Nürburgring				Ron Simons, RSR Nürburgring	Yes	
	Local	Nürburgring				Ossi Kragl, Ok-Speed	Yes	
	Local	Nürburgring				Mike Frison, Nürburgring Blogger	Yes	
	Journalist	TBD				Jens Meiners	NO	
1.4	Hyundai	Nürburgring Facility	Intro to Hyundai	New Kid on Block	4	Stephan Hoferer, Hyundai Nürburgring	Yes	
	Local	Nürburgring				Mike Frison, Nürburgring Blogger	Yes	
	Journalist	TBD				Jens Meiners	NO	
	Hyundai	Nürburgring Facility				Albert Biermann, Head of N Division	Filmed	
1.5	Hyundai	N/A	N Division Reveal	What goes on at the Ring Today	1	Albert Biermann, Head of N Division	Filmed	
	ACT 2 (Estimated TRT : 10 Minutes)							
2.1	Mercedes	Stuttgart	History	Track Construction	1	Michael Bock, Mercedes Classic	Yes	Archive: Mercedes & Duke Video
2.2	Mercedes	Stuttgart	History	First Race in 1927	1	Michael Bock, Mercedes Classic	Yes	Archive: Mercedes & Duke Video
2.3	Mercedes	Stuttgart	History	Birth of the Legend of the Silver Arrow	1	Michael Bock, Mercedes Classic	Yes	Archive: Mercedes
2.4	Hyundai	NamYang	R&D	Birth of a new Challenger Today	1	Stephan Hoferer, Hyundai	Yes	
	Journalist					Jens Meiners	NO	
2.5	Hyundai	NamYang	R&D	Clean Sheet Design	1	Mr. Oh Sun Kwon, Head of PDeN Powertrain	Yes	
	Hyundai	NamYang				Mr. Bong Joo Kim, Head of R&H Division	Yes	
2.6	Hyundai	NamYang	R&D	Rapid Prototype & Engine Build	1	Mr. Oh Sun Kwon, Head of PDeN Powertrain	Yes	
2.7	Journalist	TBD	History	Formula One Pedigree	1	Jens Meiners	NO	Can expand if needed
	Local	Nürburgring				Ron Simons, RSR Nürburgring	Yes	
	Local	Nürburgring				Ossi Kragl, Ok-Speed	Yes	
	Mercedes	Stuttgart				Michael Bock, Mercedes Classic	Yes	
2.8	Hyundai	NamYang	R&D	Engine Test (Test Bench, Dyno)	1	Mr. Oh Sun Kwon, Head of PDeN Powertrain	Yes	
2.9	Journalist	TBD	History	Crashes & Accidents	1	Jens Meiners, Car & Driver	NO	
	Local	Nürburgring				Ossi Kragl, Ok-Speed	Yes	
2.10	Journalist	TBD	History	The Death of the Nürburgring	1	Jens Meiners, Car & Driver	NO	
	Nürburgring GmbH	Track				Carsten Schumacher, CEO Nürburgring	Yes	
	Local	Nürburgring				Ossi Kragl, Ok-Speed	Yes	
	Local	Nürburgring				Ron Simons, RSR Nürburgring	Yes	
	Local	Nürburgring				Mike Frison, Blogger	Yes	

FIGURE 7.2 A Beat Sheet From "Inside The Ring".

others will be based on more concrete sources. If you can only find one minute of archival material for a particular segment, then there's no need to write a five-minute voice-over about it. You simply don't have the goods to support the dialogue. Ascribing an initial TRT to your outline forms the first factual building blocks for your project. Once you have an idea of how much *finished* content you need per subject, you can start planning on how *time* each beat will take to film.

Shooting Schedules

Having a clear idea of how long you want each topic in your program to run arms you with the necessary knowledge required to figure out how many shooting days your project needs. The goal is to create a plan that's realistic enough to bring the project to life yet bold enough to afford you the opportunity to tell the best story possible. A lot of people celebrate working 70+ hours a week, but banking on hard work alone is a terrible strategy for crafting a great factual program. Making great decisions planning the shoot allows your team to work *smarter* and more *efficiently*. If you need an entire location to support one act of your film, you might need multiple shooting days there. While on the other hand if you have a topic pop up for just a minute or two, it might only require a half day of filming or less.

Shooting schedules alter radically based on the type of program that you're creating for broadcast. Some genres require vast amounts of filming for short segments (home renovation for instance), while others can be far more efficient (list shows). The amount of time required to create a factual program can also change over time.

When we first began filming process-driven factory programs, we often spent multiple weeks inside each facility. However, as we became more accustomed to what we needed and more efficient in the field, we were able to radically trim our time on the ground.

INSIDE THE RING WORKING CALENDAR (v7 as of 8/29/15)

Month	Monday	Tuesday	Wednesday	Thursday	Friday	Saturday	Sunday
	24	25	26	27	28	29	30
	31	1	2 Book Airlines & Hotels	3	4 Team Meeting	5	6
	7 Order Currency	8	9	10	11 Carnet App Due	12	13
Sep 2015	14	15	16 TRAVEL LA to Korea	17 TRAVEL LA to Korea	18 NamYang Site Survey GEAR LEAVES LA TO DE	19 OFF	20 OFF
	21 NamYang Filming Day 1	22 NamYang Filming Day 2	23 NamYang Filming Day 3	24 TRAVEL Korea to Germany	25 Open	26 OFF	27 Nürburgring Possible DTM Race Visit
	28 Hyundai R&D // Track Nürburgring	29 Hyundai R&D // Track Nürburgring	30 Nürburgring Track CEO & Operations	1 Nürburgring Local Historians	2 Nürburgring TAXI Nürburgring to Stuttgart	3 OFF	4 OFF
	5 Stuttgart PORSCHE Historians	6 Stuttgart MERCEDES Historians	7 Munich BMW Historians	8 TRAVEL Germany to LA	9	10	11
	12	13	14	15	16	17	18

FIGURE 7.3 A Shoot Calendar From a 1 × 60 Special Called "Inside The Ring".

Every few years we also do a *Moneyball* quantitative breakdown, where we detail just how much total footage is brought into each individual episode project, how much material each specific camera rolls for an episode, and how much of each shooter's work ends up in the final programs. It's a time-consuming number-crunching process that always results in an eye-opening learning experience when you realize how much you're overshooting your films.

Rolling one hour a day less might sound meaningless, but it adds up fast once you get to the editing stage of the process. Filming one hour less per day × three cameras is 15 hours less per week, or in our case episode. Multiply that by eight or ten eps overall and you not only have a significant time savings in both the field and the edit, but also a huge storage saving in post.

Statistical modeling allowed us to rapidly trim the amount of time we spend on the road and inside a factory. Today, we might only spend four or five days filming per episode on a strictly process-based film. However, on other projects, the story defines the shoot. When we were asked to create a one-hour special for the National Geographic Channel on the famed Nürburgring racetrack in Germany, we had to build a bespoke shooting schedule based on the needs of the program. In this case it saw the crew circumnavigate the globe traveling from Los Angeles to Korea, from Korea to Germany, and then Germany back to Los Angeles.

At its core a shooting schedule is nothing more than a robust calendar, yet it influences your project's timeline and funding requirements. The more days of filming, the greater the costs involved. Producing a great factual program often comes down to building a brilliant episode in as few days as possible, and a lot of producers tend to build rather lackadaisical shooting schedules. They often don't account for travel times, equipment set-up and break-down, or meals. These are all potential pressure points that can adversely affect a crew or create angst or animosity during the shoot yet can be easily resolved with a bit of forethought.

I don't like filming for a few days, having everyone take time off and then reconvening for the next shoot days or weeks later. This sort of staccato filming style might work for some, but I believe that crews build positive momentum that stacks from consecutive shooting days. Tight and highly efficient shoots with multiple days of filming in a row help create a rhythm and positive feedback loop. Even though the crew gets tired day to day, they get faster overall because everyone learns what needs to be done for this project. Onesies and Twosies shoots always feel like you're bouncing back to square one on every new shooting day.

	Total Amount of Raw Original Footage per Camera (TIMECODE)											
	S201	S202	S203	S204	S205	S206	S207	S208	TOTAL	MIN	MAX	MEAN
	MERCEDES	ALFA ROMEO	ROLLS ROYCE	JAGUAR	CAMARO	PORSCHE	AUDI	MINI				
FACTORY SHOOT												
CAMERA A Interviews	5:02:40:12	4:43:37:20	5:13:06:16	5:23:40:16	3:37:20:12	5:00:49:04	4:05:00:16	5:54:08:08	[37 hrs]	3:37:20:12	5:54:08:08	4.60 hrs
CAMERA B Interviews	50:14:08	3:26:06:04	41:11:08	1:45:09:04	2:27:38:11	47:55:00	9:59:01	1:48:27:00	[12 hrs]	9:59:01	3:26:06:04	3 hrs
INTERVIEWS TOTAL	5:52:54:20	8:09:44:00	5:54:18:00	7:08:49:20	6:04:58:23	5:48:44:04	4:14:59:17	7:42:35:08	[49 hrs]	4:14:59:17	8:09:44:00	6.13 hrs
CAMERA A	6:46:24:08	5:29:37:00	6:52:48:00	7:06:56:00	4:12:19:12	5:57:19:20	4:51:21:12	2:11:23:08	[40 hrs]	2:11:23:08	7:06:56:00	5 hrs
CAMERA B	13:50:38:19	8:43:07:20	15:49:16:00	11:45:59:04	12:09:54:21	14:07:52:08	17:50:42:15	13:05:44:12	[104 hrs]	8:43:07:20	17:50:42:15	13 hrs
CAMERA C	8:32:44:12	6:11:14:00	12:24:16:00	9:03:26:12	9:31:12:13	9:54:55:12	4:54:47:18	14:28:52:17	[75 hrs]	4:54:47:18	14:28:52:17	9.38 hrs
CAMERA D	3:04:25:05	4:24:28:00	3:02:16:12	44:32:18	44:42:11	3:11:07:00	5:14:54:00	---------	[22 hrs]	44:32:18	5:14:54:00	2.75 hrs
B-ROLL TOTAL	32:16:12:20	24:48:26:20	38:08:36:12	28:40:54:10	26:38:09:09	33:11:14:17	32:51:45:21	29:46:00:13	[241 hrs]	24:48:26:20	38:08:36:12	30.13 hrs
FACTORY SHOOT TOTAL	38:07:07:16	32:58:10:20	44:02:54:12	35:49:44:06	32:43:08:08	38:59:58:20	37:06:45:14	37:28:35:21	[290 hrs]	32:43:08:08	44:02:54:12	36.25 hrs
TRACK SHOOT												
Track Interviews	1:49:53:19	1:33:04:07	2:01:15:01	1:23:29:16	1:42:26:07	1:33:26:06	2:20:09:04	1:01:51:22	[13 hrs]	1:01:51:22	2:20:09:04	1.63 hrs
INTERVIEWS TOTAL	1:49:53:19	1:33:04:07	2:01:15:01	1:23:29:16	1:42:26:07	1:33:26:06	2:20:09:04	1:01:51:22	[13 hrs]	1:01:51:22	2:20:09:04	1.63 hrs
CAMERA A	2:26:46:00	2:31:32:16	---------	3:09:59:08	4:23:51:06	1:10:59:04	1:23:37:08	52:17:00	[15 hrs]	52:17:00	4:23:51:06	1.86 hrs
CAMERA B	3:09:55:08	1:59:21:06	---------	5:04:16:08	4:33:54:14	2:36:35:20	1:53:09:07	3:14:17:12	[22 hrs]	1:53:09:07	5:04:16:08	2.75 hrs
CAMERA C	26:48:00	40:37:13	---------	35:27:07	1:16:05:20	17:13:00	22:56:12	17:31:12	[5 hrs]	17:13:00	40:37:13	0.63 hrs
CAMERA D/GOPRO	18:53:12	41:05:10	---------	39:40:08	9:08:01	6:25:17	10:01:17	6:03:08	[5 hrs]	6:03:08	41:05:10	0.63 hrs
B-ROLL TOTAL	6:22:22:20	5:52:38:21	---------	9:29:23:07	10:22:59:17	4:11:13:17	3:49:44:20	4:30:09:08	[47 hrs]	3:49:44:20	10:22:59:17	0.013 hrs
TRACK FOOTAGE TOTAL	8:12:16:15	7:25:41:04	2:01:15:01	10:52:52:23	12:05:26:00	5:44:39:23	6:09:54:00	5:32:01:06	[60 hrs]	2:01:15:01	12:05:26:00	7.5 hrs
ORIGINAL FOOTAGE TOTAL	46:19:24:07	40:23:52:00	46:04:09:13	46:42:37:05	44:48:34:08	44:44:38:19	43:16:39:14	43:00:37:03	[350 hrs]	40:23:52:00	46:42:37:05	43.75 hrs

FIGURE 7.4 Our Moneyball Approach to Filmmaking – How Much Footage Is Making It Into Each Film?

Shooting schedules that require multiple moves between locations add additional challenges. They also often compress time while creating more potential for crew friction. To make life easier, I always try to build as linear an itinerary as possible that always has the team moving in the same direction. Backtracking is bad for morale and a terrible use of time.

On extending travel shoots, filming early in the morning when the crew has its maximum focus almost always results in the best footage. Then you can grab a snack or meal on the way out before hitting the road and inbounding into the next destination. This way everyone gets a good night's rest before the next big shoot.

Some producers travel in the morning and film in the afternoon – and we've certainly done it when circumstances forced our hand – but it's simply not a sustainable production method. Long drives wear people out and often lead to mindless or lackluster afternoons spent filming.

Our longest multi-location multi-day shoot was a 43-day 3,200-kilometer multi-country trek across Europe to film a one-hour special on the birth of the new Bugatti Chiron Hypercar. It included a full lap around Germany, a trip down through Switzerland, Lichtenstein, Austria, and into Northern Italy, before rushing back up into Germany again. The whirlwind journey was a one-in-a-lifetime adventure that featured a new hotel room literally every night. Due to the lengthy drive times, all our card dumps and data backups were done enroute to the hotel each night. Even though the shoot was exhausting, it was also a great opportunity to refine our processes. In our case we not only built a mobile card dump station but also created a mobile battery charging station that contained all the different camera and electronics chargers in one place.

Getting Subjects to Agree

Part of crafting your shooting plan requires getting your foot in the door with the potential subjects involved in your project. Next to selling a project, convincing others to take part in your program or series is perhaps the hardest part of being a producer. Thankfully the internet is an amazing tool that can help you get the job done. You can scour the web for info on the people and companies that you're keen to connect with, track their whereabouts on sites like LinkedIn, and use a vast array of digital tools like RocketReach to snag their emails. It's never been easier to find the right door to knock on in such a limited amount of time. This also means that what was once *really hard* is now *really* easy for millions of other people to do as well. You have to out-wit and out-battle everyone else for access and opportunity.

You Have What They Want

Factual content is currently undergoing a massive renaissance thanks largely to the emergence of a whole host of new distribution outlets, yet regardless of who broadcasts the signal the key point is that whatever ends up on a television screen has a considerable cachet within our society. Think about where you typically find large-screen TVs – dead center in the largest gathering space in most modern homes. So, while the internet and online video might be all the rage for some demographics, and rightfully garners tremendous advertising dollars, TV is still a fixture for the bulk of humanity and their viewing habits. It's the warm and cozy hearth that we continue to gather around in our modern age. When you're trying to gain access, you have to remember that you have the power of television backing your project and your request. Being on television denotes a certain level of status, and if a person or company is featured on a network with a high brand value, like Discovery or Nat Geo, it is an imperator of fame and success. *You have what they want.* Your job as a producer is to use that power to your advantage.

Persuasive and Professional Emails

Some producers have an uncanny knack for sweet talking just about anyone into doing nearly anything. However, you don't have to be a superslick speaker to get your foot in the door with a potential subject or firm. The key is to be professional and concise. Be courteous and make your asks clear. You'd be surprised how many people send terrible or incoherent emails that either don't clearly articulate what they want or make an ask so beyond the realm of reality that it garners an instant "no". The recipient on the other side might get a few hundred notes a day, they're only going to respond to the ones that offer them the most upside and are penned by the most professional sounding people.

Here's a formula that has worked for me for many years.

Opening With Self-Awareness and a Common Link: I like to open cold call emails with a bit of self-awareness that acknowledges right up front that my note is coming out of the blue. Nobody likes cold call emails, so I may as well tackle the imposition first. Then I briefly describe a common professional link to quickly gain their trust.

Who I Am: Next I segue into who I am and what I do . . . Which leads me to

Why They Should Listen: I drill down into why the recipient should listen to my pitch.

Clear Ask: Then I drop the key ask – as simple and direct as possible. Make it to the point and be as clear as you can. Don't beat around the bush or as the recipient use a decoder ring to figure out what you want. Life punishes those who are vague and rewards those who are specific.

Next Step: Finally, I wrap up by asking if I can connect with them in the real world via phone or zoom to discuss the project further. So many people only want to talk via email, but humans crave live interaction, whether in person, via phone or virtually by digital conferencing. It shows that you're confident and comfortable in your own skin and that you're for real.

Here's an example:

Hi John,
Hope that you don't mind the unsolicited note; however, I see on LinkedIn that we both know Joe Thomas. I worked with him on a Nat Geo documentary project a few years back.

For the past ten years I've run a documentary television production company that specializes in telling culinary stories for global television networks.

We've produced numerous films for the aforementioned Nat Geo, as well as Discovery Channel and History Channel.

We're working on a new film about wine for the Food Network, and I understand that you're one of the preeminent viticulture experts on the West Coast. I was hoping that perhaps you might be interested in sitting down for a short on-camera interview on how the wine industry is rapidly changing.

If you have a few free minutes in the coming days, I'd welcome any opportunity to tell you more about our project via phone or zoom.

Thank you for the time,

Ted

This is a basic template that you can adjust according to need. If you want to impress upon the reader your bonas fidas, I might expand the description of your previous work, while if I'm trying to hook someone for a crucial sit-down, I might go into more detail about the project itself. Ultimately, what you want to communicate is that you're a professional who knows what they're doing and has real distribution already lined up.

The Follow-Up Chat

Getting the other side to agree to a call or video conference is the first half of the battle. Once the other side acknowledges your note and agrees to discuss it further, you know that they have an interest in your project. Now all you have to do is set the final hook. Doing that ironically requires rehashing your original intro email. Once you do that you've got to hammer home the passion you've got for the project and the opportunity for the subject. The other side will undoubtedly have questions – this is your opportunity to shine and drill down into your knowledge on the subject. Like much of producing, the more you do this, the better you'll get. It's awkward at first but becomes second nature soon after a while. The trick is to know what you want out of the call prior to taking it. This way you can direct the conversation flow toward your desired outcome.

Shooting Binder versus Shooting Bible

Most producers like being out in the field spending time on set crafting content. It's usually why people got into this game in the first place. I'm no different and generally, when I hit the road, I like to create a simple *shooting binder* for myself that includes each day's itinerary, basic location details, release forms, and an overall trip schedule. I also put a digital version in a Dropbox folder so that I can access these documents on my phone no matter where I am in the world. However, sometimes real life intervenes and prevents a producer from being in the field with their crew. In these instances, you have to effectively replace yourself and hire what is known as a field producer or field producer/director to take over your responsibilities. You want to arm this person with the best materials, resources, and insights possible so that they can succeed. After all, their success equals your project's success, which in turn is your success. So instead of creating a basic shooting binder, I produce a more in-depth *Shooting Bible* for the hand off that includes.

- All travel arrangements and crew details
- Each day's itinerary (call sheet) and shooting schedule
- All interview questions
- A list with all shooting and logistical location addresses
- Research documents
- Interviewee bios or backstories
- Program outline (TRT for each segment, footage needs, etc.)
- File naming conventions for any data dumps
- Network technical specs
- Appearance and location releases

A solid Shooting Bible is essentially a window into your mind and a navigational chart that lets any field producer understand every aspect of the project. It's not easy to craft but is crucial if you need someone else to steer the ship while you're away.

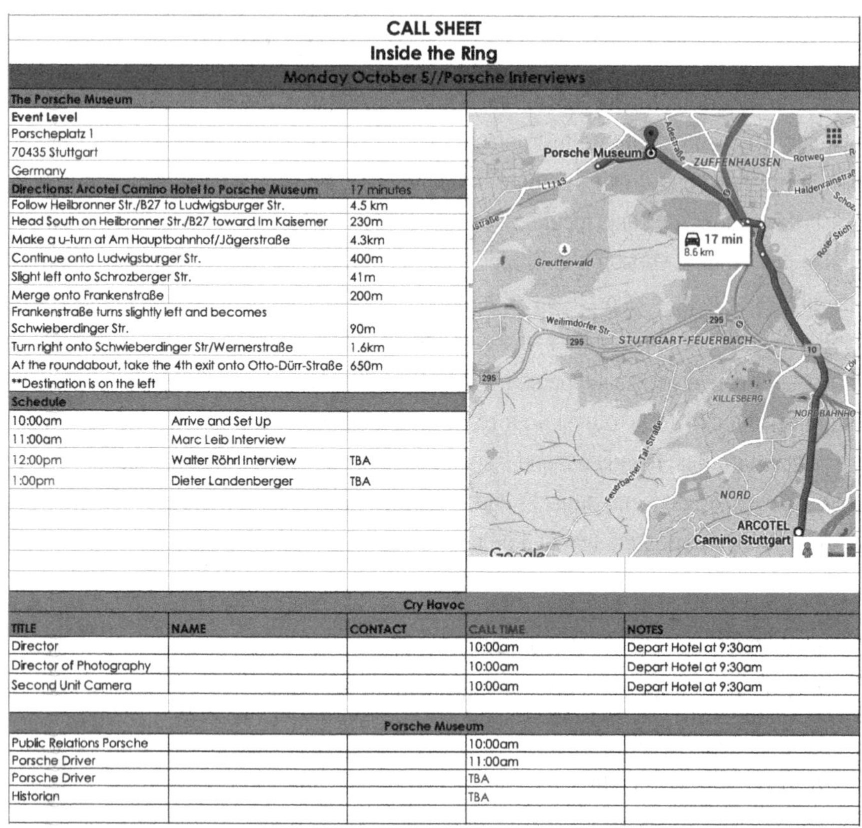

CALL SHEET

Inside the Ring

Monday October 5//Porsche Interviews

The Porsche Museum		
Event Level		
Porscheplatz 1		
70435 Stuttgart		
Germany		
Directions: Arcotel Camino Hotel to Porsche Museum		17 minutes
Follow Heilbronner Str./B27 to Ludwigsburger Str.		4.5 km
Head South on Heilbronner Str./B27 toward Im Kaisemer		230m
Make a u-turn at Am Hauptbahnhof/Jägerstraße		4.3km
Continue onto Ludwigsburger Str.		400m
Slight left onto Schrozberger Str.		41m
Merge onto Frankenstraße		200m
Frankenstraße turns slightly left and becomes Schwieberdinger Str.		90m
Turn right onto Schwieberdinger Str/Wernerstraße		1.6km
At the roundabout, take the 4th exit onto Otto-Dürr-Straße		650m
**Destination is on the left		
Schedule		
10:00am	Arrive and Set Up	
11:00am	Marc Leib Interview	
12:00pm	Walter Röhrl Interview	TBA
1:00pm	Dieter Landenberger	TBA

TITLE	NAME	CONTACT	CALL TIME	NOTES
Cry Havoc				
Director			10:00am	Depart Hotel at 9:30am
Director of Photography			10:00am	Depart Hotel at 9:30am
Second Unit Camera			10:00am	Depart Hotel at 9:30am
Porsche Museum				
Public Relations Porsche			10:00am	
Porsche Driver			11:00am	
Porsche Driver			TBA	
Historian			TBA	

FIGURE 7.5 A Call Sheet from "Inside The Ring".

Finding Great Crew

Once you've got a viable shooting plan and schedule, it's time to figure out how to bring your factual idea to life in a visual medium. Rule number one – don't even think about shooting your project yourself!

You want to go out and hire amazing teammates to help elevate your idea. Great crews are worth their weight in gold and have an ability to transform an ordinary concept into an extraordinary project. They are the technical wizards that can find creative solutions to dire problems and the people who bring the project to life on screen. As the proverb goes, "If you wish to go fast, go alone, but if you wish to go far, you must go together".

Finding exemplary crew members is no easy task. Often the best place to start is with word-of-mouth referrals. If you happen to know other producers, directors, or creatives, it's always worthwhile to mine their contacts for talented operators. If that doesn't work out, there are a plethora of digital staffing sites that can help you get the word out about your project, including mandy.com, staffmeup.com, and productionhub.com. Using these sites can be a bit hit or miss, and you'll often be inundated by intro emails; however, if you take the time to sort through the responses, you can usually find the help you need. If you have a hefty budget, you can also reach out to below-the-line agents who can help you secure numerous crew roles.

Unfortunately, the best of the best potential crew members typically charge far more than most pedestrian production budgets can afford, while the vast sea of cost-effective shooters and soundos are often too junior to do your idea the justice it deserves. It also takes time to learn exactly what you're looking for on your team and who you jive with in the field. Plus, every project has different needs or requirements, which often necessitates different crew members and skill sets.

Quite a few producers and production companies construct their field teams with crew that have come up through traditional ranks. It's a legitimate and valid way to go about staffing up a production that usually guarantees an acceptable level of final production. These folks tend to be highly competent, but they also tend to be indoctrinated in well-worn film school ideologies that often only see *the industry approved way of doing things*.

Alternatively, you can seek out less traditionally taught team members who often have more to prove. I've had great success hiring people who've slipped through the film school cracks and are less interested in the *textbook* way to do something rather than the MacGyver solution that gets the job done.

Usually, most potential shooters try to sway you with glitzy operator reels. I find these fairly meaningless because you never know who shot the images, the circumstances of the shoot, or how much time they had to get the job done. Plus, too many young shooters spend far too much time crafting beautiful images built well outside the confines of professional work. Anyone can craft a well-lit scene over an entire day, but how many can light in 30 or 45 minutes?

I'm far more interested in credit lists. In particular was an operator hired back by the same production company repeatedly, or were they a one and done wonder? If they're hired back multiple times, it immediately tells me that they have an ability to get along with people and that there's nothing suspect about their work.

When I'm sourcing crew, my biggest pet peeve is actually if someone only wears one hat or is only willing to do one job. On a factual program shoot you don't want specialists; you want Navy Seals adept at successfully completing a multitude of assignments in a rapidly changing set of circumstances.

Lots of crew members like to go all Tarantino and wax on about the depth of their filmic knowledge. Who cares? Knowing every shot in a certain feature film might sound cool at a pub, but having real-world knowledge and an understanding of human emotions is far more important for a factual filmmaker. When I'm hiring, I don't care where you went to school. *I care whether or not you can do the job. Period.*

When you're hiring your crew, it's important to clarify the following pieces of information to ensure that everyone is on the same page.

Contract Length and Timing: How long the project will last and when it will begin.

Travel Requirements and Work Environment: Where the shoot will take place and what an average day of filming involves.

Rate: How much the crew member will be paid for their services. Industry standard is a full-day rate for ten hours of work and overtime if the shoot goes past the ten hours. Typically, crew members receive a half-day rate for travel days. Conversely, you can also negotiate a flat weekly fee. This is particularly effective if you're offering multiple weeks of work in a row.

Kit: Will the production company provide the equipment, or will the crew member bring their own? If you ask a crew member to use their own kit, then they should also be paid an equipment rental fee.

Role and Expectations: Describe the crew member's role and what your expectations are for them in the field. On larger crews it also helps to discuss who each person reports to on set.

Retaining Great Crew

How do you attract and retain great crew members for factual television?

- Give them clear responsibilities
- Outline what your needs are (shots/looks, etc.)
- Give them the resources to succeed
- Finally, allow them the autonomy to deliver

It's clutch to repeatedly articulate just how much you appreciate them and their effort. You'd be amazed at how much a simple conversation can mean if worded correctly.

I learned this lesson many years ago when we produced a 12 × 30 historical recreation series for the American Heroes Channel. I sent out a single email after the first episode premiered that offered my appreciation for everyone's hard work, and it paid dividends for years.

Hi everyone,
It's been a truly remarkable year and as we get ready to watch the premiere episode of How We Got Here, I just wanted to thank everyone for your hard work, remarkable dedication and wonderful creative collaborations.
It's been an amazing run and while I'm excited about where the shows are headed, I feel even more fortunate to be able to interact with all of you day in and day out.

Landing a Dream Crew at a Budget-Friendly Rate

As a producer you walk a fine line between staying within your budget and offering enough of a rate to get a crew member to fully buy into your project. Like many things in life the cost of a crew is highly negotiable. Whatever number a prospective crew member tosses out gets counterbalanced by their need to work. So, while a shooter might say they earn a thousand dollars a day, the chances are you can get them for less if they haven't had a gig in a while.

Over the years I've found that there are a few tricks to securing a great crew and holding on to them even if your network budget can't support their talents.

Pay Your Crew Fast: A lot of production companies pay their people 60 or 90 days or even 120 days after a shoot wraps. It's totally bogus. These folks have helped create a project or series, and they deserve to be able to pay their rent or mortgage on time. I've made it a habit to put all my field crew members on direct deposit payroll, and I process payments every two weeks no matter where we are in the world. This way a team member can log into their account and see they got rewarded for their hard work.

Offer a Great Environment and Creativity: Generally, most shooters are told where to point the camera, how to frame, how to set exposure, and so on. I don't subscribe to that kind of management technique. At the outset of a project, we discuss how I envision the series and then the crew is empowered to get after it. If they see something they think is marvelous, they're encouraged to record it. I'm not in the camp counselor business, and I'm not paying people to be robots. I'm paying them to be a part of the creative process and bring their unique skills to the party.

Have a No-Jerk Policy: Life is short, and production is hard; it's not worth dealing with jerks on or off set. Worst yet bad mojo is like a virus; if one team member is disillusioned or negative, then slowly but surely everyone else will be brought down. Make it your mission to surround yourself with great team players. Not only will your team appreciate your selective nature, but the work will turn out better too.

Never Ask Someone to Do Something You'd Never Do: This is effectively *The Don't Be a Jerk Rule* in reverse. I've known producers who ask their crews to carry their bags or get to set hours before they do. That doesn't fly with me. I only ask people to do something that needs to be done and that I've done myself before and usually will do again.

Once you establish that you pay everyone quickly, offer a great environment, don't hire jerks, and you'll never ask the team to do something you wouldn't do yourself, there's one more magical carrot.

Bring the Crew Inside the Financial Tent: Generally, we live in a world where everyone is usually out for themselves financially. I've decided to stake my claim to a different kind of business model. Anyone who has worked for me for five, ten, or fifteen years has greatly contributed to the success of my projects and by extension my career. They deserve something extra for all the hard work, commitment, and repeated effort. So, I try to reward my long-time contributors with a small percentage of any project royalties, or what Hollywood movies often call *backend*. I don't recommend this solution for everyone on your crew; however, it works well for the core team that you count on the most. It's a great way for everyone to share in the glory and offer something that most production companies would never think to do. If you want your team to function like a family, you must treat them as family. If you do, they'll go to the ends of the earth to help you out, no questions asked.

Tightening Budgets

In a perfect world each successive project you land should carve out a larger budget with a network or streamer. A handful of prolific producers with hit shows can pull this off; however, most can't. The truth is that funding in this business comes in and goes out like the tide. Network budgets change all the time based on factors well outside your control such as whether the channel is going through a rebrand, how their advertising revenue projects look, and often the basic nature of the global economy. No matter how hard you try, some years are simply better than others. If you stay in the game long enough at some point, you'll be forced to tighten your spending. When this happens, it often feels like the entire weight of the cost-cutting lies solely on the producer. However, the truth is whenever the budget goes down, everyone should take a hit. It always hurts when you have to ask others to take less. Scan your budget and look for *whales*, the largest line items, and try to immediately enact meaningful change. I'm straight up and explain that our budget got slashed. Their line item is now eating up X% of the total. Make it purely about math. Some vendors won't care, but most will try to help. If they're not willing to help, then it's on you to find a new solution. Remember *everything is negotiable!* Don't be afraid to negotiate with your vendors and if need be, find new ones. Change is often scary, but it's also a powerful tool that almost always unlocks a better path.

You also need to look for new ways to downsize or "rightsize" your production. This can be as simple as cutting a planned extra shooter or can be as complicated as redefining how you're going to crew up to handle postproduction.

I ask a lot out of my vendors when it comes to rates. However, they also know that when a project pops that does have a budget, I always make sure to bump everyone up again. It's a small way to repay their kindness and engender more positive warmth on future projects.

Prepping for the Shoot

Your project has been greenlit, you've settled on a deal structure, you've agreed on a budget, created a bulletproof field production plan, and now you're ready to start principal photography. However, before you can get into the field, there are several crucial tasks that you need to tackle first. What I like to call *the pre-flight checklist.*

Insurance

It's the security blanket you hope you'll never need – production insurance. Once your project kicks over in earnest, one of the first tasks that is often required by the network is **Proof of Production Insurance**. This insurance differs from your typical personal home or auto protection because it's a short-term policy that protects you and the network against catastrophic incidents and horrific events.

There are multiple different facets of a production insurance package.

General Liability: This is your overall protection against the unforeseen or unexpected and covers the general public, companies, or individuals outside of your cast and crew.

Workers Compensation: Coverage for your crew and freelancers should they get hurt on the job. Usually, this is required by local law and typically excludes production company owners or principals.

Equipment: Protection for your gear kit should something awful happen during the shoot. These policies are very broad but often require you to tell the insurance company in advance about any extenuating circumstances. If you're filming on a boat, at a racetrack or inside a factory, you'll need to give the insurance team a heads up.

Negative Coverage: This covers the physical loss, damage, or destruction of your footage up to the amount of your total production budget.

Errors and Omissions (E&O): Typically secured at the end of the project, *E&O Insurance* protects you against copyright infringement issues, mistakes in music clearances, defamation, slander, invasion of privacy, plagiarism, and a host of other possible errors. E&O costs vary wildly depending on the type of factual program you're creating. Anything in the life-rights space or investigative arena will usually have higher fees.

Finding a reputable production insurance vendor can be tricky. There are a lot of questionable insurance brokers out there. Usually however Networks will be able to offer a list of preferred vendors upon request. Depending on the network, these vendors sometimes offer pre-negotiated rates that can save you quite a bit of money.

Picking Your Kit

When you first start out filming projects, cameras are everything. As your projects become more professional, every shooter you hire will want to film with the latest and greatest most technologically advanced camera that hit the market. In theory that makes great sense, but in truth it's a losing proposition for a factual producer who's got an eye on the bottom line. There's always a better camera, or more prestigious lens to use, but don't fall for the trap. It's not worth the spend. Stories can be told with outdated bits of kit just fine. Focus your efforts on the subject matter first and tech second. Find *the right tool* to tell your story and spend your budget on great collaborators. They're worth double the day rate on the latest camera.

> **Tools Change, Storytelling Doesn't:** The tools will continually advance during your career. While you don't need to have hands-on experience with every single one, you do need a cursory understanding of how they work and an ability to communicate what you want out of them to others. Always keep learning, inquiring, and soaking in as much knowledge as possible on the new aspects of the craft, but never become a slave to the technical aspects of production. Tech talk gets camera ops excited, but the latest, greatest image capturing device doesn't tell a story by itself. Viewers will forgive terrible quality images if they're hooked on the tale being told. Spend your time and effort on how to grab an audience.

Owning Gear versus Renting It

One of the great debates in producing is whether to own your own bit of kit. It's a philosophical divide that features two distinct camps of ardent advocates.

The Argument for Renting Gear: Some producers like to rent their gear because it allows them to keep up with changes in technology or easily switch between camera brands and packages based on each project's specific need. You only pay for the time you use the kit, and you never have to worry about where to store it or the maintenance required to keep it in good working order.

The Argument for Buying Gear: On the other side sit producers who want to own their factual filmmaking tools. Over the long-term purchasing your own kit helps you keep costs down because once it's paid off you can keep using it over and over with no additional spend. However, owning equipment also locks you into a specific camera platform, editing rig, lighting kit, and so on and has hidden carrying costs; you must have a place to store it all. Kit takes up space quickly! The downside to owning gear is that if you don't use it a lot, the costs outweigh the usage. When film equipment sits doing nothing, it tends to only lose value.

I can't speak to every producer's situation, but in my experience, it's always been better to own our kit outright. That has opened both creative scheduling and filmmaking possibilities since we never have to worry about when we send it back to the rental house. In fact, as budgets have grown tighter, owning the tools of the trade has allowed us to keep our margins up and our costs down. However, if you're going to buy your own gear, you need to be willing to run it into the ground. If you're someone who likes to trade up all the time, it tends not to be worth it. If you're OK using the kit until it absolutely dies, you'll come out ahead.

How Network's View Renting versus Buying Gear: Network budgets are based on a production renting its gear. If you tell a network that you're going to buy a piece of kit, the network will claim it as their own property. The simple work around is to buy the gear that you need and then rent it back to the production. Some networks have stricter rules about this than others; however, it's an accepted industry wide practice.

Gear Checklists

Once you and your team settle on the kit, it's time to create a **Master Gear Checklist**. This is a document that lists every single item that you own, its serial number, country of origin, carnet code if necessary, and which case it's located within. Gear checklists are a handy way to ensure that each bit of kit goes back in its correct case after each shooting day. The more you can automate this process, the faster your set-up and breakdown times will become, the less loss or damage you'll incur, and smoother your operation will run. A master gear list will also come in handy for any international travel since overseas shipping carnets require it. Some filming locations also will ask to know what pieces of kit you're bringing in beforehand, so it's often nice to already have that info already available in one document.

Cry Havoc Carnet #2

Item #	Quantity	Description	Serial #	Country of Origin	HTS Code	Box #	Weight
		PLEASE NOTE THERE ARE NO BATTERIES IN THIS SHIPMENT					
		CASE 1: 41 x 12 x 10				1	42.0
1	1	Octagonal Tuffpak Tripod Case	n/a	USA	4202.12.2050		20
2	1	Sachtler Video 18 w/ Head and soft case	18SB2237	GERMANY	9007.91.0000		22
		CASE 2: 45 x 10 x 9				2	19.3
3	1	Tenba TTP46 TriPak	n/a	USA	4202.12.2050		4
4	1	Sachtler Dolly S with wheel locks and guards	n/a	GERMANY	9007.91.0000		9.8
5	1	Manfrotto 3021PRO Tripod	n/a	ITALY	9007.91.0000		5.5
		CASE 3: 45 x 8 x 8				3	21.8
6	1	Sportube slider case	n/a	USA	4202.12.2050		8
7	1	Kessler Cine Slider with all terrain outrigger feet and soft c	n/a	USA	9007.91.0000		9.1
8	1	Kessler Parallax	n/a	USA	9007.91.0000		4.7
		CASE 4: 19 x 14 x 7				4	29.0
9	1	Pelican 1500 Slider Case	n/a	USA	4202.12.2050		12
10	1	Kessler Second Shooter controller (electronics)	SSC000057	USA	9007.91.0000		1
11	1	Kessler Second Shooter motor	n/a	USA	9007.91.0000		1.5
12	1	V-lock battery plate	n/a	CHINA	9007.91.0000		1
13	1	Parallax head	n/a	USA	9007.91.0000		1
14	1	100mm High hat	n/a	USA	9007.91.0000		2
15	1	Induro BHD1 tripod head	n/a	CHINA	9007.91.0000		1.5
16	1	Manfrotto MVH500AH Fluid tripod head	n/a	ITALY	9007.91.0000		2
17	2	Yoke to stand adapters (grip)	n/a	USA	9007.91.0000		0.4
18	1	Husky Gray bag	n/a	CHINA	9007.91.0000		0.2
19	1	100mm to 75mm adapter	n/a	USA	9007.91.0000		0.3
20	2	baby pin with ⅜ male thread	n/a	USA	9007.91.0000		0.4
21	2	3"x ¼ thick aluminum washer	n/a	USA	9007.91.0000		0.4
22	2	2 ½ aluminum washer	n/a	USA	9007.91.0000		1
23	4	Kessler ¼ x 20 knobs	n/a	USA	9007.91.0000		1
24	1	M-10 knob	n/a	CHINA	9007.91.0000		0.2
25	1	100mm ball mount with long handle and tension washer	n/a	USA	9007.91.0000		1.5
26	1	100mm tension washer	n/a	USA	9007.91.0000		0.1
27	1	USB to micro cable	n/a	CHINA	9007.91.0000		0.2
28	1	12" cat5 cable	n/a	CHINA	9007.91.0000		0.2
29	1	Canon camera control cable	n/a	CHINA	9007.91.0000		0.2
30	1	AC (Wall) power supply	n/a	CHINA	9007.91.0000		0.2
31	1	Extra pulley (Large size)	n/a	USA	9007.91.0000		0.2
32	1	Camera control cable extention	n/a	CHINA	9007.91.0000		0.2
33	1	Motor mount plate	n/a	USA	9007.91.0000		0.25
		CASE 5: 25 x 10 x 10				5	21.0
34	1	Easyrig Standard Bag	n/a	Sweden	9007.91.0000		2.8
35	1	Easyrig Vario 5 Gimbal Rig Vest	V460	Sweden	9007.91.0000		18.2

FIGURE 7.6 A Sample Gear Description List for a Carnet.

What Is a Carnet?

A Carnet is an international customs document that allows you to import and export goods or materials from one country to another. It's the backbone of the international shipping community and a key cog in getting items from their country of origin to another country for consumption. Its purpose is to stop black market equipment sales. In the factual television industry, a carnet is a crucial form that allows a producer to send equipment from your country of residence to a far-flung filming destination. If you fly from one country to another with gear, you'll need to have the local customs team sign the carnet on your arrival and again upon your departure. You can secure a carnet directly through the ATA Carnet office or you can hire a global shipping company to help you sort it out. Either solution helps you avoid headaches down the road. Some productions try to get away without carnets, but I can tell you from personal experience that doing so is not worth the trouble. Customs issues are a pain, and it's far easier to have the right paperwork on your side when an issue crops up.

Passport Check

Part of a producer's job is to have the foresight to prevent problems from turning into massive headaches. When it comes to travel, and in particular international travel, you should never take basic things for granted. This includes whether everyone on the team has valid identification prior to departure. At the start of every project, I ask the crew for a variety of data, including a copy of their current passport. The first thing you should do is check the expiration date. You'd be surprised how many people think they're in good standing yet have an expired passport. When the team arrives at the airport, I ask everyone once again if they have their passport and IDs on hand. It's often the easy things that go sideways. So, try to prevent issues before they happen. Finally, I try to remind everyone at the beginning of each week of filming, or whenever we switch host companies, to bring their ID. This is particularly critical for shoots inside of Fortune 500 companies. Some will not let you in the door without a proper identification.

Equipment Shipping

A lot of filmmakers will fly with camera equipment when working on projects in far flung destinations. They go through the trouble of hauling the kit to the airport, struggle to find porters to help them move it to the check-in counter, and then often schlep it to the oversized x-ray counter. It's a tiring process, *and you haven't even gotten on the plane yet!* Then, after a lengthy flight spent wondering if the kit made it on board prior to take-off, when you land you have to find the kit in the darkest depths of baggage claim. It's an incredibly painful way to travel, and *it burns the crew fast.* Worse yet, often the cost of shipping the gear via the airline is entirely dependent on whether you get a knowledgeable, friendly gate agent at the check-in counter or not. Some airlines will offer media discounts, while others will be totally ignorant to the concept. The difference in cost can be substantial. We've flown with kit, and in one direction the excess baggage cost us $450 total and, on the way, back it cost us $2,500. Same route, same airline, same flight, same number of cases, same kit. The only difference was the person at the check-in counter. Different countries also have different rules when it comes to baggage weight and handling. Often you can fly out of the United States with a certain number of bags and weight per case, but then have to reconfigure for the flight back. It's a total mess. After growing tired of the grind, I decided that there had to be a better way. The solution was to find a great international shipper. These companies exist everywhere and are one step beyond FedEx, UPS, or DHL. In my experience using a third-party commercial shipping company makes it easier to gauge pricing plus they can help you with any required customs paperwork. We started doing this a decade and a half ago and have never looked back. Not only is it less stressful, but it also takes the weight off a producer's shoulders and alleviates in-travel gear worries. While I'm not a fan of flying with equipment, there is one rule that's sacrosanct – *always fly with your footage in the cabin!* Never even think about checking your hard drives. The newly captured material is priceless. The producers who entrust it to others eventually pay a very steep price.

Choosing the Right Airline

Commercial airline ticket prices can fluctuate wildly between airlines. Make sure you don't just look at the cost of the airfare when booking. That's often pennywise but pound foolish. When we purchase airline tickets for crew, we always make sure to double check that the fare includes baggage. There's no point in buying the least expensive ticket only to find out that the luggage costs are double the original purchase price. We also book all our crew's travel on the same airline and force everyone on our crew to sign up for the airline mileage program. This way they can build up a reservoir of miles for personal use. A nice extra benefit for working on the project, and hopefully if we travel together enough, they'll qualify for mileage program status. It might sound like a small thing, but if you have an international shoot with several different legs, holding status in a mileage program can save hundreds of dollars per person in baggage fees and shave time off your airport experience. *Every bit of savings, whether in effort or financially, adds up.*

Kindness

Another on the road rule is to be kind to everyone you interface with at an airport or in a different country. This dovetails nicely with the no-jerk policy. When you're on the road and everyone is tired, it's easy to be cranky. Make a conscious choice not to be. You have the power within yourself to be enthusiastic and optimistic. A little bit of sunshine goes a long way. This is never truer than when you're overseas or in a foreign land. Don't be a dumb tourist. Be polite, inquisitive, and kind. Folks from other cultures want to share what makes their country wonderful.

Inside the Industry With John Hart, MFE Insurance

John Hart is a Vice President at MFE Insurance Brokerage. With over 35 years' experience in the field of entertainment insurance, he's focused exclusively on understanding the unique coverage needs of movie, video, music, and theatrical companies.

- **What exactly is production insurance, and how does it differ from traditional home or auto insurance that the general public uses?**

Production insurance is just different enough from traditional coverage, to drive the other brokers batty. Make sure you use an entertainment insurance broker. There are similar coverages but different uses of the same term, and they mean something different. I see it as my job to "translate" insurance terms into "production speak". I've made a career communicating "art speak" and "corporate speak" to the appropriate parties.

- **Can you briefly describe the different types of insurance required for a factual television production?**

You'll need Commercial General Liability (covers damages to others), Non-Owned Auto Liability, and Physical Damage (for hired, loaned or donated vehicles). A Production Package covers the Production Materials (tapes, drives, film, etc.), and it covers for rented Props, Sets, Wardrobe, Rented Equipment, Extra Expense (if something happens to the location and you need to re-shoot), Third Party Property Damage (damage to the location, subject to a Deductible), Workers Compensation, and eventually Errors and Omissions upon delivery to the distributor.

- **When it comes to production insurance, what advice would you give to an aspiring producer who's filming content for a paying client for the first time?**

You need to make sure *at the very least*, to cover the Commercial General Liability, Autos, Equipment, Location, and Workers Compensation (through a direct policy, payroll service company, or State Compensation Insurance Fund). You will need to provide a copy of the budget and the script (synopsis, storyboards, decks, etc.) to the broker.

- **What are some of the key considerations that insurance underwriters look at when determining a rate?**

Insurance underwriters base the premium on the type of project. A sit-down interview is easier to insure than a project with stunts, animals, pyrotechnics, or hazardous activities. The rates are determined by the gross production cost, post-production cost, cost of hire on non-owned vehicles and the limits of coverage. Basing the rate on the gross production cost makes sense. The more you work and the longer the production, the higher the chance of there being a claim.

- **Most filmmakers begin their careers by creating personal content in a guerrilla style, where the rules are often a bit suspect – how would you suggest that they level up and transition into a more professional insurance solution?**

You will need insurance in order to get a film permit. You will need Commercial General Liability, Non-Owned Auto Liability, a Waiver of Subrogation, Blanket Additional Insured Endorsement naming the government entity. Depending on the location, you may be able to negotiate the limits and the coverage. Realize, this is going to cost money. It's better to pay for the film permit and insurance than to take the risk of being shut down or sued.

- **What exactly is E&O insurance, and how does it apply to TV programs?**

Errors and Omissions (E&O) covers the unauthorized use of name, likeness, copyright, music, IP, and so on. It pays for the defense of the claim and pays the settlement if it gets to that. The E&O is subject to a minimum $10,000 Deductible. $25,000 Deductible is becoming an industry standard. You usually get this before delivery.

- **Production insurance applications can be a bit overwhelming the first time you go through one – are there any tricks of the trade that you'd be willing to share with first-time producers? Any areas that usually trip filmmakers up? Any places where you see people making similar mistakes?**

Make sure you fill out the application the best you can and then call the broker to go over it on the phone. It's complicated. There's a lot of detail that an experienced broker can help you navigate.

- **How has failure, or apparent failure, helped shape your career?**

I've lost more deals than I care to remember (though I do). I've learned a lot each time. I usually go to the client to ask them why they chose the other broker. I tell them that I want to know what mistakes I made, so that I can help future clients. I expect failure to be part of the process and try as I can, not to take it personally.

Hey, if it was easy everyone would be doing it. Do your homework, learn your craft, do your very best, and most of all be honest. Hollywood is a small town (really). Word gets out quickly if you are not honest. A reputation is one of the hardest things to reclaim

Don't think everyone is out to screw you. Like I said, it's a small town.

Chapter Eight

Field-Production

You originated a brilliant concept, sold it to a network or streamer, and prepped and planned your shoot. Now it's time to get out in the field and start capturing magic!

DOI: 10.4324/9781003292289-8

Great Shoots Need Great Leaders

Great shoots run like a well-oiled machine and that start at the very top thanks to a great leader. There's a thought that exists in our society that leadership is a skill you're either born with or you don't have it. I strongly disagree. *Anyone can be a leader if they choose to be.* It's up to you to take the reins and get the job done.

The best leaders I know are curious to a fault. They want to know more about the world that surrounds them. If you want to be a better leader, ask better questions, about your crew, about the tech, and most importantly about your story.

Being an amazing leader requires attempting to understand every issue from as many vantage points as possible. Making assumptions *you think* are correct isn't the same thing as *knowing* they're correct. Be careful mixing the two. Asking the correct questions is a sign of quiet confidence, not a lack of knowledge. Everyone around you has something to offer. Harness their knowledge and abilities. Questions give you options. Ignoring those around you limits your path. You don't need to know all the answers, you need to be steadfast in the ones that you do know, secure in the ones you feel are correct, and willing to ask others about the ones you don't understand.

Great leaders are also awesomely passionate. They believe in what they're doing, and they're not afraid to show it. Passion is contagious. It's a unique form of energy that people can feel. Passion is what energizes creativity. Never let it die out. The more passionate you are about your project, the more passionate others will become about it.

Confidence breeds confidence. Broadcast an unwavering sense of being in control – even if you're not. The more in-control you are, the calmer and more collective your team will be throughout the shoot. Confidence is not the same as being cocky. Nobody wants to be led by a jerk.

Leadership isn't negotiated. It's earned. Each choice you make among your team builds more trust. People will follow your vision if it's earnest and heartfelt. Great leaders don't get paralyzed from analysis. They make choices, and they never lose sight of what matters. They also fight through the hard times and constantly battle to reach the endgame.

You also need to be selfless. It's not about the credit. It's about the project. I don't care who shoots the prettiest image of the film, makes the clutch edit choice in post, or the crucial suggestion that puts the project over the top. I care about hitting the target, delivering the project on-time, and on budget to a network or streamer. *Nothing else matters.*

Leaders take responsibility. If something goes wrong, it's not someone else's fault. It's yours. Most importantly, true leaders are optimistic. They look for the bright side and aim to bring everyone along to that viewpoint.

Running a factual film crew is like captaining an athletic team, you must motivate your fellow teammates, sometimes cajole them, at other times support them and always protect them. Factual television isn't a democracy, nor is it a dictatorship; rather, it's a creative process that requires clear communication and on-point direction to craft something collaboratively.

A few of the golden rules learned from the field:

Group Discussion: There's a time and place for discussions on set. When you're right about to film a key interview or scene that usually isn't it. However, when the time is appropriate, you need to hit the pause button and learn to listen to your crew.

Be Genuine: Always be unapologetically genuine. If you want to build a great team, be a good person. It's pretty simple.

Articulate Your Thought Process: When people question your decisions, clearly articulate your thought process to unlock the knowledge that lives behind the deadbolted doors in your mind. Most crew members rarely if ever speak with a network executive. They have no idea what your conversations have been like, so the more you can illuminate *the why*, the sooner you'll get everyone on the same page.

Teachable Moments: Everyone screws up. It's human nature, and it's doubly easy to do when you've been in the field for a while. Leaders don't lose it when an error occurs; rather, they use mistakes as teachable moments for what to do next time. This not only engenders you to the greater crew but also builds powerful one-on-one relationships and fosters a positive culture within your crew.

We've had a lot of teachable moments. My favorite took place while filming in the UK. Two members of the crew took a van out for a Sunday drive. With the machine low on petrol, they stopped at a gas station and mistakenly put unleaded gasoline into a diesel machine. When they fired up the machine nothing happened. It was dead. Calamity ensued. By the time they called me they were at their wits end. However, it was an honest mistake that anyone brain dead from a lengthy bit of international travel could have made. Yelling at them wouldn't have solved the issue but jumping into the fray to help solve the problem got everyone back on track and helped ensure that they knew I had their back.

The more you bring your crew *inside the tent* and clearly explain your needs and the end goal you're trying to achieve, the better the end product will be. Factual programming isn't a solitary activity, it's a joint venture that requires a variety of diverse and talented individuals to collaborate in various ways to create something better than any of them could make on their own.

Being a great leader initiates momentum, but it takes an amazing crew to bring ideas to life. Great crews act and think like a family. They're inspired by the gig, clear on their roles and willing to lend a hand to help other members out in times of need.

Here are a few of the crew-based principals I've come to believe in.

The Crew Pyramid

There are a lot of different strategies for building your crew. Generally, I like to roll with as tight a group as possible. I believe that smaller crew allotments make you more agile and flexible in the field. Typically, I like to run with a three-person crew in addition to myself. Over the years I've honed a simple Crew Pyramid as a basic field operation philosophy.

I like to start with one **Old School Veteran**. This is someone who's been there, done it, and seen it all – a person knowledgeable not only in heady camera work but also hip to the hidden tricks of the trade. This will be the *Camera A* role.

Next, I look for a solid and dependable **MacGyver Shooter**. This person needs to be well versed in documentary filmmaking but also aiming to expand their knowledge base. They run *Camera B.*

Finally, I add one **Up and Coming Camera Op**. This is our Jack of All Trades role. Sometimes they use *Camera C*, sometimes they're on GoPro duty, sometimes they run sound. On any given day their needs adapt to the situation at hand.

The goal of the Crew Pyramid is to combine a wide variety of different life experiences in a single crew. People see things from different perspectives and learn different skills along the way. You want to be able to leverage all that various experience during your project. Age also offers a clear hierarchy, and if your younger team members are open to learning, it's a great opportunity to shape how the outfit runs. Finally, using a Crew Pyramid also prepares you for a crew succession down the road. Just like a sports team, you never know when your Topflight DP won't be available or can't make the shoot dates work, so you must proactively plan in advance. *Just as you always want to protect your network EP's interests, you also must always protect your own.*

The crew is a direct reflection of you as a producer. If you're unorganized, they surely will be too. The snippier you are with your crew, the more argumentative they'll be with each other. You want to create a crew culture that reflects your values and fosters an environment where the team knows when to speak up and when to bite their tongue. You want team members who revel in the *one for all, all for one* mindset. It doesn't matter if it's in the job description or not, they jump in to help without being asked.

Especially when no one is watching. This is how you elevate your projects. In the tiny, dark, lonely nooks and crannies on the hardest days.

On bigger productions it's easier for crew members to stick to single roles, but invariably the more that people help each other in general the faster things get done. Once you find team-first crew members, keep them as long as you can. They're priceless.

Importance of A+ Travelers

The quality of your crew can make or break your production. However, when I'm bringing new crew members on board, I'm not only looking for amazing cinematography – *I'm also looking for great travel companions.*

Bouncing around from country to country, or even county to county, with a crew is hard. It tires everyone out and often reveals people's true nature. Not everyone is cut out to eat foreign cuisine every day, sleep in awkward beds, or wake up to find a foreign language being spoken. Many years ago, I decided to flip the script and instead of focusing on the traditional Hollywood resume requirements, I started seeking out travel adventurers who like to film. This has worked out gloriously and can be distilled down to a very simple rule – *Hire B+ shooters if they're A+ travelers.*

This mantra proved invaluable during our greatest field production feat – 11 contiguous weeks filming on the road throughout Europe. Every six days we relocated to a new city or country. It was an incredibly epic adventure that not only resulted in a marvelous television series but also a uniquely fulfilling personal journey. The team and I were able to gallivant across the EU to far-flung destinations that were almost entirely off the traditional *Fodor's* travel path. Instead of seeing the usual sights, we were able to engage with all kinds of amazing people and everyday cultures. For a travel junkie, it doesn't get any better. However, while it was an inspiring odyssey, those 11 weeks spent on the road were also physically taxing. Really long filmmaking adventures are marathons that test your endurance more than your filmmaking. They're all about *patience and perseverance.*

Upgrade Your Crew

Shoots that require a lot of travel in and out of different time zones are physically exhausting. Especially if you're doing a lot of hub-and-spoke moves, starting in a small airport and bouncing to a hub before jetting to another destination. Often, you're spending days away from your friends and family and you're usually working in one time zone while your body thinks it's in another. Not to mention you're constantly moving bags in and out of hotels and picking up and dropping off new rental cars. To make the journey a bit easier I try to upgrade the crew any time I can (if it's within budget). When in doubt, book everyone into economy plus or better if there's a sale. If you want the best out of your team, you need to make life as easy as you can for them. A little bit of extra leg room on a ten-hour flight is a good way to do it. It always pays off.

Crew Buy-In

Once you have your field production crew pyramid humming, you're halfway to a great factual program or series. The next step is to get your team to believe in the project. You want them to feel as passionate about it as you do. The more buy-in they have, the better it'll turn out. You don't want the field production to feel like an ordinary 9-to-5. The best way to create great crew buy-in is to make your production feel *inclusive* and encourage opinions and ideas. Fostering great buy-in helps invigorate a shoot with enthusiasm yet is even more crucial for when things go wrong. A crew that has your back is invaluable when you're trying to sort out what to do next in a moment of crisis.

Per Diem and Meals

If there's one thing crews love to chatter about beyond gear, it's food. You'll spend as much time dealing with when and where to eat as you do discuss your content needs. It's the oil that lubricates a happy and successful shoot. Eating takes on an even greater significance for a road-weary crew. Once a crew heads back to their respective hotel rooms, the real world comes crashing in: phone calls and emails from loved ones back home, problems crop up from 5,000 miles away, and pure exhaustion sets in. Since most of a shooting day is highly regimented, my suggestion is to let the team make the culinary choices. Humans are built on free will, and lengthy shooting days offer few opportunities to display it. Dinner is a great time for a producer to take a back seat and let the team take control and make some decisions on their own.

When you're at dinner, there are two schools of thought when it comes to paying for a meal; a producer can take care of the entire bill at the end, or they can give their crew a per diem that allows the crew to be in control of a fixed amount of money for their food. Personally, I prefer the latter approach. It reinforces that the crew can make their own choices after hours and is also advantageous to the production because whenever you cover the entire bill with no questions asked the costs tend to escalate quickly. Generally, at the outset of a shoot I give each team member an envelope full of their personal per diem. This is their cash to spend as they see fit for meals, laundry, hotel Wi-Fi, and any other extraneous charges they might encounter.

Calculating per diem is more art than science. I try to find a figure that works for the overall budget but also allows for some extra profiting should crew members decide to hold a bit back for themselves. Whatever you do, you don't want to cheap out on crew food costs. There are dozens of places where you can tighten down a production budget, but squeezing your trusted field team's big reward after a hard day's work is bad for business.

Crew Conflict

Even the best crews can experience conflict. It's entirely human and natural, yet also creates a tricky situation for a producer. Tired crews often beget cranky crews, which usually leads to arguments. That's why I'm a proponent of not burning a crew by filming as long as possible every single day. I also like to make sure that there is ample opportunity for sleep. Rest is a weapon for a road warrior. Still problems and arguments arise. Often the best course of action is to let the issue go. Attention is the oxygen of conflict. When you fight a problem, you breathe life into it. However, when you starve it of attention, the problem often burns out on its own. Big problems however need quick and immediate solutions.

Conflict is always going to be part of the creative process. Getting used to it is crucial for your growth as a factual filmmaker. It's inevitable that you'll come up against obstacles and find yourself in stressful or even uncomfortable situations. However, if you can handle these moments of concern with grace, dignity, and compassion, you'll ultimately build a better foundation for your future success.

The Power of Delegation

Finding great lieutenants who can take things off your plate is a powerful superhero producer skill. The more empowered team members you can rope into your orbit, the better your project's odds of success become. A lot of young factual filmmakers want to control every aspect; however, that's a quick path to a crash and burn. *Learning how and when to delegate is the secret that unlocks the next level of creative work.*

The trick is finding crew members capable enough to do the job and who you trust to do it well. Typically, the best bet is to groom someone in-house. Hire a precocious intern or energetic assistant producer and build them up from basic responsibilities to crucial aspects of the project as they prove their mettle. Keep piling more and more key responsibilities onto their proverbial plate. The more invested you make them in the outcome, the harder they'll work on behalf of you and the project. Investment doesn't mean cost, rather it can come from clearly articulating how their role will help the project succeed. People want to know that their work is needed, respected and critical to the job at hand.

A Great #2 should be able to run the show in your stead and ought to command the respect of your field team or post production crew. They don't have to be exactly like you, nor do they have to manage the way you do. They simply need to get the job done and understand what you're asking them to accomplish.

When you find a terrific #2, an entire new world of possibility opens. Now you and your clone can be in two places at once and tackle two crucial issues at once. Eventually, this person will want to see how high and far they can fly on their own; however, for the time you have them harness their skills to increase your own headroom and potential.

Jettison Bad Apples

It takes a while to get good at hiring crew, office employees, or post-production team members. If you ever become convinced a particular hire isn't working out, pull them aside, and tell them what your concerns are and give them a fixed period of time to shape up. If they can't hack it, then you must fire them. Don't wait any longer than necessary. Usually, your team already knows this person is the weak link and can't cut it. If you don't address the problem quickly, you not only let inefficiency reign but also subconsciously tell the rest of your team that their hard work or extra effort isn't valued.

When letting someone go, you must know what you want out of the conversation before you have it. Be clear with the other person that the gig isn't working, and the relationship isn't repairable. It must be cut and dry. Take all emotion out of the discussion. You're not having a conversation. It's just over.

Another Country, Another Job

There's something magical about running a crew composed of your closet creative collaborators. It can feel a bit like a collection of Ocean's 11 masterminds meeting for the first time in months in some far-flung destination right before a big heist. There's something incredibly evocative about handcrafting a factual program or series with your closest mates that supersedes a mere occupation. If you can find a way to blend your personal interest and passions with your professional zeal, then factual television can open your life up to amazing and unusual opportunities. It can help you meet your heroes, realize your visual dreams, hang with some of the smartest and most talented individuals all over the world, and even create a life of inspired travel.

Shot Lists

Getting your director of photography and additional camera operators on the same page is one of the tougher challenges that a producer faces. It's a bit like a football coach getting their team to learn the same three or four key plays. On a narrative project, where you can create and control the entire mise-en-scène, you can develop a unified look with your DP by sharing other films and forms of art as inspiration. The factual space is a bit harder because often you have less control over your environment and subjects. This is especially true when you're dealing with regular folks in an observational manner. Often necessity dictates that you're less concerned with finding *the look* versus simply being in the right spot at the right time to capture the unfolding story.

Great factual program shooters intuitively know how to place themselves in the thick of the action but just out of the way so as not to intrude. Those sort of shooters are your stars. They need to keep their eyes up, and their head on a swivel as they survey the landscape and look for the next target of opportunity. On the other hand, highly constructed shoots rely almost entirely on a predetermined plan, having enough time to painstakingly craft the required shots, and the right tools to get the job done. There are also hybrid projects where you have some uncontrollable elements mixed with some extremely controlled settings. For example, any factual program that blends recreations and expert interviews within the moment visuals walks with a foot in both worlds.

I've always tried to offer our team a concise vision for the final film, and I've found that the best course of action is usually to show your team a few key shots from previous projects (screen grabs work well) and to share a clearly articulated game plan. This can be your network shooting outline or a simpler document that reinforces the narrative thrust of your project.

On the more controllable scenes I like to talk with the team ahead of time and crowd-source their ideas for how we might create something visually dynamic. You never know who might toss in a brilliant suggestion. Instead use this moment to generate greater crew buy in by allowing the team to own parts of the process. If you've hired the right people, they'll take the ball and run with it, often creating images that are far better than what you could have achieved on your own or micromanaged into existence. The best shooters are like topflight pro athletes; they want the ball in their hands when it matters most.

Technical Specs Are Boring

Many filmmakers breathlessly geek out about their new RED Cinema Camera's 4k or 6k capabilities and the exquisite quality of their new prime lens. Undoubtedly, we all want our projects to look gorgeous, but an expensive camera doesn't guarantee a great program or series. Often, it's the opposite. The less tools a filmmaker has at their disposal, the more creative they must become. *Gear doesn't make a factual filmmaker great.* Factual programs are about stories, emotions, and insights, not megapixels.

Get Some Rest

Sleep is the *hidden secret* to great factual television shoots. So often production companies run their crew into the ground with an unsustainable shooting schedule all in the name of shaving a few dollars off the budget. This might work once or twice but ultimately will cause you more grief than it's worth. When people are tired, bad things happen. It's that simple. Accidents occur. Gear gets broken. People say things that create larger problems down the road. Don't be that producer. Make a point of treating everyone with the same respect you'd want if you were in their shoes and ensure that everyone has enough time to get a good night's rest. Rest is a weapon. Use it.

Inside the Industry With Stephen Harrison, Director of Photography

Stephen Harrison is Director of Photography with over 35 years of experience in the factual industry. After getting his start at Australia's Ten Network, where he filmed a variety of studio and field content, he parlayed his network experience into a lengthy career filming some of the top-rated cable programs including Treasure Quest, Modern Marvels, Strange Sex, 101 Gadgets, Mega and Factories. Stephen has worked for a who's who of factual production companies ranging from JWM, Sirens Media, Half Yard, and North One TV.

- **When a producer hires you to lens a program or series, how do you get on the same page regarding the project's look and feel?**

Communication is the key. Not just talking about visual cues from reference sources, constantly talking about technology, style, formats, editing, "feel", controlling factors like location environment, time, network requirements will aid in developing a better understanding of what the Producer is dealing with and how best guide them to achieve a result they will be happy with. Communicating constantly ensures the ability to predict things and circumnavigate potential problems and even better take advantage of an opportunity. A relationship between producer and DP is incredibly important and at times can be more of a partnership as trust and openness play an integral role.

- **In your perfect world what sort of information should a producer share with you before filming begins?**

When working with a producer for the first time it's imperative to gather as much information as possible. Having visual cues like photos or other visuals can help get a better understanding of the initial "Look" the producer is aiming for, but that only gets you so far as the reality of location filming at times is very different. Developing an ongoing open and direct relationship with the producer is crucial. The more information they can give you regarding what their aim is for the program, the better: knowing what assets they have available for the production, the time frames at each location, the expected restrictions whether they be talent, location, weather, or even at times equipment usage. Even how they intend to edit it can change how you approach the shoot. Each program is unique and brings its own challenges and compromises and the more information the producer shares with you, the better prepared you will be and closer to delivering the desired product. An example from my past would be a wildlife shoot filming orangutans up close in the Borneo jungle. It will be hot, humid, and there will be constant rain. So, the camera gear needs to be protected but also knowing that humidity will be a problem so rain jackets on cameras may cause issues, so will mold on lenses and electronics. Power for equipment recharging will be available at night as will a dehumidifier. We will have access to platforms in trees to film up close and personal with the Orangutans. Which can be curious. This is a key statement . . . "they will be curious" . . . turns out they had dismantled a BBC crew's film camera the week before and they had lost their footage. The Orangutans also liked to steal tripods. So, this little piece of information allowed me to safeguard my gear [within reason] from being damaged and potentially derailing the shoot.

- **What is the best way to work with a producer to select the appropriate equipment kit for a particular project?**

Equipment discussions are many and varied when it comes to productions and depend on many factors of the project. In some cases, the production kit has already been determined and that is what it is. Other times Producers are looking for initial advice on what would be required from a list of "approved" equipment. And other times it's the dealer's choice. The Producers experience can play largely into this choice. They should know how the end project will be delivered and what the technical requirements from the Network or Streamer will be. This information has a bearing on choice of technology. This can be the difference between shooting on a GoPro or a Sony Venice. Post production comes into play also as certain camera codecs don't necessarily play well with edit systems which may have already been determined in advance. Also, certain codecs in the field are monstrously large and so not a great choice for a run and gun style shoot where large volumes of data will be captured. After these aspects have been determined to be either restrictive or not, the choice gets narrowed to style of shoot, production crew size, complexity of shots, lens requirements, environmental impacts, budget, operator experience, and even personal preference. A good DP can work with any tool, and everything has some form of compromise. Larger high-end cameras don't necessarily mean a better product especially if it requires two people to operate effectively and needs a truck load of accessories to be used for a run and gun style production. Once again, an open discussion with the producer is paramount in keeping everyone on the same page. The technical discussion is mostly in the DP's wheelhouse as it is their job to make sure the chosen tool WILL achieve what the Producer wants, provided all the information is on the table to make informed choices.

- **What are you looking for in gear that might differ from what a producer is after?**

Sometimes DPs prefer to have certain tools and technology that they absolutely have to have. Like a monitor brand/series which through experience meets their requirements and is something they feel is imperative for them to be able to do their job to the best of their ability. Sometimes they need to justify this to the Producer because of expense or size or for whatever reason. Mostly this never happens as an Experienced producer will understand that they must trust their DP to not be indulgent or exploitative of budgets. There will always be things that are required for the technical side of production that Producers are not knowledgeable of so keeping the communication window open to educating everyone on new technology can be beneficial to the advancement of the production. If something allows for the DP to do their job more efficiently, then usually it's a win-win for the production.

- **From your point of view as a director of photography, what are the attributes of a great shoot (in particular with regard to travel, crew size, talent, etc.)?**

What attracts me personally to certain productions over others tends to be subject matter and crew. There are certain subjects which challenge me technically, mentally, and physically. They tend not to fit in the usual cameraman handbook. The sweet spot incorporates the logistical and mental challenges of working remotely with limited resources, requiring a degree of preparedness and organization but also a certain mindset of capability and versatility. Working with a small multi-talented crew who can overlap one another's roles but also encourage and challenge one another. Not only does this safeguard the production's delivery but also creates an awesome production environment. While there is still the traditional hierarchy to the production, it becomes much more of a collaboration of creative minds. Whilst technology is a huge part of production, I think I tend to see it now as a series of tools. Technological advances made in the last 20 years have taken much of the overall pre-production setup work load out of production. With the expense, versatility and ready availability of this technology, setup time, crew size and equipment case count has been vastly reduced which then opens the door to more generalist production people not just specialists.

- **How does filming with talent help or hurt a shoot from your point of view?**

On camera talent can be a two-edged sword for a DP. They can aid in the shoot when there is a limited visual selection or a difficult to see element. Then the talent fills in those story line gaps. However, the other side is that you've now introduced a living breathing element to the shoot. A great example is in the perfect world we have a shot of the Grand Canyon. If it was a voice-over shot, then the DP would pick the perfect angle, with the perfect light at the perfect time of day with the correct lens. Shot done. Now introduce the Talent who has a 90-second piece of dialogue to deliver. Now comes the hard part and the decisions to be made before the actual shoot. The budget allows you 1 hour of time to shoot this 90-second piece. So, location choice must be made in relation to what the Talent is talking about. Is the light right for the background AND the talent? Is the Talent walking along the rim of the Canyon? Is it shot on a wide-angle static lens from a tripod or tracked using a gimbal? Will the weather be okay? Rain and wind now play a greater part. Will there be external elements there such as other tourists? How experienced is the Talent at walking on unfamiliar and unstable ground? What is the physical access for equipment? All of this has been decided or pre-checked on location. So off we go. The crew is Producer, Talent, DP/Cam Op. Sound op. Assistant. Take 1. Wind noise on Mic, Take 2. Cloud covers sun, Take 3. Talent forgets their line. Take 4. Bird screeches over dialogue. Take 5. Wind. Take 6. Camera lost power. Take 7 . . .

When using talent in front of the camera a certain amount of complexity CAN be introduced to the shoot. Sound and Lighting play a larger part in the shot selection for the DP. Shadows and noise can encroach and create difficulty for the Talent to best deliver their dialogue. A higher level of compromise is required from the DP as they must favor the talent, audio and lighting instead of just the final image. You now have to make certain the Talent gets their delivery correct and to the satisfaction of the producer. The sound operator has to be satisfied with the audio. When you start introducing other moving parts like second talent, or cue marks and interactive elements like in and out of cars and so on, the complexity and elements of having to do retakes increase, which then has a budgetary element. That said, when all those compromising elements are taken into consideration and using an experienced team, having on camera talent can make a shoot a pleasure and move it to the next level of quality. It introduces a whole other shooting style and elements to storytelling not just visually but also creatively for everyone including the DP, especially in relation to shot design and crew dynamics.

- **What are some of the potential landmines that a producer should look out for during field production and how might they adversely affect a crew?**

One of the largest pitfalls for an inexperienced producer is not communicating enough with your DP. Not giving them as much information as possible. The DP is there to help you tell your story. The more that individual is aware of the elements available or restricting the production, the more suggestions and solutions they can give you. Not just technically but creatively and even logistically. The more things they're aware of regarding the subject, allows them to consider the coverage selection. Another aspect would be crew harmony. Producers have their plates filled to the brim with responsibilities, especially on smaller crewed productions, but being aware of the crew harmony is imperative. This is especially important for longer shoots with higher stress loads. Keeping an eye out on crew dynamics and attitudes will ensure a smooth running and enjoyable shoot.

- **When you were starting out, what salient advice did one of your mentors share that has had the greatest impact on you and/or your career?**

The best two pieces of advice I received were, "Let people do their thing and give them space" and, "A good idea can come from anywhere, don't be afraid to try it and give credit where credit is due".

- **You've filmed all over the world with a variety of crews from different networks and production companies. What defines a well-produced shoot from your vantage point?**

From my experience the best produced shoots are those where the expectations are realistic. Where the goal is known by everyone and it's realistic with the tools and personnel provided, which comes down to pre-production planning. For the day-to-day aspects *time* is always the enemy. Realistic set up times for the required quality of the visuals is understood by all and adhered to, not just by the Producers but by the crew as well. Respect is another major aspect. Everyone needs to have respect for the roles their fellow team members play. Everyone is important. Everyone. Field production can be a difficult, stressful, anxiety riddled environment but it's also incredibly satisfying, enjoyable, challenging and character building. TV production is created by a team not just individuals and when that's understood, it makes for an incredibly satisfying experience.

- **A lot of your shooting has involved travel, are there any tricks of the trade that you think aspiring producers ought to keep in mind when planning a shoot?**

When it comes to travel while shooting, especially internationally, *time* becomes the biggest enemy. Travel time, customs, airports, baggage, case count, crew wrangling, language issues, hotel transfers, vehicle collection/loading, navigation, communication, gratuities, meals, jet lag, medical issues, and so on. So many extra elements come into play, and most of them are time related. How much time it takes to load and unload in a location, which gear is required here, does equipment require packing for shipment or just car travel? How long does it take to cross a border? They all eat into your shoot time and budget. So, considering the amount of travel, the number of locations in one day all need to be thought out a little bit in more detail than in locations you're familiar with. Moving around New York city is a lot harder with a kart load of gear than it is around Boulder Colorado. Sometimes working and traveling with a small crew is like traveling with your family. Some people like it and are good travelers, and others not so much. Surround yourself with a crew who are not only good individual travelers but who are good group travelers. In so much as they understand that you are a group, who is working in a foreign environment and are there for a particular purpose and not on a holiday. Having an understanding of group dynamics in that environment is vital.

- **From your perspective how can a producer help get everyone on the team to buy-in to the project beyond financial incentives?**

Every Producer wants to surround themselves with a crew who enjoy their work and "want" to work on their production. However, when budgets get lower, it's sometimes difficult for crew to "buy in" to the production because like everyone, they have bills to pay and taking a set amount of time away may cause them to lose out on other higher-paying jobs. So, the production is looking at other ways to incentivize a crew to take on the roles. Sometimes it's enough that the subject matter is attractive, or the style of production. Maybe it's the thought of filming in a foreign country or exotic location. Sometimes crew members may want the opportunity to work alongside certain colleagues or use a particular piece of equipment. Other times it's offering the chance to move up to a position of responsibility not readily offered, or even a CV credit. There are a myriad of incentives for crew members to agree to a production; however, those elements still must fit within the parameters of creating a cohesive crew and the incentive for one person may be a dis-incentive for someone else or causes friction for someone else on the crew. Sometimes an industry wage is the cleanest simplest option, and if someone won't do it for the money, find someone who will.

- **How has failure, or apparent failure, helped shape your career?**

Learning from mistakes made in the field is a truly important aspect for growing as a professional in the TV industry. The ability to recognize the mistake or error, analyze it, learn what went wrong and more importantly how to fix it, and move on is just as important. Mistakes happen, some are insignificant and go unseen, others can bring a production to an end. Early in my career my fear of failure made me have a death grip of control over my job. No aspect of my job went unscrutinized or left uncontrolled. Checked, double checked and triple checked. I would make certain every shot was perfect, every piece of equipment in my kit. That I had redundancies for my redundancies. Nothing would go wrong that

I hadn't foreseen. Some of this stemmed from network budgets controlling the experience level of my fellow crew members and the nature of the projects. That squeeze of control certainly allowed for a majority of problem free productions; however, it didn't always make me the best person to work with on a collaboration level. For me to guarantee delivery what I said was law and this was the way it was done. I didn't allow myself or others any freedom to make mistakes because the opportunities I was given wouldn't tolerate it. The success of the production was that I had to come back with the story 100% of the time. On the one hand my career excelled, and I was given higher and higher responsibilities and mind-blowing filming opportunities, but on the other I became aware that some of the more experienced people I enjoyed working with the most didn't really want to work with me because I was a control freak. So gradually I began to release my control and run a few more risks and be okay that should a problem occur I had enough experience and knowledge to deal with it. But even more importantly I came to the realization that I had a group of people around me whom I could bounce ideas off and come up with a solution. Soon this became the norm. Sure, I still retained a certain amount of "control" but my fear of failure had severely declined so much that I encouraged lateral thinking in every production I was involved in. This allowed for much more creative input from myself and those around me and a sense of if something stuffs up on the shoot, our abilities as professionals will allow us to rectify it and adapt. The confidence in myself and in that the people around me were also doing their best and working toward the same aim brought a whole other level to my career.

- **What is the best investment in yourself that you've ever made?**

Learning humility. Allowing my curiosity to explore. Be open for anything. Learning to listen, and when to offer advice.

- **What is the worst advice that you continually hear people giving new or young producers?**

"You are the boss". I think without clarification this is the scariest comment for a newly minted producer to be told. Producers have to be the adult in a crew. The decisions they make are so far reaching and all-encompassing that throwing a term like this can also be the recipe for disaster. I have had too many experiences where the new producer was so single minded in their micromanaging that they refused to listen to what their crew was trying to tell them and failed to see that the environment was changing so rapidly that the shoot eventually fell apart. Being the boss means you are ultimately responsible for the entire shoot and bringing home the goods. No question. That said, a good producer understands that there is a reason you have these other people in your crew. Let them do their jobs. Let them make you look good. Listen to their advice and suggestions and if it fits into your narrative, take them on and if they don't fit, thank the crew and move on. Think of the position of Producer more as a captain of a ship. You're steering the vessel filled with a crew on a journey to a far destination. How you plot the course through the storms and shoals is up to you and only you have that ability and control. It can be bumpy or smooth. Either way you're the one at the wheel, but you need those people to help you get there, because without a crew the ship never leaves dock. Being the producer also brings a certain responsibility on you from the crew. They want the project to succeed. They want the opportunity to do their best work and be safe doing it. You have that control. They want a good show as much as you do. They want to continue working. So, you have a responsibility to them to do the best job YOU can as a producer, just like they are doing in their respective fields so together you get to do it all again for the next series. Be humble. Know you can't do it without the crew, and the crew can't do it without you.

Principal Photography

It's finally time to realize a dream that originated as a loosely percolating idea and then morphed into a sellable concept. It's time to make some on-screen magic happen.

Filming Locations

On many factual projects your primary filming locations will be places that you've gained admission to during the pre-production phase. This could be a former crime scene, a subject's house, a factory, or inside of a high-profile organization. Many of these locations will be free of charge. In other instances, you'll need to not only find an appropriate filming location for your project, but also negotiate a rental rate with the property owner or manager. In major markets there are often location companies that can help you find the perfect property and broker the deal.

How to Interview

Crafting a great interview requires as much mental energy as coming up with a brilliant pitch deck. It requires detailed preparation, curiosity and an art for being conversational. Generally, anyone who's agreed to be interviewed wants to tell their side of a story – there aren't a lot of people who agree to sit down if deep down in their soul they don't want to talk. Your job is to get them to open up in as pleasant and relaxed a fashion as possible. The vast majority of people are highly uncomfortable talking in front of a camera, after all it's a completely unnatural act. The more relaxed you are, the better their performance will be.

Here are eight basic steps for capturing a terrific sit-down conversation.

Prep Work: Research everything that you can find on the person and read as many articles or books as possible. Allow yourself to become fluent in any industry specific terminology and well versed at the topic you're about to discuss. You want to have an intimate knowledge of the subject and become a qausi expert in your own right.

Questions: Next, review your shooting outline and think about where the interviewee can make the greatest contribution to the story you're trying to tell. Draft a list of questions that combines your research with what you need narratively for the project. I like to start each interview question list with a few basic warm up queries; nothing too serious nor overtly lighthearted but engaging enough to help the interviewee forget about the giant lens being jammed into their face.

I find it helpful to pre-write a bit of small talk into the beginning of my questions. This way during the interview, I don't have to spend any mental energy thinking about it and instead can use the time between a subject's answer and my next question *to listen*.

Some producers specifically tell their interviewees what to say. Personally, I'm not a big fan of that approach. It tends to look unnatural unless the interviewee is a trained actor. You can however move people in the direction of what you need by pre-telling them the answer you're after. From birth humans do a remarkable job of mimicking – it's initially how we learn to function in the world. Use this superpower to your advantage. If you state, the answer before the question most of the time the interviewee will regurgitate it in their answer. For crucial narrative turning questions, I write multiple versions of the same question and pepper them throughout the conversation. Often an interviewee will give a corporate speak filled answer the first time through, but usually if I ask a similar question later on, they will reveal how they really feel with a more honest and heartfelt response.

Interview Day: Ensure that you and your team have a decent amount of set up time. You'll find that crews always want as much time as they can have to set up, but as a producer you need to maximize your shooting day. So, you don't want to burn too much time preparing for an interview. I've found that one hour is usually sufficient for a typical three-point lighting documentary sit-down. The longer you roll with the same crew, the more set-up efficiencies you'll find and the less time you'll need.

Intro and Small Talk: When the subject arrives introduce yourself with a quiet confidence and initiate some basic off-camera conversation to warm the person up. This is a great time to drop in a few choice bits of info you've learned *about them* during the research process. People almost always perk up when you show general enthusiasm for what they're doing. It's a quick way to put the interviewee at ease and let them know that they're in good hands during the discussion. This is also a great time to remind the interviewee that this isn't live TV! If they stumble or want to restart an answer that's fine.

Release: While chatting off camera, it's a great time to save yourself future aggravation and an immense amount of trouble by having your interviewee sign an **Appearance Release**. These releases are hugely important documents because they're the legal contracts that grant you the right to broadcast someone's likeness, image and voice in your project. Without them you don't have a program. Every network

SUPERCAR SUPERBUILD - SEASON 2 11/22/15
Mercedes Interview Questions v1

Gorden Wagner (Head of Design)

Take us back to the very beginning, how did the GT project start?

Once you received the news that it was time to design a new 2-seat sports car for Mercedes Benz what were your first thoughts?

Let's talk about the lineage of the GT – First there was the 300 SL Gullwing. Its spiritual heir was the SLS AMG. And now there's the GT, which seems like the successor in an evolutionary fashion to the SLS... Can you tell us about this rich history?

Now I read a quote where you said, "It very quickly became clear to us that the Mercedes-AMG GT is just impossible to draw" – That's not something we're used to hearing from designers – What did you mean?

Often halo sportscars are harbingers for a brand's design language in the future – Does the GT represent the basis of where Mercedes is headed in terms of style?

I understand that the grill is critically important to the design & style of the machine – But haven't Mercedes grills always been a key part of the brand?

Let's talk about doors – It's hard not to when it comes to 2-seat Mercedes sports cars – I think many people are going to ask what happened to the gullwing doors?

Tell me about the exterior of the car, what is the shape trying to evoke?

In our research I keep seeing one key phrase, "sensual purity" – what does that mean?

The sportscar field has gotten incredibly complicated these days. Lots of brands offer fast machines and lots of power. Often I feel like what separates the great machines from the more ordinary ones is actually the interior. Tell us about the inside of the GT – Can you describe it for us?

I read another quote of yours where you said, "I think that the environment definitely influences creative thinking – I not only get inspired on my travels, but also by elements in day-to-day environments such as the forms of nature, architecture, art, fashion or good product design from outside the automobile industry.' Can you tell us about this?

One last quote, you were quoted as saying, "As designers we have to define the future so it is important for us to look into the future. We are already looking at 2018 concepts [and with] platforms we are looking to cars that are going to be on the road in 2030." Tell us about that?

FIGURE 8.1 A Question List From Supercar Superbuild S2

or streamer will require it as part of your final legal binder. It's much easier to get these releases signed in the field because trying to get them signed days or weeks later is one of the great pinch points in the factual program production process. It's far easier to tackle the paperwork while the iron is hot.

Organizing Releases: You can make your life much easier if you scan your newly signed release forms immediately after filming wraps each day. I like to use the iPhone app *ScannerPro*, which allows you to take a quick picture to digitize the file before saving it to the cloud for safe keeping. Once online I add a series and episode prefix to the release's filename to start the final legal binder organization process. So, for instance if I'm working on a motorcycle series and doing an interview for the Ducati Motorcycle episode, I might use "MotorcycleSeries_Duc_Name of Interviewee" as a filename structure.

Afterward, I add the interviewee's name to a project specific interview spreadsheet. The resulting list is a useful trick to track whether interview files have been transcribed and as the starting point for a future episode name and title list, which is a great document to create to ensure that there are no spelling errors in your programs.

Rolling Camera: Once you're ready to begin, the first question you should ask is the person's name, how to spell it, and their title. It's good to have a verbal record of who you're interviewing for transcription purposes. On a lengthy shoot with hundreds of interviews it can really pay off down the road when all the conversations blur together. However, if you're chatting with a famous CEO-type, you should jump right into the questions. Their time is far more valuable than yours is.

Be Conversational: The hardest part of interviewing is making the camera disappear. Once the cameras are rolling, I tell my crew not to interrupt me unless there's a technical glitch that will render the interview useless. We also don't use "action" or "cut" while filming. Usually, the DP simply taps me on the shoulder once we're recording. It's a subtle way not to break the conversational rapport you've been building.

Keep Your Ears Open: Amazingly, the most powerful weapon you have as an interviewer is to listen. Ask your question and then let the other person answer uninterrupted. Don't be so eager to ask your next question that you step over the interviewees' soundbite. You want to give your interviewee as many non-verbal cues as possible that show that you're engaged and enjoying the conversation. The best way to do that is to quietly nod or smile as they talk. Whenever the subject stops speaking, instead of immediately hitting them with the next question, take another beat and nod again.

You'd be surprised how many people will subconsciously interrupt that as the green light to continue answering the question in greater detail. This is often where the juiciest and best interview soundbites come from.

When to Break the Rules

The entertainment industry is filled with famous rulebreakers, as well as the *dead bodies* of those who broke the rules and never made it back to tell their tale. The key is to know when and where to push for your advantage. At some point on any shoot, you'll be presented with a moment when you need to cut against the grain – the question is when it's worth it?

Sometimes this is an intuitive process ("*I feel very strongly we have to have this shot*"), at other times it's purely need-based ("*We need this sequence, or we don't have an ending*"), and every so often experience dictates what to do over reason. However, just like in Monopoly, there's only a few *Get Out Of Jail Free* cards in the deck. So, you need to use them very wisely. When I was a young producer, I'd push corporate handlers to allow us to film from dusk to dawn to capture as much material as possible because I always lived in fear that we wouldn't have enough footage for the final edit. If a company rep told me we couldn't film in a particular location, I'd relentlessly circle back and hound them to break the rules just this one time. Sometimes it would work, other times it wouldn't; however, it almost certainly guaranteed that there'd be conflict on set. It took me years to learn that those one or two extra shots never make or break a project. The audience never knows what you didn't film or missed capturing in the field.

These days I only break a rule if there's something that I know is crucial to our story's success and I only deploy that card once or twice *a series*, if at all. The risk must be worth the reward and in this case, I continually think about whether it's worth burning bridges, the crew or the relationship with a brand over 1 or 2 shots. My guiding principle is always, "will anyone at home change the channel because this shot is missing?" If the answer is yes, by all means fight for it. However, if the answer is no way, then what are you fretting about?

Kill Them With Kindness

The best way to get what you need is to *kill the other side with kindness*. There are a lot of yellers and screamers and from the outside looking in it often appears that they get what they want an awful lot however appearances can often be deceiving.

The more you yell and scream your way through life, the less happy you'll ultimately be as a person and the less powerful your projects will be in the end. Negative vibes are a death sentence for a factual program or series. They infect the cast, the crew, the greater team, and the people around you like a virus. Left untreated it will destroy everything that you've worked for. The best course of action is to do the opposite. Be a good person. Be present. Be helpful. Be respectful. *Kill'em with kindness.*

Indecision Is an Assassin

You always need to know the answer to "What are we doing next?" because uncertainty is a killer. Half of that battle is simply knowing what you're trying to achieve each day and providing clear meaningful direction to the crew.

At some point in your producing career, you're going to have to either split your team to shoot in two different locations at the same time or produce a project where you can't be on-set during the shoot. In both instances your project's outcome now lies in the hands of others. *In these situations, indecision can be an assassin.*

I don't care what decision the team makes as they *choose something.* The sooner a choice is made, the sooner it can be course corrected if need be. However, standing around trying to decide what to do next is a dangerous vortex that can consume a shooting day and cost you both time and money. You may as well set your production funding on fire.

There are three core principles to decision-making.

Understand the Change: You've got to determine what needs to alter, then take a beat to bypass the easy answer so that you can find the core issue at hand.

Determine Your Plan: Once you identify the issue, laser focus on how to deal with it.

Communicate the Plan: Whatever you decide to do, clearly articulate it in a positive tone with conviction so that no one on the team doubts the solution. You can't communicate concern, rather you must arm your teammates with confidence – even if you're uncertain this is the correct course of action.

Ultimately, I'd rather empower my team to make the best choices that they can make in any moment and get the cameras rolling again. If that turns out to be the wrong choice, we'll make changes later, but at least in the meantime they've started capturing usable material and have created something of value.

Always Stay Curious

The most interesting people in life tend to be the most curious. The same holds true for factual producing – the more curious you are, the better your programs will turn out. Curiosity is what begs that one last question which unlocks an amazing answer you never saw coming. It's also what leads you to ask a handler what lies behind the locked door down the hall. When others see you're curious about what they're into, they often open up and show you new things. New options are new opportunities.

We've had multiple experiences while filming where our general enthusiasm and inquisitive nature has gained us access to even more *hidden* or *secret* locations. On one of our sportbike documentaries we were filming at Ducati Motorcycles in Bologna, Italy and doing a walk-in-talk with the company's Head Designer. The PR contact had mentioned that the designer was incredibly busy and only had a half hour interview. However, when the designer arrived, we really hit it off. Forty-five minutes into the conversation there was no end in sight. He just kept on walking us around and talking as we rolled. Then I happened to ask what was behind the door with the *no photography* sign? He slyly smiled and brought us inside an area of the facility where they kept their secret prototypes for their next new motorcycle. It was a major violation of company protocol that made for a great part of the program!

Orson Welles, one of the greatest cinematic directors of all time, called the best parts of his films, "divine accidents" and that's as true today as it was during his celebrated era.

Staying Out of Harm's Way

When you're running a crew in the field your number one job isn't to film a program, but rather to keep your team safe. While everyone wants to talk about story structure and photography, the truth is that everything else is secondary to safety. *People do amazingly stupid things when they pick up a camera.* When they're looking through a diopter, it often seems like they're removed from reality. That's great for objective filming but also incredibly dangerous for the shooter in real life. Your primary job as a producer is to make sure that you're not putting anyone in harm's way. You need to be the team's eyes and ears and keep a great overview of their activities.

Focus on the Important Stuff

Invariably when you're in the throes of the field production process, something drastic and unforeseen will come up. An interviewee cancels at the last minute, a day of shooting goes awry, a camera move you've been practicing doesn't work out as expected. When that happens, detach for a minute and ask yourself, "*How critical is this to the overall project*"?

When you feel overwhelmed, hit pause and then prioritize and execute. When multiple issues are cropping up all at once, take a step back and look at the situation from as global a view as possible. Assess all the various issues you're dealing with and then choose the one that will make the greatest impact and then *solve that problem first*. If you try to multitask and solve everything all at once, you'll fail. Instead, solve the biggest issue first and then each successively smaller problem until you find an overall solution.

No one has ever changed the remote, and therefore potentially impacted the ratings, because of something that's 29 minutes into a show. *Focus on the important stuff and unabashedly discard the meaningless part of the process.*

Sharing Bad News

Another great lesson that I've learned is that no matter how much you want to *will a project to succeed*, unfortunately there will be times when circumstances simply don't go your way. By nature, Producers are fixers. We aim to bring order to chaos. Yet even though we feel an innate ability to bend problems into solutions, there are times when something crops up that's so far beyond repair that it's impossible to fix. You can lose a crucial location, find out the key archive is too expensive, or discover that the access you had secured has fallen through. When this happens, you need to deliver the info as quickly as possible to your network EP. The most successful people get on top of trouble immediately. Putting your head in the sand does no one any good. Every minute matters during a potential crisis. Holding the info back wastes everyone's time and invariably leaves your EP with the impression that you were the problem. Don't beat around the bush. Don't bury the lede. Don't obfuscate. Just lay it out there. People don't want to feel like they need a decoder ring to understand what you're trying to communicate. Once you've stated the problem, give it context. Keep it short and be clear. Then offer some background on how it happened and why. Don't give excuses. Take responsibility. Nobody wants to deal with a whiner. Network EPs have dozens of fires to put out each day; don't be their biggest problem. Instead, be proactive and offer potential solutions. If you don't have any good ideas, ask for help. Trust me, your EP would much rather have you asking for their assistance now than find out later that you knew you needed it and didn't have the guts to seek it out. If you or your team's actions are responsible, then fall on the sword and apologize. Show empathy for the mess that the EP now must deal with on their side. Once the crisis has passed, spend some time reflecting. What could you have done differently to prevent the issue? How could you have reacted faster? What could you have done to prevent the issue from coming up in the first place? Giving bad news is never fun; however, it can be a powerful learning opportunity that offers tremendous growth possibilities.

Production Proverbs

Below are a few random field production thoughts that have helped me during my career.

Measure Twice, Cut Once: Think logically and be calm. Take emotion out of the equation and try to be as levelheaded about what lies in front of you as you can be.

Get Ahead and Stay Ahead: If you start keeping up on the small tasks early in the process then you'll make your life one-thousand percent easier on the backend. This is especially true of paperwork, card ingesting in the field, and checklists.

Be Naïve: Find a way to ignore negativity and instead focus on the promise of what you and your team can achieve. There are no bulletproof plans, no hard-and-fast ways to do anything, and we all bring something different to the table.

Don't Be Jaded: The lack of enthusiasm is the quickest way to turn the magic of factual producing into a dull 9-to-5 job. Stay present and optimistic.

We're Not Curing Cancer: You got into factual television because you thought it was fun. Keep reminding yourself – too many people take this gig far too seriously. If someone is paying you to produce a factual program or documentary that's pretty awesome.

Make Everyone 85% Happy: Producing factual television is a multi-disciplinary skill set that requires numerous different creative individuals to come together around a single idea. It's nearly impossible to please everyone. Make everyone 85% happy and everybody is happy.

It All Works Out in the End: Field production can be extremely stressful, particularly on a shoot with numerous moving parts. In these instances, it's easy for you and your crew to feel overwhelmed. I always try to take three big steps back. If you have a great team, no matter how stressful it gets, *somehow it all works out in the end.* This is a mantra that I've repeated thousands of times.

Getting a Jump on Post

By now most factual filmmakers are accustomed to capturing their field material in a digital format using a tapeless camera. It's common to pull data cards as you shoot and either digitally transfer, or dump, the cards while you keep working. Some producers use an on-set Digital Intermediate Technician, or DIT, to do the job. Others prefer to do it themselves on small-sized crews. It's a great way to start the ingest process; however, a lot of producers primarily focus on copying their field footage and often miss one of the fastest ways to get ahead of the post-production process – **Field Transcripts**.

Encoding a low-resolution QuickTime file from the field for transcription is one of my favorite time saving hacks to speed up the script writing process. Instead of waiting to get back home or to your production office, you can get ahead of the post-production tidal wave while still in the field by sending these low-rez files directly to a transcription service. Often, I start by assigning each film, or episode, a specific prefix. Then I add it to the beginning of every low-rez file name. Later on, during post there's no confusion where the file lives or which episode it was intended to be used in. Next, I'll track every file I send to a transcription house using a spreadsheet. Typically, it's a simple document that includes the name of the file, the person interviewed, the date it was

Aston Martin				**TRANSCRIBED**
Andy Palmer	CEO	SCB_A_0500.MXF	English	Y
Marek Reichmann	Head Designer	SCB_A_0532.MXF	English	Y
Marek Reichmann	Head Designer	SCB_A_0533.MXF	English	Y
Marek Reichmann	Head Designer	SCB_A_0534.MXF	English	Y
Marek Reichmann	Head Designer	SCB_A_0535.MXF	English	Y
Steve Waddingham	Historian	SCB_A_0543.MXF	English	Y
Nick Mynott	CAD Modeller	SCB_B_0161.MXF	English	Y
Nick Mynott	CAD Modeller	SCB_B_0162.MXF	English	Y
Chris Roffin	Aerodynamicist	SCB_B_0219.mov	English	Y
Chris Roffin	Aerodynamicist	SCB_B_0220.mov	English	Y
Chris Roffin	Aerodynamicist	SCB_B_0221.mov	English	Y
Matt Becker	Chief Engineer (In Car)	SHGINF_S001_S001_T026	English	Y
Marek Reichmann	Head Designer (Coffee House)	SCB_A_0699.mov	English	Y
Marek Reichmann	Head Designer (In Car)	ASTON3_S001_S001_T001.MOV	English	Y
Philip Cooden		SCB_A_0757.mov	English	Y
Philip Cooden		SCB_A_0759.mov	English	Y
Philip Cooden		SCB_A_0760.mov	English	Y
Philip Cooden		SCB_A_0761.mov	English	Y
Philip Cooden		SCB_A_0762.mov	English	Y
Philip Cooden		SCB_A_0763.mov	English	Y
Andy Barnett		SCB_A_0770.mov	English	Y
Andy Barnett		SCB_A_0771.mov	English	Y
Andy Barnett		SCB_A_0772.mov	English	Y
Andy Barnett		SCB_A_0773.mov	English	Y
Andy Barnett		SCB_A_0774.mov	English	Y
Andy Barnett		SCB_A_0775.mov	English	Y
Andy Barnett		SCB_A_0776.mov	English	Y
Matt Becker	Chief Engineer	SCB_A_0811.mov	English	Y
Nikki Rimmington		SCB_A_0920.MXF	English	Y
Nikki Rimmington		SCB_A_0921.MXF	English	Y
Nikki Rimmington		SCB_A_0922.MXF	English	Y

FIGURE 8.2 A Typical Field Transcript List.

SUPERCAR SUPERBUILD
CRY HAVOC PRODUCTIONS
JOB TITLE LIST for LOWER THIRDS
(Subtitles, Captions, Text Identifiers, Chyrons)

Episode Name: **Rolls Royce Wraith**
Episode Number: 5

Name	Title
Brian Staite	Manager, Leather Manufacturing
Michelle Lusby	Colour & Materials Designer
Alice Strachan	Team Leader
Glen Corbett	Wraith Product Manager
Martin O'Callaghan	Production Manager, Woodshop
Simon Baldey	General Manager, Assembly
Joshua Liles	Embroidery Specialist
Lee Silter	Bespoke Manufacturing
Irena Hlimesova	Headliner Install
Martin Norbury	Headliner Install
Lukatz Vlen	Line Associate
Ben Benford	Team Leader
Mark Court	Coachline Specialist
Stephen Horscroft	Manager, Test and Finish
Rob Bashford	Bespoke Manufacturing
Andrew Ball	Global Communications Manager
Michael Bryden	Bespoke Designer

FIGURE 8.3 A Name and Job Title Doc.

sent, whether it was sent and if it has come back as a finished transcription word doc file. All the sent files are color coded yellow; all the received files are marked in green.

This simple yet powerful tool not only tracks the interview QT files but also can become the basis of a name and title list. When a shoot wraps at a specific location, or with a specific company, I copy all the names from this document and send it to the press contact and ask them to double check the full names, spelling and appropriate lower third graphics titles. This is another way to help ensure that no one is mis-identified in the program or series.

Post-Shoot TRT Outline

Another field production hack that I love to employ is to craft a **Post-Shoot TRT Outline**. I try to do this while the shoot is still fresh in my mind and before we get to a new location. It is a bare bones outline of what just went down, where I try to detail the basic topics that we've just filmed and ascribe a projected total running time (or TRT) to the eventual resulting segment based on how I feel the shoot went. Essentially, this is an updated version of the TRT outline created during the pre-production phase, only it's now directly connected to the footage we've captured in the field.

Lamborghini Aventador SVJ		
MINUTES	TOPIC	Acts
5	Teaser / Set-Up	Act 1
5	Design	Act 1
4	Engineering	Act 1
5	CFK (Carbon Fibre)	Act 2
5	Engine	Act 2
3	History	Act 2
4	Nürburgring / Simulation	Act 3
3	Action & Beauty	Act 4
8	Factory Build	Act 5 & 6
2	Finishing	
0	Handout	Act 6

FIGURE 8.4 A Post-Shoot Outline Constructed After Filming at Lamborghini.

This basic outline then becomes the backbone of the remainder of the writing and post-production process. An assistant editor will use the document to make selects reels. Based on the assigned TRT they know how much energy they should devote to that selects reel and how long it should run. Weeks or months later a writer can review this same document before starting the script. It helps give them a quick insight into how much time to dedicate to a specific topic in the program. This way the writer doesn't pen pages and pages about a topic you don't have the goods to cover. Finally, the film's lead editor can review this list before beginning to cut and hopefully avoid overusing the same images too many times in the edit. In the end the purpose of the post-shoot TRT outline isn't to be too prescriptive but rather to help communicate how the field production portion of the project went to the people who weren't in the field. Like many other aspects of life, the clearer and more open you can communicate, the more engaged everyone on the team will be and the less siloed they'll feel.

Milestones and Cost Reporting

As your project moves through the various stages of production and eventually final delivery, you'll eventually hit the various payment milestones that the network has agreed to at the outset of the project. When you do, the network's production manager will ask you to generate a *cost report*. This is a document that reconciles what you've spent versus what you have left in the budget and allows the PM to see exactly where you are financially at any given time before they release more funds.

Cost Report April 15, 2011 Factory Series DESCRIPTION	CURRENT COSTS	ESTIMATE TO COMPLETE	TOTAL EST'D FINAL COSTS	BUDGET	(UNDER)/ OVER BDGT
Salaries-Producers Unit					
Acct: 1100					
Executive Producer	$4,000.00	$12,000.00	$16,000.00	$16,000.00	$0.00
Producer/Writer	$3,500.00	$10,500.00	$14,000.00	$14,000.00	$0.00
Associate Producer	$2,000.00	$3,000.00	$5,000.00	$5,000.00	$0.00
Associate Producer/Annotation	$0.00	$1,500.00	$1,500.00	$1,500.00	$0.00
Researcher	$500.00	$500.00	$1,000.00	$1,000.00	$0.00
SUBTOTAL	**$10,000.00**	**$27,500.00**	**$37,500.00**	**$37,500.00**	**$0.00**
Salaries-Director's Unit					
Acct: 1150					
Director	$9,000.00	$0.00	$9,000.00	$9,000.00	$0.00
SUBTOTAL	**$9,000.00**	**$0.00**	**$9,000.00**	**$9,000.00**	**$0.00**
Salaries- Field Prodution					
Acct: 1200					
Director of Photography	$7,500.00	$0.00	$7,500.00	$7,500.00	$0.00
2nd Unit Photographer	$6,000.00	$0.00	$6,000.00	$6,000.00	$0.00
Field Audio Technician	$4,500.00	$0.00	$4,500.00	$4,500.00	$0.00
Grip/Gaffer	$4,500.00	$0.00	$4,500.00	$4,500.00	$0.00
SUBTOTAL	**$22,500.00**	**$0.00**	**$22,500.00**	**$22,500.00**	**$0.00**

FIGURE 8.5 A Standard Network Cost Report.

Inside the Industry With Robert Angelo, Executive Producer

Robert Angelo is an Emmy-winning Executive Producer who co-created *Leno's Garage* for NBC.

- **What advice would you give to a film school student entering the "real world"?**

Network, assist, and pitch! Network every chance you get from independent projects to industry events. The more time you spend on a set, in a writer's room, or in a post house the better chance you have to connect with future partners and colleagues. Assist someone that has the job you want. You will learn the ins and outs of the business through a lens of experience. Finally learn how to pitch ideas to others. Selling your concepts is something you will need to hone throughout your career. Good luck, stay creative and never give up on your dream!

- **When you were first starting out in your career, what was the best advice you ever received from a mentor?**

My first internship was with a post-production and special effects facility. I worked on a movie called "Monkey Bone" and a few commercials for Universal Studios. My boss was Jamie Hyneman, who would go on to launch the TV show MythBusters. Jamie and his team taught me how to look for innovative solutions. The majority of the workday was spent discussing how the team was going to accomplish a difficult task. I remember leaving work and getting onto the bus and spending the entire drive home thinking about various ways to accomplish the same task. At the heart of the lesson was that the team working together, engineering a solution led to more successes than failures. Find your team, hone your craft, teach others, and be humble.

- **You spent many years at the network level, how would you describe network thinking?**

A large network is always prepping for the next big hit. Either in pre-production, post, or during a full-blown marketing blitz, the whole company is always pulling the same direction. It is strange to witness at first but after a few cycles, you get into the rhythm and flow of the development process. The thought process is to do everything in your power to help create a hit show. From development, marketing, and fan engagement you are part of a larger team trying to launch content that resonates with a broad audience.

- **What do you think are the most important traits a producer should cultivate?**

Often students focus on the hard skills needed to do the job while overlooking the soft skills. Working with talent, publicists, lawyers, and upper management is often where I see young producers have trouble. Knowing and articulating the goal of the project and forming a consensus is your main task. Learn how to bring people together and you will go further than the average producer.

- **Producers tend to live in a state of constant "hustle" – how do you handle it, and/or what advice would you offer to young producers?**

There will always be enough work for a competent producer in the entertainment field. Take the time to find your pace. The correct environment exists, and experience will help inform what works for you. Learn about basic content cycles in film, television, and streaming. This will inform staffing ebbs-and-flows, development opportunities, and production supply chain. Find your niche and have fun while creating.

- **How has failure, or apparent failure, helped shape your career?**

To some, failures can be debilitating, for others rejection is a motivator. Everyone you meet will have some form of self-doubt. The goal is to rise above those fears of failure and progress a little bit each and every day. Your past experiences will help to inform your future decisions so stay true to your gut instincts.

- **How broadly based should a young producer's knowledge be in the various disciplines involved in filmmaking?**

I believe that a producer should understand the context of each job on set. This will help you make informed decisions. Time management is extremely difficult as a creative producer. My advice is to learn what your teammates are doing and how long each of their tasks takes. Setting realistic expectations and keeping the creative processes in mind while producing is always key to a successful project.

- **What is the best investment in yourself that you've ever made?**

Take time off! There was a period of time while I was working at a big TV network, and I didn't take any time off. I worked for six years straight on a huge transition that took a mental toll on me. Making sure to take care of yourself is paramount to a successful career. Take time away from your projects and relax. More often than not you return fresh with new ideas and solutions.

Chapter Nine

The Post-Production Process

With a collection of brilliant footage in hand it's finally time to start the **Post-Production** phase of the project. This is when all the magic that you've captured in the field is finally ready to be merged together with a powerful script into a brilliant viewing experience.

Post is where we give life to the work.

It's the language that we speak and the place where we weave our tales. Master the post-production process and you can do incredible things. Learn how to scale it and you're well on your way to becoming a dependable network provider.

DOI: 10.4324/9781003292289-9

Scripting

Script writing for factual television is a combination of entertainment, education and penning punchy lines that engage the viewer. Like episodic narrative television, there are a number of different formats you can use for the script. They all more or less achieve the same end result. You simply need to find a format that you feel comfortable using for your initial draft.

I'm a fan of rather traditional A/V scripts, where you describe the visuals on the left and the audio on the right using a three-column table. The first column is the cell number, the second the video assets, and the third is for the text of the interview sound and narration.

When I initially sit down to craft a factual program, I don't start with a blank sheet of paper and try to write the actual script from scratch. That's a great way to inspire writer's block! Instead, I begin by crafting an **Interview Transcription Breakdown**. This is a simple thematically driven document that groups the interview soundbites by category or subject.

ICONS OF AUTO **6/28/21**
JEEP - ROUGH CUT SCRIPT v1

8	OPENING TITLES	OPENING TITLES
9		**FROM BATTLEFIELDS TO SUBURBAN DRIVEWAYS, FOR OVER THREE QUARTER OF CENTURY THIS REMARKABLE CONSTRUCTOR HAS FOUGHT WARS AND HARD TIMES TO BECOME A DRIVING FORCE IN THE AUTOMOTIVE LANDSCAPE...**
10	Derek Powell A008R005_210616WR 08:40:14:14	Jeep really ties into the fantasy of the sense of adventure that everybody wants to have, and the great thing about Jeep as a whole is that these cars are indeed capable of taking you on that adventure //
11		**TODAY JEEP IS A GLOBAL NAME YET IT'S EPIC STORY IS FULL OF BRAVE DECISIONS, BOLD BETS AND HARD CHARGING DREAMS...[2]**
12	Tony Quiroga A009R005_210616PY 12:07:36:13	Jeep is one of the strongest American brands // born out of the world war two // they've been ahead of the curve on SUVs and SUV popularity. //

FIGURE 9.1 A Sample A/V Script.

I'll often start by pulling up the original Post Shoot TRT Outline and use its topics as a starting point. Then I'll review all of the episode's corresponding interview transcripts and pull out the most salient soundbites and copy them into the most appropriate sections in the Interview Transcription Breakdown. Often during this process new categories will emerge, and fresh structural ideas will reveal themselves.

As I copy and paste the sound on tape (or SOT) from the interview transcripts into this new document, I make sure to enter the name of the interviewee, the name of the QuickTime file and the timecode for the soundbite. This information is sacrosanct. If you mess this part up now, the editors will have a heck of a time finding the footage. Bad code crushes productions.

Distilling the interviews into one master document gives you an opportunity to start sorting which soundbites play the best off each other and often allows you to make quick narration notes as you go along. It also gives you a terrific 360° overview of your total interview sound so that you don't write yourself into a corner later on.

Once the interviewee sound is pulled, it's time to refresh yourself with your initial research, your original shooting script and the pre-production outline. Finally, we're ready to start the heavy lifting of scripting the show and writing the voice-over narration.

The Broadcast Clock

Every network uses their own **Broadcast Clock** for their programs. This is a unique and specific structural format that all programs or series need to follow in order to comply with the network's broadcast standards. Of all the paperwork that a network will send a producer, the broadcast clock is one of the most critical because it defines your project's structure. Some channels like to have 4 acts per hour, others might want 5 or 6 per hour. The broadcast clock also establishes another key structural requirement – the minimum and maximum act lengths.

Writers have to plan their scripts around the broadcast clock. If we're telling a linear observational documentary inside of a factory, aka a process-genre show, I know that we'll start the program at the beginning of a build and then finish the film with the conclusion of the manufacturing process. However, what I don't know is how we'll get from Point A to Point Z. The broadcast clock helps determine the beats in the middle and the amount of time that we can send on each narrative arc. During the writing phase it's crucial to pay attention to the network's clock because there's no

GUIDELINES FOR PART BREAKS – Programmes of 44'00 (1 hour) [can under-run by 15secs but must not over-run 44 minutes]

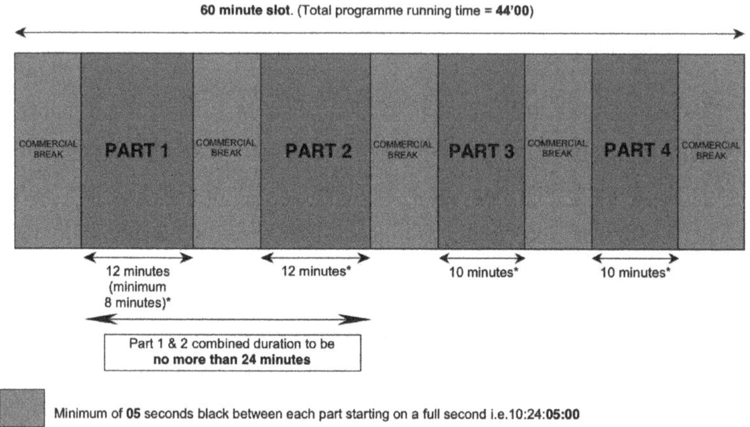

FIGURE 9.2 Discovery's 4 Act/44-Minute Broadcast Clock.

point to writing a brilliant 15-page act if the network's run time requirements only allow a ten-minute segment. You don't want to have to spend extra time cutting your script down to time.

The broadcast clock is hugely important for linear networks, but less necessary for streaming services that don't run advertisements. Generally, they don't have the same hard-and-fast timing rules. On the other hand, AVOD services are closer to conventional television due to their commercial breaks.

Writing Voice-over Narration

The voice-over style is different in every genre of factual television. Classically constructed docs with an omnipresent narrator use voice-over, or VO, to connect the dots between each expert's soundbite, while on a reality competition series the VO might only be used sparingly to fill in the small holes between *in-the-moment* scenes. I like to think of the narrator as the play-by-play announcer in an NFL football broadcast while the interviewees are the color commentators offering their opinion or insight. Great VO sets up the SOT that comes next.

Some networks also like their programs to *Signpost* the interviewee soundbites. This is a fancy way to describe a 2,400-year-old Aristotelian "triptych" presentation approach: *tell the audience what you're going to tell them, say it again, then tell the audience what they just heard.* It's an effective tool to ensure that the entire audience moves along with the program's narrative.

A typical script sequence might go something like this.

Narrator: Introduces new idea.

Interviewee: comments on or explains the idea.

Narrator: Highlights the idea again, tells you what you just heard and then adds new information, before transitioning to next soundbite's commentary and starting the process over again.

There are many different philosophies for crafting great narration and your network EP will have their own take on the channel's preferences. Personally, I like to keep VO in an active, present tense while trying to keep the vocabulary energetic and conversational but not too wordy or overly educated. Big words sound fancy, but in factual narration they're often taxing on a listener's ear. The more complex your lingo, the quicker you'll lose part of the audience. Instead try to be conversational and make your project as *accessible as possible.*

Great VO also lets your experts be experts. Don't get sucked into superlatives. They scream infomercial or paid placement. Try not to rely on the narration doing the heavy lifting explaining things – it's much better to have interviewees describe the details. After all, they're the experts!

Writing a script can be daunting and there are definitely some writers that obsess over each line or cell in a script as they painstakingly build it day by day. I'm a much bigger proponent of *moving fast and breaking things* along the way. Rough drafts are rarely perfect and it's much quicker to just get your ideas down on paper before revising it to perfection.

Ernest Hemingway supposedly once said, "*write drunk and edit sober*". Whether that's true or not is up for debate, but the general sentiment is pretty spot on. Blank pages are your worst enemy and revision is your friend.

In addition, scripts are living documents. They change as you go through the post-production process. Things need to be added, other items need to be cut, often you

SUV SUPERBUILD – CHEVROLET SUBURBAN 5/26/21
ROUGH CUT SCRIPT *v10*

100	SLX_1B. DESIGN_1936 CHEVROLET SUBURBAN.MOV 1935-CHEVROLET-SUBURBAN-CARRYALL.JPG W35HV_CT002.JPG SUBURBAN-80-YEARS-OF---.MP4	**THE SUBURBAN'S STORY STARTS IN NINETEEN THIRTY-FIVE...** **AT THE TIME THE UNITED STATES HAS A POPULATION OF JUST ONE-HUNDRED AND TWENTY-SEVEN MILLION PEOPLE...** **A U.S. POSTAGE STAMP COSTS JUST THREE CENTS...** **AND CANNED BEER GOES ON SALE FOR THE FIRST TIME...**
101	Jim Fleming A040C003 170731YX 10:29:05:23	// At it's // introduction it was really kind of // a covered pick-up truck. // Then, as people used it // it became kind of synonymous with utility //
102	1935 CHEVROLET SUBURBAN 155854.JPG 1935 CHEVROLET SUBURBAN 194661.JPG 1936 - 133004.JPG 1937 CHEV SUBURBAN151076.JPG	**THE INITIAL MACHINE IS EXTREMELY BARE BONES, COMBING A PICKUP TRUCK WITH A STATION-WAGON...** **LITTLE DOES ANYONE REALIZE JUST HOW PROFOUND THE CONCEPT WILL BECOME...**
103	Scott Evans A044C001 170901D2 00:51:27:14	// If you look at all of the vehicles that are being put out in the 1930's you didn't have nearly the range that we have now. You had Sedans // You had trucks // and you maybe had // some luxury cars // (00:51:46:13) The Suburban // was trying a new thing. //
104		**THE AUSTERE NATURE OF THE MACHINE FITS THE ERA...**

FIGURE 9.3 A Typical A/V Script. The Yellow Highlights Are Footage Notes for the Editors.

have to make adjustments to hit the specific broadcast clock requirements. Don't be too precious with your words, phrases or soundbites. Learn to kill the excess fluff and trim your dialogue to its core.

Scripting to Time

The more often you write factual scripts, the sooner you'll find your own **Minutes Per Page Pace**. Generally, I find that an energetically edited episode script tends to underrun the total run time (or TRT) of the show. So, one page in one of our supercar scripts typically equates to just over one finished minute of content. For a 44-minute show our final scripts usually come in right around 40 pages. There are obviously a lot of variables to this formula; the speed of your expert's speech, the narrator's pace, your editing team's use of montages and even the type of music that you choose to use. Non-native English speakers will almost always slow your pace down as well since they're searching for words more often. The closer you can bring your script to time right off the bat, the faster your edit team will be able to cut the show and get it to time.

The Frankenbite

What happens when you don't have the perfect soundbite for the next section of your script? You can either reframe your narrative and revise the voice-over or create a *Frankenbite*. A Frankenbite is a Reality TV convention that takes different words or phrases from multiple takes or interviewee answers, reorganizes them and creates a new manufactured soundbite to tell a different story. The Kardashians might never have said the dramatically tinged line of dialogue you think they did. Instead, the story producers and editing team might well have recast their worlds to create a different sentence or implied meaning. Every documentarian or factual producer has to decide their own comfort level with frankenbiting. Some readily use them in their arsenal, while others strongly object to their inclusion in films and programs. It really depends on which side of the isle you sit on when it comes to journalistic integrity. Personally, I'm not keen on radically changing someone's verbal intent; however, I am a fan of going in to clean up an interviewee's lexicon. Someone can be a brilliant speaker but sound less than intelligent if they mix up a pronoun or trail off at the end of sentence. Rearranging their words ever so slightly can make their statements more powerful and more succinct without altering their meaning.

Paper Edit Reviews

Some network EPs require a **Paper Edit Review** before actual editing can begin. This is an opportunity for the EP to review the script and ensure that you're on the correct track before any monies are spent editing. The intent is on point and as an advocate for not overspending I love the idea; however, in practice it can be extremely challenging. Factual programs are a visual medium and even the best visualizers often have a hard time judging a project without seeing the supporting imagery.

Editing

Once there's a finished script, it's finally time to get cracking with the edit. Few parts of the factual television process can shape the project quite as much as the act of assembling hundreds if not thousands of divergent clips into one coherent story.

Editors Are Rockstars

Editors are the rockstars that bring the footage to life and help shape it into a watchable final program. On a basic level editing is the language and syntax of visual content. It's the vocabulary that gives documentaries and factual programs form, pace, and style. Great editing brings a story to life and helps accentuate its power. Bad editing on the other hand is immediately obvious. It'll stop the viewer dead in their tracks and usually subconsciously convince them to change the channel. *Often, it's easier to see or hear a mistake than it is to appreciate the nuance of a great edit.* There is an artistry to editing that takes years to master. Like great woodworkers who hand cut their joinery, highly skilled editors play a Tetris like game on their timeline, deftly piecing stories together in tight ways that sometimes defy traditional thinking.

Some producers, like myself, who come from strong editing backgrounds, build systems that leverage their institutional knowledge and house style to help make the process as efficient as possible. Other producers are fonder of dropping boxes full of field hard drives off and asking their editors to *find the story* for them. There's no one way to do it, but there are more *efficient ways to do it.*

I would strongly encourage any aspiring producer to learn a basic working knowledge of editing. It will help you communicate with your post team and help inform your decision-making in the field. Editors turn into great producers, directors and camera operators because they tend to think about *sequence* and how the pieces will fit together later on.

Gut Reactions: When you watch down an edit, if something repeatedly bothers you about it you need to figure out what it is and change it. Your initial gut reaction is almost always correct. Always listen to it.

Choosing the Correct NLE

One of the larger decisions that you'll face at the outset of post is which Non-Linear Editing Software (or NLE) your team will use. These days it's an Avid versus Apple versus Premiere smackdown. Each has its own unique advantages, and some editors are more fluent in one platform compared to another. They're all basically the same – they're the tools we use to tell our stories.

Conversations about which NLE has the most amazing feature set aren't really important. What is critical however is stability. Editing software that crashes is an emotional killer. Once you live through that process once you never want to repeat it. Usually, NLE's have a preferred editing codec. I'd strongly advise you to *transcode* all of your material into the same codec prior to editing. While these days it's easier than ever to mix multiple different formats on the same timeline, in the long run it usually comes back to bite you. Feed the NLE the QuickTime format it likes and keep it happy from start to final finishing.

Finding Great Editors

The best way to find an awesome editor comes down to personal recommendation or online job board postings on sites like Mandy.com, Staffmeup.com or ProductionHub.com.

When I interview an editor, I rarely care about their *reel*. Just like when you interview camera operators, you have no idea who actually cut it or where the images came from. I much prefer to hear about their experiences working on other projects, whether they've edited multiple projects with the same producer or production company, and their thoughts about the technical aspects of the project.

Here are a few of my key questions for editing interviews.

What type of shows or films have they edited? Do they have long-form experience or is their background only in short form new media and online content? Ideally you want to find an editor with broadcast experience but that's not always required if the editor you're interviewing is highly organized, highly engaged and hungry to prove themselves.

What kind of style are they used to cutting? Most editors see a timeline in a certain way and cut accordingly. It's very rare to find an editor that can cut flashy, high-performance material and then jump into slow moving drama. Usually, it's one or the other.

Have they worked on broadcast documentaries before? Are they familiar with a broadcast clock and quality control standards?

How do they approach an edit? Organization is paramount. Editors have to understand how to properly set up projects, the workflow process, ingesting, file organization, the differences between NLEs, versioning and plethora of other tasks.

How long does it take them to craft a one-hour program? Getting a sense for an editor's sense of turnaround time is crucial to their longevity within your organization. Frequently this is the greatest point of confusion. If an editor expects to have six weeks to cut a one-hour program but you expect it to be done in five weeks, there's going to be a problem.

When interviewing a prospective editor, I also like to drill down into *how they organize* as opposed to why they might organize. Two of the best editors that I ever hired showed up to their interview with excel spreadsheets from their previous gigs and showed me exactly how they set their projects up. I hired both on the spot and each was a fantastic addition to the team because they approached each edit with a *plan*. The truly great editors don't just assemble your project, they elevate it. The best of breed can read a script, internalize it, and *feel it* in their edit. They take the basic gist and find a way to tell the story in a better way that you couldn't have possibly imagined.

Post-Production Playbook

As we organically grew during our first decade in business post-production was a word-of-mouth affair. I did a lot of editing myself and tended to verbally describe our workflow to any editor that we brought in to help. However, once we moved into series work, I quickly realized that this sort of verbal transfer of knowledge didn't work. There were too many editors to bring up to speed at once, and too many different interpretations of how I wanted the system to function. This caused a great amount of confusion. In particular my most trusted editor, Terren Lin, was spending an inordinate amount of time helping everyone else instead of focusing on his own creative pursuits or tasks. Too much knowledge resided in the minds of just a few talented people and was far too compartmentalized. *The solution was to create a company post production playbook.*

Handbooks are powerful tools. Look at McDonald's success. Regardless of how you view their food, you have to admit that it's rather remarkable that no matter where you are in the world, a Big Mac tastes like a Big Mac. This isn't by chance. It's the result of having a great system and a brilliant playbook that gets every employee on the same page even if they're thousands of miles away from each other.

Our playbook started as a very basic Word document and slowly morphed into something more substantial over time. Eventually, this manual moved into the cloud and now lives on Google Docs. Subsequent editors have added their own thoughts, processes, and revisions, which has ultimately broadened the playbook out even further. Best yet is a document like this creates institutional knowledge that's shareable in the future. Today, whenever onboarding someone new, their task is to review the playbook.

Crafting your own playbook is fairly simple. Just start by describing your own editing process from start to finish for someone who has no knowledge of how you work. What steps do you take when you start? How do you set up your project? How do you organize your material, etc.? The goal is to arm a potential editor with the knowledge to open up a project that they've never seen and instantly be at home sorting through it. When you go a level deeper, you can start detailing the editing style that you're after, the plug-ins that you use, the way you deliver cuts for review, any required passwords for applications or online tools.

The Importance of Systems

After one particular vexing project that required a number of late night edit sessions, I made a vow that I'd never allow anyone on the team to miss dinner with their family. That's our cardinal rule in post. *Everyone goes home at 5 pm, every single day, with no late-nighters, no mad rushes before a deadline, and no scheduling stress.* Trying to suss things out late at night is a sure-fire way to end up in the danger zone.

The key to enacting this sort of mandate is to build great systems. Every minute that you can save throughout the entirety of the project will add up to massive amounts of time later on. This is how you create a stress-free environment and a stress-free factual program or series.

Building a great system begins by implementing a robust workflow with defined rules and staying on top of organizing your digital assets. We start by coding all footage as it's ingested. Whenever a card comes in from a shooter it's immediately downloaded and then a prefix is assigned to each resulting folder of information. Naming conventions are crucial to creating order in chaos. Define a structure and stick to it.

Our basic ingest naming convention hasn't altered in years and it makes finding files extremely easy – *Date_Series Nickname_Episode_Camera_Card #*

After ingest a corresponding excel sheet is crafted by the Producer or DIT that lists.

- The card name
- The date the card was filmed (often in the card name)
- What project it is connected to
- The camera used
- What was filmed that day (in broad strokes)

Once back in the office, each card is brought into Avid Media Composer in its own bin that corresponds to the date and name of the card on the excel sheet. The Assistant Editor then takes the Post-Shoot Outline and creates bins based on each topic before

BENTLEY CONTINENTAL Gen 3		Subject
012819_SCB_Bentley_5D_01	Canon 5D	Promo Photos
012819_SCB_Bentley_Atomos_01	A7S / Atomos	Engine Beauties
012819_SCB_Bentley_CamA_01	FS7	INTS, Engine Build, Design
012819_SCB_Bentley_CamA_02	FS7	INTS, Engine Build, Design
012819_SCB_Bentley_CamB_01	F5	Engine Build
012819_SCB_Bentley_CamC_01	FS7	Engine Build, Exteriors
012918_SCB_Bentley_5D_01	Canon 5D	Promo Photos
012918_SCB_Bentley_Atomos_01	A7S / Atomos	Metrology
012918_SCB_Bentley_CamA_01	FS7	INTS, Final Assembly, Designer INT, Car Beauties
012918_SCB_Bentley_CamA_02	FS7	INTS, Final Assembly, Designer INT, Car Beauties
012918_SCB_Bentley_CamB_01	F5	Final Assembly, Metrology
012918_SCB_Bentley_CamB_02	F5	Final Assembly, Metrology, INT
012918_SCB_Bentley_CamC_01	FS7	Final Assembly, Metrology
012918_SCB_Bentley_CamC_02	FS7	Final Assembly, Metrology
013019_SCB_Bentley_5D_01	Canon 5D	Promo Photos
013019_SCB_Bentley_5D_02	Canon 5D	Darren Day (Interior Designer INT & Drawing)
013019_SCB_Bentley_A7S_01	A7S / Atomos	Wood Shop Ronin & Jib, Engine Factory, Final Assembly, Car Beauties
013019_SCB_Bentley_Atomos_01	A7S / Atomos	Wood Shop Ronin & Jib, Engine Factory, Final Assembly, Car Beauties
013019_SCB_Bentley_CamA_01	FS7	Wood Shop
013019_SCB_Bentley_CamA_02 - Design	FS7	Darren Day (Interior Designer INT & Drawing)
013019_SCB_Bentley_CamB_01	F5	Wood Shop
013019_SCB_Bentley_CamC_01	FS7	Wood Shop
013019_SCB_Bentley_CamC_02 - Design	FS7	Darren Day (Interior Designer INT & Drawing)
013119_SCB_Bentley_5D_01	Canon 5D	Final Assembly, Leather Shop
013119_SCB_Bentley_A7S - ATOMOS BACK UP	A7S	Final Assembly, Leather Shop
013119_SCB_Bentley_A7S_01 - NOT A BACK UP	A7S	Leather Shop - 1 shot
013119_SCB_Bentley_Atomos_01	Atomos	Final Assembly, Leather Shop
013119_SCB_Bentley_CamA_01	FS7	Final Assembly, Leather Shop INT
013119_SCB_Bentley_CamA_02	FS7	Leather Shop
013119_SCB_Bentley_CamA_03	FS7	Leather Shop
013119_SCB_Bentley_CamB_01	F5	Leather Shop, Engineering Center
013119_SCB_Bentley_CamC_01	FS7	Leather Shop, Engineering Center
020119_SCB_Bentley_5D_01	Canon 5D	Promo Photos
020119_SCB_Bentley_CamA_01	FS7	INT, Lineage
020119_SCB_Bentley_CamA_02	FS7	Lineage
020119_SCB_Bentley_CamB_01	F5	Paint Shop
020119_SCB_Bentley_CamC_01	FS7	Paint Shop
020119_SCB_Bentley_CamC_02	FS7	Building Exteriors

FIGURE 9.4 A Field Card Log From Our Nat Geo ULTIMATE SUPERCAR Series.

duplicating and sorting the ingested cards footage into their appropriate topic derived bin. These new files will now become the working digital copies. This way no matter what happens next, we can always find the original field material if we need to.

The Power of Checklists

Inside our post-production playbook are a series of Checklists and Cheat Sheets that range from basic import settings to project hierarchy, and finally export details for color correction, audio mixing and music scoring. These checklists help dummy proof the process and remove as many technical glitches as possible from the editing workflow.

		ROUGH CUT - VIMEO UPLOAD FOR NAT GEO REVIEW
✓	Step	Task
		TIMELINE PREP
	1	Show start at 01:00:00:00 in 24p
	2	Timecode Burn in 24p
	3	TPT should be 45:30:00 in 24p (With Act breaks)
		SLATE
	4	All timings in 24p
	5	TRT should be 44:00 min
	6	Labeled "ROUGH CUT"
		EXPORT FROM AVID
	7	Mark in at the first frame of the slate; Mark out at final frame of show (No black at end)
	8	Enable all tracks
	9	Use export setting ROUGH CUT TO VIMEO
		> Check "Use Marks" and "Use Selected Tracks"
		> Export as an Apple ProRes 422 Proxy
		> Check "Prepare for Internet Streaming" with "Fast Start" selected
		> Aspect ratio 1920 x 1080
	10	Set destination as "Respective project folder > 3. Exports > ROUGH CUT > For Vimeo"
	11	Name it "SCB_S1_*Episode Name_Date*_24p_ROUGH CUT"
		COMPRESSOR
	12	Load avid Proress 422 Proxy export into compressor
	13	Use preset "HD 720p"
		UPLOAD TO VIMEO
	14	Select password protection with the password

FIGURE 9.5 One of Our Export Checklists.

However, over time I began to realize that these simple lists served a much larger purpose – they're incredibly powerful tools that allow people to unleash their creativity.

A famous racer once told me that every rider has 100 cents of focus while they're piloting a motorcycle. When you first start out you spend most of this money keeping the machine upright, avoiding danger and obeying traffic rules. However, once you get more comfortable you spend less coinage on basic tasks and free up funds for more advanced pursuits like increasing your speed, leaning into a corner, or even putting your knee down on a racetrack. Editing with checklists and cheat sheets works exactly the same way. *The less you have to focus on the mundane tasks, the more mental space is available to be creative and do the hard stuff.*

Checklists and Cheat Sheets give you the time to think about the edit, to craft a better show, to come up with fresh ways to push the product forward. Checklists free you from the nuts and bolts of editing and off-load the "gotcha" moments. If you follow the cheat sheets, you'll never have a technical problem during the eleventh hour.

Creating a powerful checklist is extremely easy. Simply write down all the necessary steps required on any repetitive task in their order of execution. This way any time you have to do the same task again, all the needed knowledge resides in just one place. This is particularly useful for repeated activities such as timeline set-up or export settings that can take a lot of time to troubleshoot if done incorrectly.

Creating Selects Reels

A lot of producers spend vast amounts of time and energy talking about having a great workflow but ironically only apply it to the field production of their project. Once the material lives inside the editing software, often it's up to an editor to figure it out. I like to call this the *Box of Tapes* approach to editing, as in "*Hey Editor, here's a box of tapes!*". That's not a very time efficient way to get things done. Especially on a series with a lot of material.

We go about things a little bit differently.

After we capture material in the field, we send the raw footage hard drives to the editing team along with a corresponding card log. The editing team then dissects the log and builds their own **Shot Footage Outline**. This is a simple document that lists all the various scenes we filmed grouped by theme. This outline brings order to the field footage chaos. Instead of a box of disorganized tapes or cards, our editors create

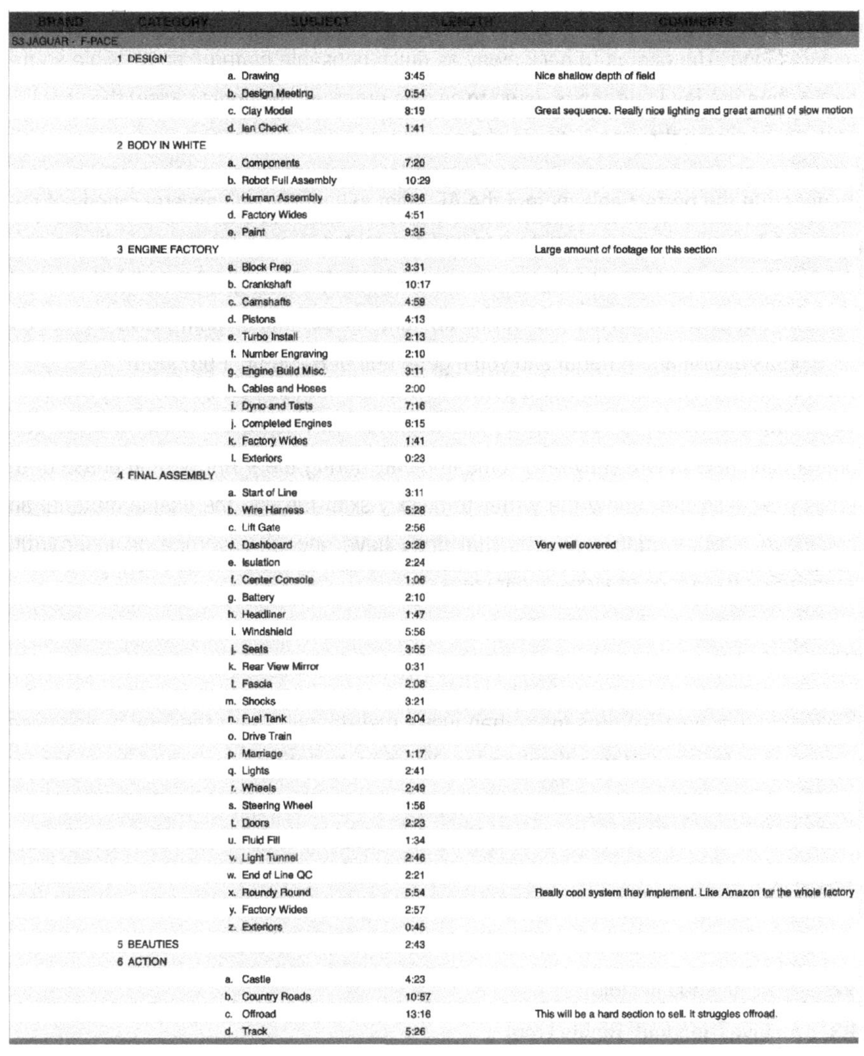

BRAND	CATEGORY	SUBJECT	LENGTH	COMMENTS
S3 JAGUAR - F-PACE				
	1 DESIGN			
		a. Drawing	3:45	Nice shallow depth of field
		b. Design Meeting	0:54	
		c. Clay Model	8:19	Great sequence. Really nice lighting and great amount of slow motion
		d. Ian Check	1:41	
	2 BODY IN WHITE			
		a. Components	7:20	
		b. Robot Full Assembly	10:29	
		c. Human Assembly	6:36	
		d. Factory Wides	4:51	
		e. Paint	9:35	
	3 ENGINE FACTORY			Large amount of footage for this section
		a. Block Prep	3:31	
		b. Crankshaft	10:17	
		c. Camshafts	4:59	
		d. Pistons	4:13	
		e. Turbo Install	2:13	
		f. Number Engraving	2:10	
		g. Engine Build Misc.	3:11	
		h. Cables and Hoses	2:00	
		i. Dyno and Tests	7:16	
		j. Completed Engines	6:15	
		k. Factory Wides	1:41	
		l. Exteriors	0:23	
	4 FINAL ASSEMBLY			
		a. Start of Line	3:11	
		b. Wire Harness	5:28	
		c. Lift Gate	2:56	
		d. Dashboard	3:28	Very well covered
		e. Isulation	2:24	
		f. Center Console	1:06	
		g. Battery	2:10	
		h. Headliner	1:47	
		i. Windshield	5:56	
		j. Seats	3:55	
		k. Rear View Mirror	0:31	
		l. Fascia	2:08	
		m. Shocks	3:21	
		n. Fuel Tank	2:04	
		o. Drive Train		
		p. Marriage	1:17	
		q. Lights	2:41	
		r. Wheels	2:49	
		s. Steering Wheel	1:56	
		t. Doors	2:23	
		u. Fluid Fill	1:34	
		v. Light Tunnel	2:46	
		w. End of Line QC	2:21	
		x. Roundy Round	5:54	Really cool system they implement. Like Amazon for the whole factory
		y. Factory Wides	2:57	
		z. Exteriors	0:45	
	5 BEAUTIES		2:43	
	6 ACTION			
		a. Castle	4:23	
		b. Country Roads	10:57	
		c. Offroad	13:16	This will be a hard section to sell. It struggles offroad.
		d. Track	5:26	

FIGURE 9.6 The Post-Production Team Selects Reel Outline From an Episode of SUV SUPERBUILD.

specific bins in Avid that correspond to each *footage bucket* in the outline. Then as material is ingested, it's sorted directly into a thematic bin. So, if B Cam films material of an engine build, that material is placed in the engine build folder (or bin in Avid parlance).

Once the sorting is completed, the editing team then starts cutting **Selects Reels** from the footage in each folder or bin. A selects reel is a straight cut-based sequence that uses only the very best footage for a particular subject or category. The TRT of each reel is based on the loose Post-Shoot TRT Outline. Ideally no reel is more than eight minutes long. The goal is to hack away as much unusable material as possible so that by the time the lead editor sits down to cut the program, they only review the very best of the best material to use in the final program.

To generate the perfect selects reel the AE team will go through several rounds of revision and tightening down prior to handing the material over. By the time that they're done, the lead editor might only have 5 hours out of the 50 original field hours to use in the edit, but every single second will be brilliant, usable and on point. Give a great editor 5 hours of brilliant material and you'll get a hell of a one-hour program!

When done correctly Selects Reels are a terrific way for a Producer to keep post-production costs down. They also come in handy during the script writing phase of the project because they allow the writer to quickly skim through the usable material and helps avoid over-writing segments that don't have enough coverage or underwriting scenes that have tons of awesome images.

Timeline Layout

Saving time in post requires more than just a well-thought-out schedule. It also needs a clear plan for your editing timeline too. Years of evolution have led us to a standard timeline layout where every track is dedicated to a specific type of content.

VIDEO

V1 Interviews

V2 B-Roll (Filmed in Field)

V3 Archive (Handout, Rights Free)

V4 Archive (Handout, Rights Free)

V5 Stock Imagery (Licensed)

V6 FX Shots & Overlays

V7 Act Breaks (Slugs for timing)

V8 GRFX – Full Screen & Lower 3rds

AUDIO

A1 Interview sound

A2 Narration

A3/4 Archive/stock sound

A5/6 Music

A7/8 Sound FX

The beauty of the system is that it organizes madness. Every video or audio asset has a specific home on the timeline. This makes it extremely easy to find exactly what you're looking for whenever you need it and during the rough cut and fine cut stages it lets you immediately know exactly where the show stands – are you close to completion, or do you have miles to go?

Cleanly laying out your timeline also allows you to easily export the metadata from the various tracks to track costs. For example, you can export the archival track and input it into excel to figure out what your licensed footage fees are running nearly instantly. An organized timeline also saves you money in color correction and audio mixing. Most audio engineers budget an entire day to clean up an editor's timeline; however, if you do it for them that's money that can stay in your pocket. This system also allows for super-fast archive, graphics or music logging creation when you get to final finishing because all the necessary materials for each log live on a single track.

Editing to a Broadcast Clock

The biggest difference between editing for broadcast and an online platform like YouTube is the need to adhere to the broadcast clock. In a traditional one-hour factual programming slot, the actual program content is usually 44 minutes with the remaining 16 minutes reserved for commercials. This means that a producer has to deliver a 44-minute edit, typically broken down by a number of acts. When editing to a specific broadcast clock, you have to remember that every choice made in Act 1 has a ripple effect on every Act that follows. If you run long in Act 1, then Acts 2–4 will be very short.

Finding Amazing Collaborators

While editing often gets the glory, the post production process is far more expansive than just assembling raw footage into meaningful sequences. Graphics and music both play a key role and offer the opportunity to elevate your production while layering in the glossy sheen of higher-end production values. Poorly lensed programs can often feel rather high-end if the accompanying graphics are richly textured and well animated.

Discovering terrific creative collaborators to help fill in your knowledge and proficiency gaps isn't always easy because it requires a brutally honest self-evaluation as well as the ability to verbalize your deficits to others. Then you have to cast a wide and broad net to find someone to shore up the skill sets you or your team lacks.

Initially, you can begin by using pre-built graphics from websites like Envato or Music from a plethora of low-cost online library sources. Both offer terrific launching points for most projects. However, they're rarely enough for true broadcast factual programs or series.

To take the next step, you often need to track down talented graphic artists, GRFX studios or music composers. You can start with referrals from colleagues within the industry or advertise on industry websites like Mandy.com, Staffmeup.com or Productinhub.com. I also like to engage with local universities. Most have digital creative programs that offer Adobe After Effects, 3D Max and Pro Tools courses, which means that they have students learning their craft. You can also search the net for below the line agents who specialize in repping these sort of talented individuals.

Once you identify the key outside vendors for your project, it's a good idea to follow up every important conversation via a summary email. The goal is to clearly define what you just spoke about so that there's no confusion later on. This simple hack will help you avoid 90% of the problems that plague productions.

Vendor/Supplier Follow-Up Email Steps:

- Remove all fluff
- No more than 250 words max
- Use bullet points to summarize
- Explain deliverables and expectations

Always remember that should anything go wrong this is your paper trail!

After you find your core team members, do everything in your power to hold on to them. The shorthand that you'll develop is priceless and the more that you can appropriately offload to the people that you trust, the more time that you'll have to focus on what you do extremely well. For example, I don't speak music particularly well and have no idea what a beat or a measure are or how to symphonically describe sounds. I find it much easier to describe what I'm looking for by referencing a combination of existing scores such as asking for a sound that evokes "The Bourne Identity mixed with Gladiator". Not surprisingly it took me ages to find a composer who spoke my particular musical language. Thankfully, many years ago I was introduced to a composer named Peter Karr and hired him for a project. Once I saw how he translated my inept music language into a beautiful score that totally elevated our project, he became a true ride or die component of all our projects.

Archival and Stock Footage

Archival footage is one of the great foundational pieces of the documentary genre going back to the dawn of the medium. Great footage from the past can help illuminate a subject as well as offer context when compared to its shiny modern day ultra-high-definition or 4k counterpart. Similarly licensing **Stock Footage** can be a terrific solution when you're in a bind and don't quite have the correct imagery for the story that you're telling. While both are highly useful, they can also be incredible budget busters too. The trick is to properly track them and squeeze as much bang for the buck out of each licensed image or clip.

There are many ways to track down amazing archival footage or stock imagery to use in your productions. The easiest method is to search a wide range of mainstream footage houses such as Getty Images, Shutterstock, AP Archives, or the Corbis library. These are just some of the big stock names however there are hundreds of other footage libraries available online where you can secure material. You can also drill down even further and search university libraries, local television stations, and public institutions as well. There's all kinds of terrific hidden footage residing in random locations and there are Associate Producers and Stock Footage Researchers who excel at tracking it down. Some networks even have their own footage repositories, like Discovery Access, where you can leverage clips from previous factual programs.

Sourcing the material is just part of the challenge for a producer. Archive and Stock also tends to come with a hefty price tag. Many sites will state their prices on their websites. The ones that don't will have rate cards available if you call or email. If you're willing to guarantee a certain amount of spend at any of these repositories, you'll be able to negotiate considerably better rates. These houses are used to haggling, so it behooves you to ask if they'll take less. Remember it's all negotiable.

Typically, once you find the footage that you want to license, you'll be able to download a low-res proxy file of the material. These digital files almost always use boring alpha-numerical file names. They're not only utterly useless in a Non-Linear Editing System but problematic when tracking down which footage house the file originated from. Our solution is to add a prefix to every archival asset at the finder level prior to ingesting it into the editing system. When a project starts, we build a spreadsheet to track all the archival sources used in the production. Each vendor is given its own unique three-character abbreviation. Then every file that comes from that source gets tagged with this three-letter code. For instance, any file that we download from Getty Images gets tagged GET_, or if we're using material from the Library of Congress, we add LOC_ to the beginning of each file. Once ingested, this makes it super easy to know exactly where the file came from and who owns it.

Using someone else's material tends to come with a cost. Some can be relatively cost-effective while other footage can be brutally expensive. On the low end there are some smaller stock companies that either charge a monthly subscription fee for an all you can eat buffet of footage or a per clip flat fee based on resolution; SD clips are one price; HD clips are a bit higher and 4K files are the most expensive. However, if you buy in bulk, they will often lower their unit price. On the opposite end of the spectrum are sports leagues, which are notorious for charging hefty usage fees that can run upward of US$30,000 for just a few seconds of material.

Generally, most stock houses charge by the second, usually rounding up or down to the :15, :30, :45, or full minute. These institutions tend to offer a price break if you agree to buy a certain minimum number of minutes from them.

Over the years I've found that the best way to keep track of licensing costs with these houses is to pull the actual timecode for the licensable material straight out of your NLE system and import it into a spreadsheet to gain an instant understanding of your usage and current costs. Our workflow is to export the footage usage from the timeline as a CMX3600 file. Then we wash the resulting file through a stand-alone timecode sorting program. I'm a big fan of EDL Ease for Mac OSX. The application kicks out a tab delimited text document that can be imported directly into Excel or Sheets. Now you can sort the names for the files with the stock house prefixes that you established earlier during import and quickly total the timecode usage for both the individual files and your entire spend for a specific stock house. Our *How We Got Here* historical recreation series literally had hundreds of stock footage sources over the course of the series 12 episodes. So, I built a bespoke archival spreadsheet that utilizes a variety of custom formulas to help track the usage and fees.

HOW WE GOT HERE ARCHIVE COST REPORT					EP 101 - VONBRAUN						
								Ep Budget			$ 13,500.00
								Archive Total			$ 7,090.50
						00:15:06:16		TOTAL COST			$ 6,409.50
CODE	**Archive**	**Type**	**Cost**	**Notes**	**Frames**	**Total TC**	**Count**	**Sub-Total Cost**	**Minimum**	**Cost Per Sec**	**Total**
***	HONORARIUM										$ -
BBC	BBC News	Clip	$ 360.00	*check rights	0	00:00:00:00	0	$ -	$ -		$ -
CRP	Critical Past	Clip	$ 225.00	Schauer 10% discount	0	00:00:00:00	0	$ -	$ -		$ -
DIA	Discovery Access	Clip	$ 10.00	FREE	5261	00:02:55:15	46	$ 460.00	$ -	$ 2.58	$ 460.00
EFO	efootage.com	Clip	$ 249.00	$49-$249 depending on clip	0	00:00:00:00	0	$ -	$ -		$ -
FED	Federal Archives	Clip	$ -	FREE	1816	00:01:00:18	2	$ -	$ -		$ -
FMC	Ford Company	Clip	$ -	0 Licence fee, fee to transfer non-digitized assets	0	00:00:00:00	0	$ -	$ -		$ -
FRD	Ford Company	Clip	$ -	0 Licence fee	0	00:00:00:00	0	$ -	$ -		$ -
GET	Getty	Clip	$ 262.50	260-340/clip or Subscription	1438	00:00:47:28	3	$ 787.50	$ -	$ 16.16	$ 787.50
HSC	Hearst Castle	Clip		FREE	0	00:00:00:00	0	$ -	$ -		$ -
IST	iStock	Clip	$ 150.00	$150 clip (Getty) (20% with Heather Tanning)	0	00:00:00:00	0	$ -	$ -		$ -
NEW	Newseum.org	Clip			0	00:00:00:00	0	$ -	$ -		$ -
PBS	Public Broadcasting System	Clip			0	00:00:00:00	0	0	0		0
PDO	Public Domain	Clip	$ -		1621	00:00:54:01	54	$ -	$ -		$ -
PRE	Prelinger Archives	Clip	$ -	FREE	151	00:00:05:01	5	$ -	$ -		$ -
REA	http://www.reaganfoundation.org	Clip	$ -		92	00:00:03:02	3	0	0		0
SHU	Shutterstock	Clip	$ 66.00	~66/ clip	4324	00:02:24:08	13	$ 858.00	$ -	$ 5.85	$ 858.00
THF	thehenryford.com	Clip	$ -		0	00:00:00:00	0	$ -	$ -		$ -
USA	US Army	Clip	$ -	FREE	0	00:00:00:00	0	$ -	$ -		$ -
USD	US Dept of Defense	Clip	$ -	FREE	0	00:00:00:00	0	$ -	$ -		$ -
USG	US Federal Government	Clip	$ -	FREE	423	00:00:14:03	14	$ -	$ -		$ -
VBX	Video Blocks	Clip	$ -	$99 Monthly Pricing	29	00:00:00:29	0	$ -	$ -		$ -
INA	Internet Archive	Free	$ -	FREE	2701	00:01:30:03	82	$ -	$ -		$ -
LOC	Library of Congress	Free		FREE	0	00:00:00:00	0	$ -	$ -		$ -
NAR	National Archives	Free		FREE	1281	00:00:42:21	0	$ -	$ -		$ -
NAS	NASA	Free		FREE	4177	00:02:19:11	149	$ -	$ -		$ -
APA	AP Archives	Second	$ 60.00	Waiting on DCI Price	288	00:00:09:18	17	$ 1,020.00	$ -	$ 104.48	$ 1,020.00
BPA	British Pathé	Second	$ 25.00	Min. $500	0	00:00:00:00	2	$ 50.00	$ 500.00		$ 500.00
CNN	CNN Archive	Second	$ 39.00	$39/ sec per DCI Deal	0	00:00:00:00	0	$ -	$ -		$ -
CRB	Corbis (Footage)	Second	$ 72.00	3/sec per clip min	0	00:00:00:00	0	$ -	$ -		$ -
FIL	F.I.L.M. Archives Online	Second	$ 35.00		0	00:00:00:00	0	$ -	$ 1,000.00		$ -
FRA	Framepool	Second	$ 49.00	$49 /second	0	00:00:00:00	4	$ 196.00	$ -		$ 196.00
HIF	HistoricFilms.com	Second	$ 45.00		0	00:00:00:00	0	$ -	$ 500.00		$ -
NBC	NBC Universal	Second	$ 50.00	$45-$55 per second	0	00:00:00:00	0	$ -	$ -		$ -
PEF	Periscope Film	Second	$ 35.00	30 second price break	0	00:00:00:00	0	$ -	$ -		$ -
PLI	Producer's Library	Second	$ 30.00	`	0	00:00:00:00	10	$ 300.00	$ -		$ 300.00
UCL	University of California Los Angeles	Second	$ 90.00	~90/ Second	0	00:00:00:00	2	$ 180.00	$ -		$ 180.00
WPA	WPA Film Library	Second	$ 38.00	thought $38/sec -- has w/ $500 licensing minimum	164	00:00:05:14	59	$ 2,242.00	$ 500.00	$ 403.29	$ 2,242.00
APA	AP Archives	Still	$ 100.00	over 8 stills	639	00:00:21:09	4	$ 400.00	$ -		$ 400.00
AUT	Autofocus	Still		Should be marked Ford	0	00:00:00:00	0	$ -	$ -		$ -
BAN	The Bancroft Library	Still	$ 55.00	$0 license / $30 per scan	0	00:00:00:00	0	$ -	$ -		$ -
BPK	BPK Gate	Still	$ 375.00	$375/image	0	00:00:00:00	0	$ -	$ -		$ -
BRI	Bridgeman Art	Still	$ 195.00		0	00:00:00:00	0	$ -	$ -		$ -
CRB	Corbis (Stills)	Still	$ 200.00	1-10 $195 // 11-20 $175 // 21+ $150	0	00:00:00:00	0	$ -	$ -		$ -
DWM	Dead Wood Magazine	Still	$ 20.00		0	00:00:00:00	0	$ -	$ -		$ -
EDB	Ed Buckbee's Personal Collection	Still			0	00:00:00:00	0	$ -	$ -		$ -
FMC	Ford Company - STILLS	Still	$ -	FREE	0	00:00:00:00	0	$ -	$ -		$ -
FSH	forgottenshow.net	Still			0	00:00:00:00	0	$ -	$ -		$ -
GET	Getty - STILLS	Still	$ 147.00		211	00:00:07:01	1	$ 147.00	$ -	$ 20.55	$ 147.00
GFG	German Federal Government	Still		NOT A SOURCE	0	00:00:00:00	1	0	0		0
NAS	NASA	Still		FREE	2262	00:01:15:14	19	$ -	$ -		$ -
HBH	Historic Black Hills	Still	$ 50.00		0	00:00:00:00	0	$ -	$ -		$ -

FIGURE 9.7 A Sample Cost Tracking Spreadsheet for Archival Material.

Typical stock contracts allow you to reuse the material you license within the same program (or series) as much as you want at no additional cost. This is why you see a lot of programs that repeat the same stock footage shots over and over again. It's a highly cost-effective way to burn total running time (TRT).

Once you determine how much material you're going to use from a particular stock footage house, the next step is to negotiate the best rate. Usage is the first pillar of the final cost; usage rights are the other. Most networks and streamers require you to obtain a very specific set of rights that grants them the ability to broadcast the footage *in all markets and territories, in perpetuity, in all media, known or unknown.* Basically, the network or service wants the right to air the film for as long as they can use any new technologies that might emerge in the future. If that's too costly for your budget, sometimes convince a broadcaster to let you acquire a ten-year term license instead.

The trick to using archive footage well in a factual program or series is to find a balance between the narrative storytelling needs, the associated costs involved, and the total running time required. Spending huge sums of money on a 6-second clip you see one time might make for a great program but it's bad business. You need to either unearth a more cost-effective clip or reuse the footage to bring its cost per second down.

Staying on Schedule

The post-production phase of a project is all about crafting a realistic schedule at the outset and then sticking to it as you work your way toward final delivery. Larger productions employ a specific person to do this called a **Post-Production Supervisor**, and it's their responsibility to keep tabs on where all the various facets of post are at on a daily basis. On smaller projects producers can manage the process by themselves and easily stay on top of the process if they build and utilize great systems. On our traditional automotive programs, we don't leave anything up to chance. Every week is accounted for, and every day has a set goal. Generally, I like to budget for an editor to have four weeks to put together a 44-minute rough cut. They start with the already-to-time assembly cut and have twenty 8-hour days to build out a show. That translates to just 2.2 finished minutes per day. Any editor worth their salt ought to be able to do that with ease.

Slow editing is the death knell of factual filmmaking. We once produced a one-hour special for Nat Geo Asia about the famed Nürburgring racetrack in Germany. The gent I hired to edit the film turned out to be a procrastinator. He spent the first of his four allotted edit weeks laying out music in the timeline without editing any footage. This put us behind the proverbial eight-ball and meant that he had just three weeks to cut the 44-minute show. A lot of late nights ensued. He was a good friend, and I gave him the benefit of the doubt thinking that *this was his process*, but as I watched him only jump into action once there was a looming deadline, I realized that his procrastination not only was creating a rushed edit but was also raising the agitation inside the entire office. Everyone seemed on edge. In the end it was a painful experience, but it taught me a valuable lesson – you want to hire editors who keep an eye on the clock and stay ahead once they've got a time advantage.

To ensure that everyone stays on schedule, it helps to hold a **Daily Review** of what everyone has edited at the end of each day. Over time I've found that this helps create a very positive sense of camaraderie among the team and helps everyone stay on target. A positive by-product is that it also adds a bit of peer-pressure to perform. Nobody ever wants to be seen as the weak link. Best yet, it often helps offer creative inspiration. When a young editor sees a well-constructed sequence or montage in someone else's edit, they often attempt to either replicate it or better yet one-up it the next day. As a producer there are a lot of different ways to inspire your team; however, the best motivation tends to come from creating an environment where *team members want* to impress *their teammates of their own volition*. This also puts the sage veteran editors on notice that there are youngsters nipping at their heels. Just like in sports, *competition breeds a better end product.*

After enough group watch downs, eventually the entire edit team will begin to speed up their output on their own. Instead of cutting 1 or 2 finished minutes per day, they'll

SUPERCAR BUILD S1: EPISODE BREAKDOWN

	BENTLEY	ASTON	PAGANI	LAMBO	PORSCHE	FERRARI
INGESTING STAGES						
Create Project	YES	YES	YES	YES	YES	YES
Copy footage from FT to RS drive	YES	YES	YES	YES	YES	YES
AMA Link footage in project	YES	YES	YES	YES	YES	YES
Transcode footage in project	YES	YES	YES	YES	YES	YES
Sort footage into categories	YES	YES	YES	YES	YES	YES
Finish SLX Reels for all footage	YES	YES	YES	YES	YES	YES
WRITING						
Written Script	YES	YES	NO	YES	NO	YES
EDITING STAGES						
STRINGOUT	YES	YES	NO	YES	NO	YES
ROUGH CUT	NO	YES	NO	NO	NO	NO
FINE CUT	NO	NO	NO	NO	NO	NO
PICTURE LOCK / NETWORK APPROVAL	NO	NO	NO	NO	NO	NO
FINAL QC PASS	NO	NO	NO	NO	NO	NO
SCRIPTS						
ANNOTATED SCRIPT	NO	NO	NO	NO	NO	NO
NARRATION SCRIPT	NO	NO	NO	NO	NO	NO
AE GRAPHICS						
LOWER3RDS (Cut in)	NO	NO	NO	NO	NO	NO
BUMPERS (Cut in)	NO	NO	NO	NO	NO	NO
SLATE (24p) (Cut in)	NO	NO	NO	NO	NO	NO
CREDITS (Cut in)	NO	NO	NO	NO	NO	NO
MUSIC (PETER)						
EXPORTED TO	NO	NO	NO	NO	NO	NO
RECIEVED FROM	NO	NO	NO	NO	NO	NO
CUT IN	NO	NO	NO	NO	NO	NO
GRAPHICS (SOMATIC)						
Maps and Opening Title Downloaded	NO	NO	NO	NO	NO	NO
ARCHIVE MATERIALS						
Order Car Company Archive	NO	NO	NO	NO	NO	NO
Additional Shutterstock Needed	NO	NO	NO	NO	NO	NO
Shutterstock Ordered	NO	NO	NO	NO	NO	NO
FINAL TIMELINE PREP						
TIMELINE CLEAN UP	NO	NO	NO	NO	NO	NO
CLEAN COVERS	NO	NO	NO	NO	NO	NO
VO RECORDED	NO	NO	NO	NO	NO	NO
VO CUT IN	NO	NO	NO	NO	NO	NO
SOUND (SALAMI)						
AAF EXPORTED	NO	NO	NO	NO	NO	NO
720p Reference EXPORTED	NO	NO	NO	NO	NO	NO
Sound Package SENT	NO	NO	NO	NO	NO	NO
FINAL SOUND CUT IN	NO	NO	NO	NO	NO	NO
COLORING (CLINTON)						
AAF w/ 2 Tracks	NO	NO	NO	NO	NO	NO
TEXTLESS PR 4444	NO	NO	NO	NO	NO	NO

FIGURE 9.8 A Series Post-Production Checklist.

Editing

cut three or four finished minutes. They'll see the pace that their teammates are cutting and without realizing it slowly raise their own output to match. This not only keeps your project on schedule but as a by-product saves a producer money in post!

Managing the post-production process for a producer is often like being an air-traffic controller who surveys the skies to keep flights safely on track. You have multiple people that you have to keep on schedule, and you need to coordinate their deliveries while constantly staying updated on where the various elements of the project stand. We like to track each episode's progress inside of a single document we call the **Post-Production Breakdown**. It's a color coded excel sheet that clearly defines each program's route through post from start to finish and its current status. By housing all the information in one place, you can give it a quick glance and immediately know where the team is at in the process.

Inside the Industry With Jacinda Davis, Executive Producer

Jacinda Davis is an Emmy award–winning producer who focuses on True Crime.

- **What advice would you give to someone entering the "real world" who wants to produce their own content for a network like Discovery or Nat Geo? How would you suggest they start their career?**

I think it's important to get hands-on experience. Apply to production companies that are producing content that interests you. Your education doesn't stop when you graduate, in fact, in many ways that's when it begins. Listen, observe, ask questions – every job is a learning experience. And there is no one position that is more important than another. Every role is vital to the production and should be treated that way.

- **After you've been hired on and initially told the brief about the program, what are your first steps to bring the project to life? What are the initial mission critical issues you try to tackle first?**

I tackle every production like a research project. I read books, articles, and primary documents. I want to learn everything I can about any given topic. It's important to know enough to have a meaningful conversation with the people you book. Whether it's a nuclear physicist or a victim of crime, you can't call someone up and ask them for an interview if you don't know the story inside and out. But at the same time, always remember you are not the expert. A natural curiosity about the subject matter goes a long way. After I feel like I know the subject matter, I try to figure out the story – what is the hook? What is the point of the production, and who do I need to tell that story? I'm using "I" here, but it's always a collaboration. From pre-production through final delivery, it's a collaboration.

- **It has always struck me that one of your gifts is an ability to convince people who might not be fully keen on being interviewed to tell their story – any tricks of the trade for convincing people to sit down for an interview? (If it's helpful, perhaps you can describe how you initially engage a prospective interviewee, what you say via email or on a call, etc.)**

Before I reach out to anyone with an interview request, I try to see the request from their perspective. What would motivate them to say no, what would motivate them to say yes? Always remember that this is about them, not you. Never forget – your most valuable tool is your ability to listen, truly listen, in an open, curious, receptive way. Most people do want to tell their story – but only if they sense that you are willing to hear them out, on their own terms. Finally, don't be afraid of silence – just wait for them to fill it.

- **Over the years are there any particular kinds of systems or checklists that you've found to be particularly helpful to keeping a project rolling smoothly?**

I live by to-do lists and production calendars. Mapping out when things need to be finished and the steps needed to complete each task is essential in managing a project. But because a million things can go wrong in production – from canceled flights to flat tires – you also have to be able to adjust as needed. It's like a game of Tetris – how do I get all these pieces to fit together no matter what's thrown my way?

- **For those that don't readily know how to access or obtain archival footage, what are your best practices to find, source, and secure amazing material to use in your programs?**

I like to start by seeing what's out there. What material has been used in other projects, what material pops up in a simple Google Search, what material do I know exists based on the topic? For example, is it an event I know was filmed? And from there I backtrack – who owns it and who might have filmed it? The traditional "archive houses" are a great place to start. Casting a wide net but also including specific or unique search terms will usually yield good results. But I also like to look for "never before seen material" like home video – things you can only get from the people who are personally close to the story. You never know what you might find if you don't ask.

- **Archival footage can cost a tremendous amount – how do you keep the spend under control?**

Budget ahead of time. It's essential to know the exact licensing terms you need for the project and how much it will cost to license material with those terms. And don't be afraid to negotiate. Ask for a discount, or bulk rate. Most places are willing to work with you, but it's best to negotiate up front. Of course, it's a guess as to how much archival material will actually make the cut, but I always overestimate so there aren't any surprises.

- **As a producer, how does episode quantity affect your preparation or field production? (e.g., do you take a different approach for a one-off special versus a mini-series versus a long-running series)?**

Interviewing people for an hour-long show is different than for a six-hour show. But in both cases, it's the same approach. I map out the story arc ahead of time and by doing that I know exactly what beats I need each interview to cover. I put a great deal of effort into mapping out those beats very specifically in writing before the interview. A six-hour show will obviously need more material than a one-hour show. Those interviews will generally be longer and will go into more depth. But whether it's a one hour show or multiple hours, it's essential to immerse yourself in the topic. Some of the best material comes from the things you don't anticipate . . . but if you don't know the topic well enough it's hard to navigate the interview when those moments pop up.

- **How has failure, or apparent failure, helped shape your career?**

I learn something new with every project. And also, from the people I work with. And in that sense, you can't fail. You can't fail when you're constantly learning and growing. If you find yourself in a place where you feel like you have all the answers, then either you don't really know what you're doing, or it's an indication that it's time to call it quits.

- **What is the worst advice that you continually hear people giving new or young producers?**

That's tough. I don't generally hear bad advice being given to new producers. But I guess when it comes to interviewing people I do sometimes hear – if the question makes you uncomfortable or if you think it will make the interviewee uncomfortable then don't ask it. The problem is, asking hard questions is part of the job. The only way to get the story is to ask hard questions. And I think some producers get that confused. I work a lot in the true-crime genre. If I'm sitting across from a convicted killer and don't ask the tough questions, I'm doing a disservice to everyone involved. You aren't there to do anything unethical but just because a question is hard, doesn't mean you don't ask it. It's knowing how to ask it and when to ask it . . . and that takes experience. But don't be afraid to ask.

Types of Edits

Editing is the process of manipulating your field material and other visual assets to create a final program master. It's a powerful storytelling tool that done correctly can compel the audience to feel very distinct emotions. Yet lurking behind the flashy cuts is nothing more than basic math.

The process of editing a factual program for broadcast features four key stages.

The Assembly Edit

The *Assembly Edit* is the initial stage when you put your program together on a nonlinear editing (NLE) platform timeline. This is when you build the foundation for your project. The more solid the base, the better the edit.

I see a lot of young editors dive right into assembling their footage, with little regard to a project's final running time or act structure. That's a good way to *overcut your total running time*. It might seem daunting when you face an empty timeline, but the truth is that every choice you make directly affects the remainder of your timeline. Every cut is precious and every montage crucial to your eventual timing, rhythm and pace.

If you edit without constraints, you often end up with a stunning 50- or 60-minute cut that then will need to be hacked down *to make time*, which is a fancy way of saying it fits within the network or streamer's total running time requirements. Most one-hour factual TV programs have 44 minutes of total content. The remaining 16 minutes are filled with commercials. If your initial edit is 60 minutes long and intended for a 44-minute programming slot, then you've edited an additional 36% of content that will never make it to air!

That's not only a waste of time, effort, and energy but also budget. Financing is a finite resource, and you only want to spend it on the parts of the project that make it *into* the final program master. Paying an editor to cut extra finished minutes that never see the light of day is wasteful.

The solution is to employ a more thought-out approach similar to how a general contractor systematically remodels a home. Editing a factual program is just like renovating a house; You can move the walls around inside and change the finishes, but the basic guts are defined by the exterior walls. In the case of a broadcast documentary those walls are the network's broadcast clock.

Here's our battle-tested solution: Once the rough draft of the working edit script is completed, we immediately record a temporary voice-over track and have the narrator read the script at the same pace that we want the final narration to be tracked. Next, the edit team takes the rough cut script, the temp voice-over, and the key interviews and begins laying a very basic structural edit. This cut isn't about pretty pictures or glorious b-roll, but rather exclusively about the dialogue and timing.

We've come to use a very simple timing formula.

- Cut in Interview Soundbite
- Add 3 seconds of Black
- Cut in Voice-Over track
- Add 1 second of Black
- Cut in next Interview Soundbite
- Rinse and Repeat

This ensures a consistent pace for every program and allows for reliable act timings.

When this initial audio-driven assembly edit is completed, the edit team's next task is to log the act timings. They're quickly checked against the network's requirements, and if any alterations are needed, they take place *before* any b-roll or music is added to the timeline. This guarantees that the episode is *on-time* when it's handed off to the lead editor for the rough cut. With the lead editor freed from structural or timing issues, they're free to spend their creative and emotional capital cutting the best episode possible.

The Rough Cut

Once the Assembly Edit is completed and the program is on-time, you're ready to begin the fun part – the **Rough Cut**! This is the editing equivalent of a working written draft, your initial pass at crafting the perfect program and ultimately will become the first version of the documentary or program that you will share with a network or streamer. All of your creative energies have led you to this point and the quality of what you build and deliver will directly affect how easy or hard the remainder of the process is.

Some production companies deliver rough cuts that have holes because they're still filming or haven't had time to track down key footage. I'm not an advocate for this approach. Delivering a 100% airable rough cut that features all of your lower thirds in place, LUTs on all the footage, and as many final graphics as possible helps a network

EP *see the vision* and not get hung up on *what's missing.* Also take a beat to give the rough cut program one more watch. The difference between good and great is often one more revision. An extra run through a cut often adds an additional layer of polish that will separate your project from others. After reviewing a rough cut your network EP will send you a set of notes and in my experience the more polished the initial cut is the less notes you'll receive and the sooner you can wrap up the project.

One-Off versus Series Editing: When you're crafting a one-hour special or self-contained long form documentary film you have the pleasure of building something that stands alone. If you're fortunate enough to land a series, then you're going to be playing a very different game – *series are all about repeatable storytelling.* Format reigns supreme in the series world. You have to be able to make a great hour of television and then do it again, and again, and again. In many ways the difference is akin to the TV Chef versus Restaurant Chef paradox. Often your ego wants to be a TV Chef – someone who creates an amazing meal made exclusively for four people to enjoy in a unique culinary moment. However, to be a successful Restaurateur, you need to be able to make 6, 8, 10, or 12 brilliant meals, exactly alike, over an entire season. It's a very different kind of artistry. One that is both more commercial and more commoditized.

On one of our first big series, I made the mistake of letting the edit team tackle the initial cut of the first episode on their own. What they created was very different from what I had envisioned, yet by the time that I realized it there was no time left to alter course. In effect I put the look and feel of the series in the hands of others without offering them a concrete vision for what I actually wanted. I thought the script alone was enough, but it wasn't. The resulting edit was beneath my expectations, yet the momentum of the series forced us to move forward. It was heartbreaking to watch that particular cut being uploaded because I knew in my heart that we could have done better. The experience taught me a very valuable lesson and forever altered how I approach series editing.

Whenever you land your first series, *you either need to cut your first episode yourself or have your very best and most trusted editor put it together for you. You have to build a perfect blueprint for others to follow.* The first episode of a freshman season is a mini-pilot. You have to put more energy into this episode than all the others combined. It sets the tone, the style, the look and the structure for everything that follows and is crucial to the success of the series in the network's eyes.

The Fine Cut

The next step in the process is the **Fine Cut**. This is your chance to polish the initial working draft of the program and is your opportunity to respond to the network EP's notes. While working on this edit you have to balance giving the network what they've asked while also protecting the integrity of your project. Just as the sun always rises, it's almost assured that you'll object to at least one or two of the network's main notes. If you have a logical and truthful reason to fight it, then go for it. However, it's often best to try and meet the Network halfway as long as it won't adversely affect your overall vision.

Handling Network Notes: Crafting a factual program is a war of attrition. The initial edit is the most creative step in the process. However, it doesn't happen in a vacuum with unlimited resources. Eventually the source of your funding, otherwise known as your boss, will weigh in with their notes. Some network EPs give great notes that are highly specific and clearly articulate what they like or what they don't like. These folks are a dream to work with and easy to please. Other times, you won't be quite so lucky. Unfortunately, vague notes are often a part of this business.

I've always looked at the note receiving process as a fluid situation built on give and take. When I receive a new set of notes, I try to immediately identify the core issues that connect them all and set out to address that issue first. Is there a hidden subtext to the concerns? Is there a common thread that ties them all together? Once you sort that out you can move on to tackling the individual notes.

You also have to take any objections with a grain of salt. Your network EP might have been interrupted 12 times while watching your edit. They might have had a family emergency crop up last minute or a phone call they had to take. They're human, and sometimes it's hard to separate external feelings from the note-giving process. So don't get down on negative notes. It's just part of the process. When you come across a note that you vehemently disagree with, it's OK to fight for what you believe in. You have to stand up for what you think is correct, and while you might not ultimately win your argument, as long as you present a clear rationale for why you believe that the note isn't valid, no one can fault you. There've been many times I've stood up for something in one of our projects only to have the network EP say, "That's a great point, I don't know why I had a note" or "You're right, let's keep it in".

Picture Lock

Once the Fine Cut is completed, you're on your way to wrapping up the program. Your next major milestone is a **Picture Lock** cut. As the name implies, this edit aims to lock the final program in place so that you can move on to the narration stage. This is essentially a ready for air edit that incorporates all of the network's previous notes. The goal here is give the network EP one last chance to review the edit for any final thoughts.

S&P Review: Throughout the editing process there's a second type of review and note giving process known as the Standards and Practices review or **S&P Review**. This is when the broadcaster's legal team weighs in with their thoughts on the project. Every net runs the process differently, some have their legal department weigh-in at each edit interval while others only review once the film is nearly finished. Either way the rationale is fairly the same – depending on the country there are strict rules that govern over-the-air transmissions. These rules guide everything from product placement to logo usage. If you've ever seen a show on your TV where someone's t-shirt or hat is blurred out, you have the network S&P department to thank. Some of their decisions are legal related, while others are actually about advertising. At most networks the S&P decision-making process is kept entirely separate from the editorial team. So, your network EP won't hold much sway over the S&P department team or any potential verdict. Generally speaking, what S&P says, goes. There are specific, if rare, cases where you can fight back or negotiate – though it usually has to come from your network EP to move the needle.

We once battled with Nat Geo's legal department over a point of view shot filmed from atop the hood of a Porsche Panamera. The car was in a full drift around a corner on a racetrack and you could see the track's iconography fully reflected in the hood. It looked like a book-matched mirrored image, where the top and bottom of the frame were identical copies. However, smack in the middle of the hood sat the Porsche Crest. Legal felt we were highlighting the brand's logo too much. They asked us to cut the shot. Our network EP thought that it was a travesty given the quality of the image. After a great deal of back and forth, everyone finally agreed to trim the clip down from 13 seconds to 7 seconds. In the end 144 frames caused a week's worth of back and forth!

Uploading Cuts and Review Tools

Most networks have their own digital portal where they want completed edits to be uploaded. Some offer built in note taking tools, while most are simply basic FTP platforms. There are however some new Web 2.0 tools that can augment and help the review process. In particular, Adobe's Frame.IO platform is a lifesaver for multi-stakeholder reviews. It allows each contributor to detail their own thoughts with exact timecode stamps while at the same time being able to see anyone else's notes on the project. This works extremely well for non-network projects; however, most broadcast nets still prefer you utilize their own in-house systems.

Inside the Industry With Terren Lin, Founding Partner at Snacktime Creative

Terren Lin is an Emmy award–winning producer and editor who has hand-crafted a wide range of content. He's worked on everything from *Jay Leno's Garage*, to Discovery Channel motoring series as well as launch Motor Trend's flagship *Head 2 Head* series on YouTube.

- **What advice would you give to a smart film school student entering the "real world"?**

Don't work for others for free too often. That's what film school is for. Projects that want you to work for free will likely not have the capital needed to provide polished "reel worthy" footage. While building your reel is important. In today's world, there are other avenues to acquire work for your portfolio. One of the things that impresses me is when job candidates with little experience "will" a reel into existence using found footage. In many cases, the footage obviously did not belong to the interviewing editor, but they were about to weave a story or exemplify a sense of their editing style using it.

- **How would you suggest a young filmmaker begin their career if their goal is to eventually edit original programming for a broadcast network?**

Learn the technicals of the craft. This means all the jargon that comes with television engineering (NTSC, PAL, telecine, de-interlacing, etc.). It's not as fun as the creative but important if you want to be perceived as someone who is serious about post production. Traditionally, you'd work your way up the ladder as an assistant. Many careers have begun with AE's cutting inconsequential scenes on broadcast shows before graduating to full episodes. With television, it's all still rooted deeply in the limits of established technology. Be prepared for the system to be rigid.

- **You've edited everything from Broadcast TV to Digital first content and New Media videos – how do you view the difference between them?**

I usually think of new media as commercials or music videos. Fast paced with a concentration on high quality visuals, anything goes. Experimental, narrative, doco and everything in between. With Broadcast . . . there are more boundaries to work within. The biggest hurdle is considering time limits and structuring a piece around that (pre-determined act breaks and total running times to consider). It can be difficult to stretch a piece to fit into a 60 min presentation which contrasts with digital where the TRT is whatever feels right.

- **What are some of your best practices when editing for Broadcast?**

Preparation and pre-production is everything. Be prepared to work cross functionally with folks who specialize in one thing (story producer, broadcast engineers, colorists, sound designers, etc.), it takes a village. Whatever your task is, it's more concentrated and singular. It may seem like there is less freedom, but the freedom lies in that the weight is not all on you to do everything. Make sure your organization is tight. No two editors will work exactly the same so consider your cross functional colleagues as well. Any post pro professional should be able to open up your project and figure it out in 5 minutes or less. Apply feedback from the end of the timeline and always watch down a cut in full before sending it along to stakeholders.

- **Do you have any core tenants to editing that you feel young editors should focus their energies learning? (Style or techniques that you think are missing in today's creative community?)**

Today's editors have plenty of style, especially when browsing social media platforms. Aside from techniques . . . I feel it's more important to wrap one's head around speed and forward progress. It's very easy to fall into a state of paralysis by analysis, just start with a single decision on the timeline. To push past that creative wall, find that one perfect cut. It could be a matched action shot, a shot that feels perfect as it falls on a musical beat . . . whatever. Then anchor the rest of the timeline around that decision, it will all fall into place.

- **How do you approach storytelling and structure when editing? Do you have any core beliefs about editing for TV? (For example, a reliance on nat sound or a certain kind of editing style?)**

In broadcast, the acts are almost pre-determined for you based on the timing of act breaks. Naturally, an editor will want to be flashy and show off all the cool techniques they've learned. All that style doesn't not make up for lack of substance. Mature editors realize that they need to be invisible to the viewer, especially when filling 30–60 minutes worth of screen time per episode. Over several episodes. Regardless of timeframe (7 seconds to 3 hours), a piece should be clear and easy viewing for the audience. You never want to exhaust them, and the audience should not have to work too hard to understand the piece. If the audience is "working", it should be because the filmmakers intended cerebralness as part of the experience.

- **How do you engage a network executive or stakeholder in the project when delivering cuts?**

Keep your emails short and concise when addressing anything in the edit, easily digestible, and referenced. Ain't no one got time for a college dissertation! Let the work speak for itself; they're likely going to want to start watching it down as soon as they can. Lengthier discussions can happen once they've digested the piece. Remember, they likely have other edits on other projects to watch down as well.

- **What do you think is the most important part of the post-production process? Any specific areas that you think young editors commonly under or overthink?**

When you hit a creative wall, don't let it paralyze you. Move onto tightening other aspects. Every little improvement adds up to give confidence in your decisions. Also . . . don't spend 80% of your time making the opening sequence awesome only to have the rest of the edit rushed. It's a common mistake among new filmmakers.

- **How do you manage and navigate potentially hundreds of hours of footage for a series?**

Systematically with patience. Scrub through it and start chunking it out. Make large piles of related footage then move into granular organization. The key thing is not to be overwhelmed, just start somewhere and be disciplined about it. Part of an editor's job is to intimately know the footage and continuously whittle away until the best footage makes it to screen. Hopefully, you have AEs, so you're not fried by the time you have to get into the creative aspects.

Chapter Ten

Delivery and Exhibition

As you work your way through the various editing stages, you'll be moving your project step by step toward the finish line. Yet there are still a handful of important moments to go!

DOI: 10.4324/9781003292289-10

The Annotated Script

If you ever thought that once you left university you'd be done with footnotes, think again. Once you have a Picture Locked show, it's time to hand in your **Annotated Script**. The annotated script is basically a term-paper for your project. Most networks require you to cite where every fact in the program originated and include a short quote pulled from the source so that the network annotator can quickly review it. The length and severity differ by network and typically you don't have to annotate soundbites, since presumably the people talking are experts on your program's subject. The real focus is on the narration. The annotator's job is to ensure that the voice-over is factually accurate. They hold the power to kill whatever narration they deem is incorrect or unsupportable. It's a noble and important job for a network that cares about truth.

You'll find that network annotators come in many different forms; the really good ones act more like collaborators, helping to research and often suggest alternative ways to write narration that will pass the review process.

ULTIMATE SUPERCAR – PORSCHE TAYCAN 5/23/21
PICTURE LOCK ANNOTATED SCRIPT v5

3	1:00:25:00		**NOW AS THE ELECTRIC VEHICLE ERA DAWNS, PORSCHE'S FAMED PETROL-SPORTING FUTURE IS IN DOUBT...** *I suppose one could argue that the petrol sporting future for all marques is "in doubt." Probably not much doubt, but still.*	*THERE'S A HUGE RISK THAT EVERYONE IN SILICON VALLEY WILL BE LAUGHING AT PORSCHE IF THIS CAR DOESN'T WORK. – JASON CAMMISA TRANSCRIPT 21:59:41:06* *BUT ONE CAR STANDS OUT ABOVE ALL THE REST AS THE SINGLE MOST ESSENTIAL VEHICLE I MUST DRIVE IN 2019: THE PORSCHE TAYCAN. A LOT IS RIDING ON THIS OTHERWISE HUMBLE FOUR-DOOR SEDAN. OR STARTERS, THIS IS PORSCHE'S FIRST MOVE INTO GENERAL-PRODUCTION ELECTRIFIED CARS (THE 918 SPYDER HYBRID DOESN'T COUNT). AND IT'LL PLAY A CRUCIAL ROLE IN THE VOLKSWAGEN LINEUP AS VW EXECUTES A PLAN TO BECOME MORE AGILE WHILE IT FACES BIG SHIFTS IN THE CAR INDUSTRY.* HTTPS://WWW.AFR.COM/LIFE-AND-LUXURY/CARS-BIKES-AND-BOATS/PORSCHES-ELECTRIC-TAYCAN-IS-THE-MOST-IMPORTANT-CAR-OF-2019-20190102-H19M7K
4	1:00:33:00	Bernd Wūrsching	// We're trying // to produce a new // iconic car //	
5	1:00:38:00		TO CREATE A NEW ICON AND FEND OFF NEW COMPETITORS, THE MARQUE GAMBLES THREE QUARTERS OF A BILLION DOLLARS TO BUILD THEIR VERY FIRST EV...	*IT TOOK AWHILE—YEARS, IN FACT—BUT PORSCHE ON WEDNESDAY MARKED "THE START OF A NEW ERA" BY FINALLY INTRODUCING THE HOTLY ANTICIPATED PRODUCTION VERSION OF THE ALL-ELECTRIC CONCEPT THAT WOWED THE CROWD AT THE 2015 FRANKFURT MOTOR SHOW. DUBBED THE TAYCAN, THE NEW SEDAN, WITH A BASE PRICE TOPPING $150,000, TAKES AIM AT THE TESLA (TICKER: TSLA) MODEL S. DELIVERIES WILL START BEFORE THE YEAR'S END.* HTTPS://WWW.BARRONS.COM/ARTICLES/PORSCHE-JUST-UNVEILED-A-HUGE-THREAT-TO-TESLAS-HIGH-END-ELECTRIC-SEDAN-51567627187 *PORSCHE ALSO SAYS IT WILL SPEND MORE THAN $760 MILLION AND ADD 1,000 NEW JOBS AT ITS STUTTGART-ZUFFENHAUSEN FACILITY TO PRODUCE THE ALL-ELECTRIC SPORTS CAR.* HTTPS://TECHCRUNCH.COM/2019/09/04/PORSCHES-ALL-ELECTRIC-EVOLUTION-FROM-SKETCH-TO-MISSION-E-CONCEPT-TO-PORSCHE-TAYCAN/
6	1:00:47:00	Jason Cammisa	// The question in my mind is whether the Porsche electric vehicle will be as good //	

FIGURE 10.1 A Page in an Annotated Script.

Easy Annotations Being During Scripting: The best way to make the annotation process go smoothly is to start citing facts while writing your script. If you wait until the end, it's a very laborious process that often requires you to scour the internet to find the articles that support your work. It's much easier to know exactly where you pulled the information from to begin with.

Final Narration Record

If you're working on a dialogue-driven film with a narrator, once you've completed the editing and have gone through all the network review phases, including any legal reviews, you'll eventually end up with a locked script. *Now it's time to record the final narration!*

Voice-over artists are the hidden stars of the factual creative community. Selecting the correct voice can be a highly subjective discussion; however, the right narrator can truly separate a project from the competition.

Often a producer will have to direct the narrator during a Voice Over Session (VO session). This can be extremely tricky. Up until now you've only heard the edit with the temporary VO track and often it's easy to unwittingly fall in love with its pace, style, tone, or inflection without realizing it. The first time you hear another voice reading the script can be jarring; however, it's also hugely inspiring. This is when your project starts becoming a real program.

During a recording session I try to give basic and direct notes. You don't want to overcomplicate the process nor require the narrator to decode your direction. I tend to ask for a "faster" or "slower" read, more emphasis placed on a certain word or phrase, or often a "bigger or more emphatic" read. Since you picked the VO artist based on their voice, there shouldn't be very much discussion about the *sound.* However, if you use any *character* actor voice-over artists, then you might need to help shape the dialect.

For example, our long-time translator voice is also a Hollywood cartoon dialogue artist who can read with multiple different accents, including Italian, German, and Spanish. Sometimes he'll inadvertently slip from one accent into another, and it's my job to keep him honest to the ethnicity that he's portraying in the script.

Overall keep the experience light and fun to get the best results.

Audio Mixing

Once the final voice-over is laid into the master program timeline, you're finally ready to export your audio for mastering. You'll send the resulting audio files to an Audio Engineer typically via an AAF or OMF file. The engineer will then begin working on the **Final Audio Mix**. Their key responsibility is to ensure that the program's final audio mix meets the network or streamer's quality control standards and doesn't exceed any peak audio levels. Once the wrap up the audio mixing, the engineer will send you back a variety of audio tracks for your final finishing. While viewers at home are often familiar with listening to 5.1 or stereo audio, few realize that all television programs are actually made up of a multitude of additional *audio stems*, or audio files. These additional tracks allow a broadcaster to *version* the project for different markets, changing the main narrator to a local voice and sometimes dubbing the dialogue of any non-native speakers.

Color Correction and Mastering

Once your edit is locked, the narration has been recorded, and your audio is fully mixed, it's time for the **Final Color Correction and Mastering**. In most factual programs, color correction usually equates to legalization. Your colorist's job is to ensure that none of the colors are out of spec and that your black levels are correct so that your film passes the Network quality control process. Some higher-end programs or series will also feature a "look". This is similar to Hollywood movies, where the director of photography pushes the colorist to develop a unique feel for the film's color palette.

In the factual or documentary world the look is seldom determined by a director of photography (DP) since they're usually on their next gig by the time a project rolls into coloring. Usually, any look discussions fall to the producer. Over the years we've had a few projects that featured a specific visual style where we pushed the shots toward a blue or daylight balanced feel. While it's a fun way to separate your content from the pack, it's debatable whether it makes the end product any better versus the extra time invested.

A fully color-corrected program is now ready for final mastering. Back in the day this used to be a simple process of laying the show back to tape: first with ¾" tape, then Beta SP, followed by Digi Beta, and finally HDCAM or HDCAM SR.

These days it's far more complex as the number of required deliverables continues to expand. The international market continues to broadcast in 50i/25p, while North America still transmits at 29.97/30p. This means that somewhere in the distribution chain a time-base conversion sub-master has to be made. Networks used to do this, but today it typically falls on the producer or production company instead. To accommodate both the global markets and the North American market, we film our projects in 23.98p. This has turned out to be the best middle-ground format for making clean conversions to either major time-base and usually means that for a global project we'll deliver four QuickTime files per episode.

- A fully Texted 23.98p QuickTime
- A Textless 23.98p QuickTime
- A fully Texted 25p QuickTime
- A Textless 25p QuickTime

The key to multiple time-base file deliveries is to pick which time-base is your master early in the project. Since our primary market tends to be Europe, we're often editing 23.98p footage to a 25p/50i clock. We set-up Avid Media Composer to keep a 25p/50i timecode-burn up all the time while editing and use this clock to correctly cut for the eventual 25p master QuickTime. That means that during the edit, the timeline's actual 23.98 time-base is useless. All of our crucial decisions are informed by the 25p/50i TC burn-in. It might sound complex, but in reality it's fairly simple. Instead of using the 23.98 timelines built in timecode, we're simply replacing it with another set of numbers. Once the 23.98 sub-master is converted to 25, the **Start of Program** (SOP) and act breaks all line up exactly where they're supposed to on the new master. No matter how many format conversions you plan to make, there can only be one master timecode cut to the broadcast clock. So, you have to judiciously pick which one is king.

For many years we had our color correction done at a major Hollywood post-production facility because we thought it was too complex a task to trust others. But then we had a quick-turnaround project come through for a foreign division of an international network group and the post-facility dropped the ball. They missed all of their deadlines and the project nearly missed its broadcast date. This ultimately burnt our relationship with the network client. It was a horrific turn of events, yet today I'm thankful for the experience because it forced us to look for new solutions. This led us to a series of boutique colorists. Just because a final finishing facility does all the big Hollywood series, doesn't mean it's the right fit for your project. Our latest boutique colorist does *even better work* than our previous supplier and has a much lower overhead. They're far more responsive and *also* creatively engaged in the projects. So, it's both better and a creative win. I'd strongly encourage others to seek the most like-minded colorists, not the biggest or the industry perceived "best".

The Network QC

When the audio mix is completed, the colorist will combine the final picture with the final sound mix into a single master digital QuickTime file and upload it to the network or streamer, where the platform's engineering staff will run a **Quality Control Check** or "QC". Ideally your film passes on the first go; however, it's not uncommon for the **Network QC Department** to find some minor faults with your program. If and when that happens the QC department will send you a very specific *fix-it* list of required changes. Don't fret. This happens all the time and is no big deal.

A decade ago, the Network QC process used to be a highly complex affair that was full of mystery. Today, it's a bit simpler thanks to the advancement of modern multi-territory flat-screen televisions. Back in the day if your colors were out of spec, it could actually damage a traditional tube or CRT television. To stop that from happening, networks put new programs through rigorous QC evaluations. Someone from the QC department would literally watch every frame and grade them. When they were done, they'd send this report back to the project's producer asking for corrections. The evaluation form was built on a four-point scale. A four was a noted issue but passable while on the other end of the spectrum a one required an immediate fix. Since the process was shrouded in confusion, producers would have to pad their budgets for the cost of potential fixes since any changes are not the network's responsibility.

These days, QC departments are much more lenient, and most nets and streamers put all new programs through quality checks via an automated system. The pass/fail range is much wider thanks in large part to the ubiquitous of flat screen TVs. Since newer TVs don't use transistor tubes, the chance of one blowing up because of bad colors or a strange frame rate is highly diminished. The Network QC departments can still ask for alterations, but they're typically much smaller issues such as graphics that spill into the network's bug zone (the area where the network fades on or elevates their logo during the broadcast).

Just like other parts of the factual process, QC reports can be *negotiated*. Sometimes they'll call out issues that you simply can't change. It's not uncommon for a QC team to note poor quality uprezzed historical archival material. However, there's often very little that you can do to increase the footage's resolution. The footage might have been shot on film sixty or seventy years ago and has been transferred to so many different video formats over the years, before eventually being digitized, that no one even knows where the original source material is anymore. In a case like this you usually want to start a conversation with the QC team and explain that the footage is editorially motivated and therefore worth a waiver. Most departments will grant such an exception.

Inside the Industry With Tom Maydeck, Sound Mixer C.A.S.

Tom Maydeck is an Emmy-winning audio sound mixer and designer.

- **You've mixed audio for a wide range of different types of visual content including theatrical films, animation, narrative television, and factual TV. How do you view the difference between them?**

Although there are certain universal audio practices which an audio professional has as a foundation for any project, it is vital to understand how each is to be viewed by the public. A film is to be enjoyed in a medium to large room with a large screen and sound system, while a television project is to be watched at home in someone's living room or even on a laptop using ear buds. The final mix for film won't work for television without certain adjustments being performed first. Contain the dynamic range as the broadcast medium will suffer with distortion otherwise or streaming networks suppress the mix with heavy handed compression. Know that there are different industry standards for dialogue level in a film versus in a television show and networks will reject your work if you don't deliver your mix correctly.

- **Do you have any core tenants when it comes to audio mixing for Broadcast?**

Television and streaming broadcasts are intended for the home listening environment. Generally, the playback volume is somewhat lower than the reference level I mix, and the ambient noise from the household can mask elements of the mix. This is to be expected, and all I can do is make sure that the dialogue can be heard at all times. Dialogue is always most important since it is how the story is told.

- **How do you navigate mixing for the experience versus ensuring that the dialogue and subject matter can be heard fully?**

Make sure you study the HAAS Fusion Curve. Simply stated, this is a vital resource which shows how listening to your mix at different volumes can produce different outcomes. Before any of my mixes leaves the studio, I do a final watch down on a stereo television at a volume less than what I used to mix the project. It is simple insurance, and it works well for me.

We live in a world with many different TV standards (HD flavors, frame rates, etc.) and numerous forms of distribution (over the air, cable, internet, streaming, etc.) – how do you mix a piece of content so that it plays correctly on a large screen TV with a killer sound system as well as a small CRT TV with built-in speakers?

This is something I encounter in all of my mixes. I do build my mixing templates with buss assignments for the folding down to the smaller formats, and it does much of the work for me; however, it still requires a listen in case a tweak or two is needed.

- **How do you like to interface with a producer on a project? What defines a good audio mixer/producer relationship in your eyes?**

I always welcome any early communication with the producer. Getting his or her focus on what they hear in their head is vital to getting my mix close to their expectations. However, with television turnaround getting shorter these days, many of my broadcast mixes are my solo interpretation of how I think it should be mixed. The producer comes in and hears the mix after my pass and hopefully likes it!

- **Is there anything that a producer can do to help make the audio mixing process better or more efficient?**

A great producer takes the time to understand the processes that support his work. As television programs are visually edited using computer based systems, the project comes to me with multiple tracks built with dialogue, music, and sound effects placed against the picture. Having those tracks organized by groups is always welcome.

The Final Legal Binder

After you deliver the final finished edit it might feel like you're done; however there's still one more important step in the process left – the final legal binder.

Decades ago, this was an actual physical binder that producers would have to FedEx to the network for review. Today's legal binder is a bit easier and consists of a collection of digital documents that you typically upload to a broadcaster or streamer's production management portal. The purpose of the binder is to prove that you have the right to use all of the elements in your project.

There are seven main categories of a documentary legal binder.

Releases

We live in a litigious society. People sue for all kinds of reasons these days. That's especially true in the television industry. Before a network or streamer will broadcast a project, to avoid any future complications they'll want to ensure that all the footage contained within the program or series has been properly acquired.

There are two basic ways that a producer can prove their footage is unencumbered. First, any footage that you originate yourself in the field must correspond to a signed **Location Release**. This is a document that grants you the right to film at the specific location. Second, for any still images or film/video that you don't own or didn't originate yourself, you'll have to supply a signed **Materials Release** from whoever owns the materials rights. A materials release is a legal contract that states that you've secured the right to use the footage for a certain period of time, in certain forms of media, for a negotiated rate. In a perfect world you want to obtain worldwide usage rights, in all media (known and unknown), in perpetuity, for as little cost as possible.

Acquired Material Logs

The next mission critical document is an **Acquired Footage Log**. This is typically a spreadsheet that pinpoints where the licensed material lives within your program. This document lets a network know who owns the material, how long it's been licensed for use, and in what media it's allowed to be used.

Graphics Log and Contract

Similar to the acquired footage log, the **Graphics Log** lets a broadcaster know where all of the on-screen graphics sit within the program. It's an essential document in today's global viewing world. Typically, foreign networks and channels want to *version* each project to fit their specific market. The easiest way to do this is by changing all of the on-screen text to their native language. The graphics log tells a network exactly where any lower thirds name identifications, full-screen graphics, or graphical elevators exist *and* where to find clean replacement images or plates on the master QuickTime file.

Appearance Releases and Log

Once you have a graphics log, you can tackle the next piece of the puzzle, the **Appearance Releases and Log**. This document defines who appears in your program, typically in order of appearance, and helps define the order of the appearance releases in the final legal binder.

Talent Agreements

Similar to an appearance release, any show that features a host or paid contributor requires a signed **Talent Agreement**. This document is essentially your contract with the talent to host the series.

Voice-over Agreement

If you have a narrator in your project, you'll need to provide a release or contract for their work as well.

Music Cue Sheets and Contract

The network or streaming service will require you to put together a **Music Cue Sheet**. This spreadsheet lists every piece of music in your project, its length and usage, as well as who composed it and their performance society. This single document is the basis for how musicians and composers get paid royalties for their tracks when they're broadcast over the air. In addition to the Cue Sheet, you'll also need to provide a Contract with your composer or music library that states you have the right to use the recordings.

End Credits

Television and documentaries in particular hold remarkable allure. Especially if someone can get their name attached to a broadcast project. As a producer you can use this sentiment to your advantage, and in particular when it comes to your credit list.

Every network is different, but typically a producer is granted between 30–50 name slots on the final credit roll that runs at the end of the program. With the exception of the really big specials or series, few projects need all that space. *These slots are actually a tradable asset* and a resource for a producer. In fact, it's one of the great hidden currencies in the documentary space. Especially when it comes to your crew. Everyone always wants a better title. Young shooters want to be known as Directors of Photography. Young Assistant Editors want to make the jump to full Editor. Bumping your team up is an easy give. It makes them feel better and often creates more buy-in for the overall project. The best part is it costs you absolutely nothing, yet the payoff is tremendous.

Airdates

Once you send in the final legal binder you've just completed your project! It's time to sit back and appreciate the journey that has seen you climb your first factual programming mountain. Surviving a factual program whirlwind can feel like jamming a decade of decisions into a year. It's a heart pounding series of non-stop creative choices, a constant battery of problem-solving, and an amazing time spent with your closest creative collaborators. Take a beat to let the trek and accomplishment sink in.

Networks control when a new program or series is scheduled for broadcast. Usually, they'll give a producer a heads up about the air schedule, though you should keep an eye on it too by doing weekly internet searches after you've delivered the air master QuickTime files.

There are few uniquely positive and proud feelings quite like seeing your program hit the screen for the first time. It often takes a village to make it happen and a hell of a lot of hard work. *Celebrate the victory* and savor the moment!

Chapter Eleven

Forging a Factual Career

It's not entirely uncommon to feel the pangs of regret when a project comes to its natural conclusion. Many creatives lose their mojo after wrapping up a big project. This is a normal and a form of post-project depression. TV projects take so much out of you that it's only natural for your body to need a recharge. Don't fret if you feel stuck or unable to creatively engage. Disengage and then slowly work your way back into the fold as you ramp up for the next project on the horizon.

As you start to begin to think about what comes next, here are a few suggestions that might help you on your own journey.

DOI: 10.4324/9781003292289-11

Get Comfortable With Being Uncomfortable

If you want to become a prolific producer, and run your own productions, you need to be willing to push yourself into an uncomfortable place. Learn to embrace uncertainty and push back self-doubt. They're the arch nemesis of progress and a quick way to lose your way – instead, focus on cultivating your skill as a creator.

Success in this business comes from solving content problems. You can create a little bit of content that appeals to a wide range of viewers; you can create a lot of content for few people or produce massive amounts of content for as many people as possible. Each path has its ups and downs, and being a professional producer means living with a fluid career path. You never know what each day will bring, let alone what might transpire in any given year. Producing requires daily triage as new needs will emerge, clients submit new requests, and pitches constantly need to be written to land new work. Every day starts with the best intentions, but it's up to you to keep it in order and keep yourself sane. Yet that's also the allure to the gig – the constant juggling of priorities is part of the attraction and part of the drug. No two days are ever the same. If it isn't uncomfortable, you're not at your limit. And if you're at your limit, then you're not really living. As Oscar Wilde wrote, "To live is the rarest thing in the world; most people just exist".

Selling the Next One

An indie producer or production company has got to always be continually hustling for dollars. You can never stop thinking about idea creation or funding. They are your oxygen and your life mana. As they're fond of saying in Hollywood, *you're only as good as your next one!*

The really good creators work their way toward balance by landing both a summer and fall series. This way one project can be filming while the other is in post, and vice versa when the seasons flip. Running two series at the same time has a number of benefits. It allows you to keep the team you've spent years building employed over an entire calendar year. This minimizes your staffing turnover and also means you'll spend less time onboarding new talent. Two series per year also gives your team some security. That's a rare thing in the mainly freelance-driven factual programming industry. Finally, running a fall and a summer series is the best way to mitigate the financial impact you'll feel from the loss of a series or renewal.

For many intrepid factual producers, there's no greater creative challenge than reaching the point where multiple networks entrust you to run projects at the same time. It's a hugely inspiring professional moment, yet to pull it off you have to lean into the challenge. For first-time producers making the jump into two-series life, there's no greater trial by fire. Your time is stretched to the max and your ability to oversee every detail is consistently tested. Now's the time to reap the rewards of building a great factual producing foundation with bulletproof systems, amazingly talented creative collaborators, and clear delegation. This is when all that time spent building your team's buy-in pays off the most – because now the hard work *really* starts. There's nothing that quite compares to essentially running two separate start-up businesses at the very same time. The best time to prepare for running multiple projects concurrently is *before it actually happens.*

Figure Out Your Superpower

Everyone has a great gift. Some people are highly compassionate; others are visionaries; some have highly analytical task-oriented minds. Perhaps you speak "actor" really well or have a very clear mind for sequential storytelling. Early in your career, mastering one "hard" skill is crucially important. This is the first stone that you lay in your factual programming foundation. Learning it inside and out will allow you to get your foot in the door and scale your role as you grow more proficient. Figure out what you do best and become the expert that everyone in your circle goes to for help on the subject. Once you know your superpower, you can leverage it into bigger and better projects. Later in your career, you can transition from the initial hard skill you've mastered into broader soft management skills.

Art of Self-Promotion

If you never dare to self-promote your own work, you run the risk of being a magical and mysterious secret production entity that only a select few people appreciate. We spent far too many years producing great work without anyone outside of a small circle of commissioners knowing it. To gain exposure you have to proactively pitch your own story, and to gain awards you have to enter as many contests, categories, and festivals as you can. For many creatives this is an unnatural act. We want our work to stand out on its own merits. However, the world doesn't always work that way, and it's ultimately in your best interest to be your own cheerleader.

What's Your Calling Card? Every producer is uniquely qualified to make at least one particular type of content. Figure out what it is and tell the world about it.

Create Noise: Getting noticed requires making newsworthy events a regular part of your weekly, monthly, and yearly plan. Find a way to get *others* to tell the world about your work.

Embrace New Media: Today, there are dozens of great ways to get your message out online. Figure out your medium and exploit it to the best of your abilities in order to tell your success story.

Play the Awards Game: Enter as many contests and film festivals as possible. Once you win an event, use it to reiterate your producing experience, success, and ability.

Celebrate All the Victories: People like to hire winners. Commissioners want to hire the best of the best. Success is intoxicating. So, celebrate the wins in public.

Circle of Competence

Billionaires Warren Buffett and Charlie Munger are famous for referencing the importance of topflight financial managers knowing their boundaries. They call it the *Circle of Competence*. If the entire world's knowledge base was expressed as a circle, an individual's Circle of Competence would be a small circle inside of it. The space between the two is the danger zone. You build your Circle of Competence over time. The more you learn, the larger your circle of knowledge becomes. To become an epic producer, you have to define your own circle and identify what you do well. At the same time, you have to be honest about what you don't do well too. The really good producers determine what they know and spend their time laser focused on just those topics while humbly admitting to everyone else that they need help elsewhere. If you're a visionary, hire a great general that can be your execution-focused field producer. If you're great in the field, find people to partner with who can elevate your pitches. If you have a vision but lack the chops to cut it together, find a great editor to bring your story to life. Be ruthlessly honest with yourself and brave enough to admit your limitations.

Prepare to Pivot

Once you decide to dive into the entertainment industry in earnest you have to learn to come to grips with its volatility. *The only constant is change.* The best producers and documentarians learn to adjust on the fly and more importantly when it comes to the business of being a filmmaker. Thoreau once wrote, "Not until we are lost do we begin to understand ourselves", and that's entirely true of this profession. From funding and finances to technology and workflow, you have to keep an open mind and continually learn to morph your game. Every time you think you've found firm footing, chances are that something unexpected is about to emerge that will shake you to the core. Factual television producing is a lifestyle choice that requires you to think three steps ahead while dealing with immediate crises. This is particularly true when it comes to personal finances. Keep your living costs down and you'll have more flexibility to chase your dream projects.

The Measure of Success

You can't always predict the value of your work. The world is a big place and there are numerous arbitrators of worth. That's fine. It's not your job to judge your own work. You can't control how many people see your film or how your series does in the television ratings. Your job is to pour your heart and soul and passion into it and to master your craft the best you can. Success ultimately is knowing that you gave it everything that you had. As Shakespeare penned, "Cowards die many times before their deaths, the valiant never taste death but once".

Forging a career in the factual television industry can often require making a Faustian bargain when it comes to the relative calmness in your life. If you want certainty and security while staying close to the factual industry, you might well be better served to get a network executive gig. On the content creator side, you have to learn to live with wild ups and downs that range from living a true freelance existence where you never know when your next paying gig is going to hit all the way to the masochistic process of pitching your brilliant ideas until a project pops.

Just a few years after founding my production company, we found ourselves looking at a dwindling bank account and a lack of sales prospects. Life felt bleak and the situation was dire. We had one last meeting set up at TLC's LA offices in Century City. We went in and pitched our hearts out. The two female development exes patiently listened to our ideas yet seemed to be baffled why two gearheads would pitch them lifestyle programming. Literally every dart that we threw on the wall missed its target. When we left, I knew we were doomed. It seemed inevitable that a corporate bankruptcy was in our future. The slow-moving crosstown car ride back to the office was solemn and depressing. The air sat so heavily inside the cabin. There wasn't much left to say as we headed down Santa Monica Boulevard–and then out of the blue something magical happened. The phone rang with a District of Columbia area code. It was an executive producer from Discovery's HD Theater (which would later rebrand as the Velocity Channel and then eventually the Motor Trend network). They wanted to know if we could produce a new motoring series for them. It was an amazing stroke of last-minute luck when the chips were all in and we were down to our last card and a great example of how you simply never know when luck will strike in this business. Undoubtedly, through the course of your career you'll face an emotional career rollercoaster ride.

Some years are better than others. Appreciate the triumphs when they happen while peacefully acknowledging that they may not last. At first it can be a scary, daunting, and unsettling way to go about a career; however, the more you do it, the more accustomed you'll get to the cyclical nature of the process. I've learned to live by a simple mantra: "This Is the Life I Chose".

The Business of Business

Crafting factual programs and series is a risky profession where you compete against thousands of other storytellers who are all aiming to share their own stories. When you're young, you have nothing to lose and everything to gain by chasing your dreams – so think big and aim high. Later in life making bold decisions and big bets on yourself gets harder, so dive into the deep end as quickly as possible.

You don't need the flashiest computer or camera, a fancy office, or a new production vehicle. Keep your expenses low until you're more established. When it comes to office space, don't fall into an ego trap. Never upgrade your space until you're busting at the seams for six months straight.

Producing factual television is the ultimate form of entrepreneurship – your ideas are your sustenance. A producer's very survival is intrinsically tied to their output. So, take every opportunity as they come and learn from each one. When someone asks if you can do something, always say *yes* and *then* go figure out how to do it. There's always someone that you can call on for help or a website you can research for info.

Plenty of people will tell you that safe and secure jobs are better, but as a friend once said, "ships sit safely in the harbor, but they're built for the open seas".

Reels, Revenues, and Relationships

Regardless of whether you're a contract work-for-hire producer or happen to run a small production entity, you essentially live a freelance lifestyle. That means you'll always need to hunt for work and rarely know where your next gig is going to come from. Sales aren't independent acts; they build on each other. The more you sell, the easier the process becomes, and always remember that business is about making a buyer or client's life easier.

Always remember the "**3 R's**":

- **R**ecent Work
- **R**evenue
- **R**elationships

Recent Work: Your most recent work is almost always your best calling card to convince new clients to jump on board new projects.

Revenue: There's only so long that you can work for pennies. To succeed in this business, you need to make sure that every gig you take makes you more money than the previous one you took.

Relationships: No matter how digital the world becomes, relationships still rule the television and documentary business. If you can solve your clients' content problems, you'll forge a strong and everlasting bond that will grow over time as they'll look to solve their future programming needs.

Keep a Balanced Outlook

By nature, filmmakers are intrinsically optimistic beings. In some respect you have to be given the remarkable tumult involved in the process of taking an idea through the various steps to completion. There are literally hundreds, if not thousands, of ways a project can go wrong. Yet as creatives we repeatedly ignore those potential setbacks and instead focus on the final vision of the project *because we believe*.

The trick is to always appreciate that nothing is ever as good or bad as it seems. When life is good and networks are buying your projects, appreciate the positivity but also realize that things probably aren't as good as they seem. Conversely, when the going gets tough, allow yourself to some critical distance – nothing is equally as bad as it seems either.

The Japanese have a term called *Ikigai* (pronounced "eye-ka-guy") that strives to balance the spiritual and practical portion of your life. It is the balance found at the intersection of where your passions and talents meet the things in this world that people need and are willing to pay a creator for.

It roughly translates to "reason for being" and is an all-encompassing way to view life. Ikigai isn't simply about your work, money, or success – it's about the full global view of your existence: the balance and harmony in your life. To find it is to master the wild and turbulent seas of the factual filmmaking industry and its lifestyle. This is the nexus of passion and practicality, and a path toward a rewarding life.

Loving the Life

Some of my earliest memories are running around TV news control rooms unabated because I was blessed to grow up immersed in a television household, which helped foster an intuitive understanding for the power of television.

As a second-gen television producer, my first mentor was my father. He spent most of his career as a broadcast journalist producing the nightly news for a variety of stateside television networks. At the zenith of his career, he was anchorman Peter Jennings' personal producer at ABC's flagship *World News Tonight* newscast.

Nearly every week my old man would gallivant across the country, and sometimes the globe, chasing breaking news. He used to kindly say, "When news breaks, we fix it", and he meant it. He felt a strong duty to inform the general public of what was going on around them. In my eyes his travels were adventures, and it was mind-blowing to think that a network would pay someone to travel the world seeking truth. It was an amazing Indian Jones-like life where adventure was never far from your keyboard.

Yet I also saw that Broadcast Journalism, or *Big J*, felt stuffy. Everyone wore fancy suits and constantly debated the latest *New York Times* article, no one seemed to have an interesting hobby or a strong marriage, and the stories about corporate politics were intense. On the other hand, factual entertainment relied on the same insightful truth-telling skill set yet in a lengthier and more relaxed manner. Ever since I've been extremely fortunate to spend my entire life chasing amazing stories. It hasn't always been easy, but I've also been very lucky to never feel like I've worked a day in my life. There's a tremendous opportunity to love life when you can combine your passion with your professional path. *This is an industry that allows you to chase your dreams.*

However, to chase those dreams you have to constantly put yourself out there again and again, or as Steve Jobs once said, "You gotta act. You've gotta be willing to fail; you gotta be ready to crash and burn. If you're afraid of failing, you won't get very far."

Importance of Mentors

The best producers cultivate as many great mentors as possible. When I enrolled at USC Film in Southern California, I didn't know what I'd find. Most of the curriculum was feature film focused; however, Professor Jack Oswald turned out to be a tremendous factual filmmaking teacher. He owned his own production company in Pasadena, California, and specialized mainly in industrial documentaries. At the time, his biggest client was *The Rose Parade*. Watching him up close taught me several invaluable lessons about running a small business, and I continue to utilize many of his core concepts today, including paying crew quickly, allowing creative collaborators the room to run with their ideas, and looking beyond a potential employee's resume to see their potential. However, mentors don't just exist on the production side. I've also been very fortunate to learn countless lessons from *buyers* as well.

The first great buy side mentor was Steve Burns, who at the time was the general manager of the Science Channel. He later went on to run the National Geographic Channel and recently was awarded a lifetime achievement award by the World Congress of Science and Factual Producers.

The first time we pitched Steve, we truly believed that our ideas were an amazing fit for him and the new Science Channel mandate. After all, each concept not-so-cleverly used the word "science" in the title, so how could they possibly fail, right? Steve patiently listened to the presentation as I passionately described two or three ideas. He kept nodding his head, so I thought we were on track, but once I finished, he sat back and calmly told us that our concepts were absolutely terrible. My heart just sank. But then a beat later he said, "but I really like the two of you, so what do you like to do for fun?" My old man mentioned that we like tinkering on things that had engines. Steve quietly nodded and then said, "great let's do a film about that". We left the meeting unsure of what exactly had just happened, and a few weeks later someone from Business Affairs called up to say they heard we were doing a project together and then asked, "what is it about?" And that's how we sold our first factual program. It's a classic example of how being passionate can pay off in ways you least expect it.

Admittedly, it was also a very unique moment in time. The Science Channel's parent company Discovery Communication was in the midst of transforming from a small concern into a massive factual programmer with global reach. Their ratings and revenue were skyrocketing, and they were looking to fill hundreds of hours of programming. Back then a simple conversation could kick-start a project all by itself, and commissioners made programming decisions based on gut hunches. Today's factual industry works a bit differently thanks to a reliance on focus groups, analytics, and big data, which help programmers make informed bets on what the audience wants to watch.

While I'll always remember the sale, what truly changed my life is what came next. Steve rang us up to talk about our *film* and the kind of filmic documentary language that he wanted to see on *his channel*. I'll be eternally grateful for the discussion that ensued because it radically shaped my career. Steve loved sequential storytelling that used BIG wide shots to establish the scene, inquisitive medium shots to draw the viewer in, and brilliant close-ups to capture what the human eye normally misses. This basic W/S, M/S, C/U sequential construction lies at the heart of most Hollywood movies and has been a cornerstone of our projects through the years. There's a unique power in sequential editing, and it requires a great deal of footage, or *coverage*, but when done right it tells a story all its own – without sound, music, or dialogue or narration. In fact, when you're struggling with a sequence, one of the best tricks is to turn the audio off and see if the pictures alone can tell the story by themselves.

Steve also wanted us to arm the audience with *take-away information*. These are the little surprises and facts that make for good water cooler discussion the next day at work or the moments when someone asks, "did you see this?"

Finally, Steve was a major proponent of great on location sound. This is one of the great underserved parts of both documentary filmmaking and factual television, yet terrific natural sound can transform a decent doc into a riveting experience.

Many years later when Steve moved to the National Geographic Channel, we continued our collaborations and were introduced to a gent named Michael Welsh who handled the network EP role on our Nat Geo U.S. work. He oversaw our work for the channel and became perhaps the greatest network collaborator I've ever dealt with. While a lot of EPs offer vague notes or toss out wild ideas, Mike has always been exceptional at watching down an edit, rolling up his sleeves, and offering concrete thoughts on how to improve the end product. He made clear suggestions and at times even rewrote the script to offer unambiguous direction. Mike transcended the typical network EP/production company relationship, offering insight and guidance that helps craft an hour for their specific audience. Mike is a firm believer in not pandering to the audience. One of his big pet-peeves is not over *sign-posting* a script. This is when you tell the audience what they're about to hear, allow them to hear the information, and then tell them once more what they just heard. It's a well-worn convention of factual television yet often also forces you a producer to dumb down their program in order to appeal to as wide an audience as possible. Mike always gave the audience more credit than most, and it showed in his work.

Many years later we were introduced to another executive on the international side of Nat Geo named Stephen Hunter. Working for Stephen wasn't easy; however, I'm continually grateful for the experience and the lessons that he taught me. He asked a lot out of us but also forced me to elevate my abilities and in doing so level up the work. Stephen was the first net execs to try and summarize what made a great process-based factual program. He drafted a three-page production manifesto that spelled out exactly what he was looking for in precise terms. He called it the three-legged stool approach that highlighted the process, the plot, and the characters involved. He wanted us to follow how something comes together (the process) and discover what is at stake for the company (the plot) and what is at stake for the people involved (the characters). It was a brutally simple analysis that still works today. This clear directive was a professional game changer because it offered a clear articulation of the expectations.

Stephen also hellaciously pushed me to be a better filmmaker. He firmly believed in advancing the story with interesting POV shots, great lighting, and terrific *actuality sequences*. The more *in the moment* the project feels, the more *real* it seems for the viewer.

When it came to the actual editing of our programs, Stephen pushed me to explore the edge of the envelope. He'd seen a few triptych frames in a demo reel I'd cut and when he viewed the first edit for a new batch of docs that were cut straight, he wondered aloud where the multi boxes had gone? It was a valuable lesson: When someone sees a style in your demo reel, you should assume that's why they're hiring you.

However, Stephen's great ask and perhaps the most difficult challenge I've ever faced came in a factual program he hired us to produce about MV Agusta Motorcycle. It was a small boutique brand of high-end Italian sportbikes run by a father–son duo. The father had just passed away when we filmed with them, and now the son had to take over the business, or it would fail. It was a compelling and unusual narrative for a petrol-based doc, and in the initial rough cut, we made the decision to jump right into the story by showcasing Giovanni, the son, picking up pieces of the business as he takes over. Stephen felt this was the wrong narrative choice. He thought we should hook the audience on the strong bond between father and son and wanted us to open the film with their relationship in the present tense. There was just one problem – *Claudio, the father, was dead!* It was the most *Hollywood-like set of notes* I've ever received. Stephen asked us to bring Claudio back to life through the first act even though we had no footage of him while he was alive. It was a remarkable challenge that I fought tooth and nail; however, in the end Stephen was right. The emotional payoff was much stronger – and more importantly Claudio's passing at the end of Act 1 begged the audience to ask, "What happens next?" There are few tools in a filmmaker's toolbox quite as powerful as making an audience wonder *what happens next*?

Each program we produced for Stephen elevated me as a factual filmmaker, and his continual pressure to search for *even* better storytelling *accelerated* my abilities. In the end that's what you really want from a mentor. You want them to push you toward greatness and view the work with enough critical distance to allow you to realize the film's potential. To this day I feel an amazing amount of gratitude for all the late nights, hard work, and difficult lessons that helped shape me and my career. Stephen's lasting gift isn't a specific skill or technique but rather that he elevated my ceiling without me knowing it. What I thought was tough suddenly wasn't quite so hard, and I realized that I had unearthed the capacity to handle even *more challenging* creative endeavors. If you're lucky, you'll encounter a similar EP in your career. Once you're pushed past your comfort zone and forced to expand your creative headroom, you'll find that projects that once seemed daunting suddenly seem easy, and what you really crave is to be pushed to your limits once again. There's something addictive about seeing how high and how far you can push things. A similar phenomenon exists in automotive and motorcycle racing. The first time a pilot goes 150 miles per hour out on a race track, it seems blazingly fast, and their vision can barely keep up. Yet the next time they hit the same speed, it doesn't seem nearly as fast or quite so dangerous because the mind has an amazing capacity to catch up. Now to get the same epic endorphin rush the pilot needs to crank it up a notch and push themselves to go *faster*.

Once you develop a close relationship with a mentor, you should seek them out and ask for some 1–1 time. Make it clear that you're not looking to sell them anything but rather are seeking some of their guidance. Generally, most folks are flattered that you consider them successful enough to seek council from. Plus, if you never ask, you'll never gain their insight. The worst thing they can say is "no". When you chat with them, ask precise questions:

- What are other producers doing that you're not doing?
- What do they look for in a pitch or project that catches their eye?

- How can you elevate your game to the next level?
- What do they attribute most of their own personal success to, and how can a producer help them in their own career quest?
- What should you stop doing? (e.g., What is wrong with your game?)

It's shocking how few people take the time to ask the big fishes in the pond for advice.

Specialized Factual

By nature, producers are inquisitive individuals with a natural curiosity that often allows them to lend their creativity to a wide range of factual subjects. The ability to combine your personal and professional passions can elevate your project to an even higher standard *and* give you a leg up on the competition. Working on a project that blends your love of storytelling with the activities or interests that you're personally drawn to is a tremendously powerful way to unlock the story within the story. An intuitive understanding of a subject allows a creative to hit the ground running and gives you a powerful insight into what fans of the subject matter crave.

Our first *big break* was extremely lucky because it propelled us down the path of motor-driven storytelling, and the subsequent knowledge we've built allows us to enter any auto-filmmaking situation with an innate understanding of the story that we're trying to tell. Since we started as motoring fans, we have a very clear idea of what the adrenaline-filled horsepower-crazed fan base expects and admires.

After spending two decades filming inside hundreds of design studios, engineering facilities, car factories, and sub-supplier shops, we've earned a PhD in how complex products and machines are made. Our preexisting interest gave us an entree to learn the language of the industry. This genre-specific knowledge grows over time and becomes a tactical advantage. It makes you more efficient every step of the way.

Whether it's scuba diving for an oceanic film, roaming the outback in a nature doc, or celebrating culinary experiences, there's a real tangible value to building your brand at least partially around the things in life that you love.

Appreciating the Wins

Sometimes, being a factual content producer can feel like a death by a thousand cuts. The network might be on your case about deliverables, your subject or talent might be rethinking their participation, the unique access that you secured might fall through, the newly revised shoot dates won't work for one reason or another, or perhaps you've got typical small business issues chasing you at any given moment. Yet no matter how emotionally taxing it might *feel*, you need to take a deep breath and appreciate just how lucky you are to be working on a broadcast project. Getting any kind program on the air is a Herculean task – so take a minute to celebrate the little victories along the way.

Our brains are designed to keep us in survival mode, and humans generally obsess over the negative. Thousands of years ago perhaps this helped our species stay alive. Today, our continued focus on negativity tends to overwhelm our positive influences and emotions. However, with a bit of practice you can learn to focus on the good in every experience. Keep doing that and you can rewire your brain so that you only allow the positive moments inside and keep the negative clutter out. Professionally producing factual programming is a magical ride full of splendor if you're willing to open your eyes and take it all in for what it is.

Once you start having a bit of success, it's easy to think that you and your work will rocket to stardom; however, continued progress is never linear. Humans love the notion of consistent and gradual 1–2% improvements, but that's incredibly unrealistic. Worthwhile progress often occurs through spontaneous and thrilling leaps into the unknown that are usually followed by extremely long stretches where it feels like you're stuck in quicksand. Some days you give it your all and nothing happens. Other days you chip away and unexpectedly unearth gold. You just never know. So, when it feels like you've hit a plateau, there's often far more going on under the surface as you build up the base of your skill set and harden your foundation in preparation for your next launch.

I find for myself this is particularly true while writing or editing. Some days the best I can muster are a few pages. Other days, I fall into a creative zone where it all comes easy, and I can knock out lengthy segments with ease. Being a great factual producer is all about taking great nonlinear parabolic leaps forward.

> You have power over your mind – not outside events. Realize this, and you will find strength.
>
> – *Marcus Aurelius, Meditations*

What I'd Do Differently

The lessons, rules, and thoughts detailed so far have been accumulated over two decades spent filming factual programs all across the world. I've been one of the lucky people who can honestly say that they haven't worked a day in their life and my entire career journey has felt like an adventurous way to forge a unique path. I strongly believe that the best way to learn factual television producing is by jumping into the deep and just doing it. Naïveté is a powerful tool when harnessed appropriately. Twenty years ago, when I jumped out of the airplane without a proverbial parachute, I honestly had no idea if I could actually build a career within the industry. All I had was a dream and a stern belief that I could do it. Along the way I've certainly eaten my fair share of glass and would be the first person to tell you that this isn't the easiest lifestyle choice. It is however hugely rewarding and a brilliant way to see the world on someone else's dime.

Generally, I'm not a backward-looking person; however, in the context of writing this book a few things do stand out that I wish I'd done differently.

For starters I didn't appreciate the need to scale quickly enough. When we first started out, I saw the factual industry through a fully handcrafted and bespoke lens. The programs and documentaries that I aspired to create were one-off handcrafted films. However, that's not how our society consumes content or what networks and streamers crave. They want repeatable, returnable, scalable series. In retrospect I should have focused on how we could ramp up to series orders as quickly as possible. Instead, I spent too long believing that great work alone would eventually get us there. It ultimately did, but it took years longer than it should have.

We were also too slow on the sales front and spent a decade caught in a vicious in field production/post-production/sales cycle rotation, when in fact we needed to be selling the entire time. *Nothing is more important than sales.* Whether you aim to produce broadcast and streaming content, industrial films, agency work, or YouTube videos, selling is the most important part of the gig.

I also should have delegated much sooner. Once you decide that you're going to invest in someone and teach them how you run a project, it makes no sense to keep them on the bench as you wait *for the right project* to hand over the reins. You have to act swiftly and with determination. I spent too long worried about how each project would make or break our reputation. The industry is far more commoditized than most factual filmmakers realize. A lot of the industry discourse that flows around highlights unique one-of-a-kind films that *breakthrough*; however, the vast majority of the global content system is greased by returnable projects.

Finally, defining the type of factual programs you want to make is easy, but selling your vision is not. I was super fortunate to blend my personal passions with my professional one. This has been a blessing and a curse. I've been able to become an expert in a very specific segment of the factual landscape, yet I'm also typecast by that expertise as well. If I could go back in time, I'd make a more concerted effort to branch out into a greater diversity of factual genres. You want to become known for being great at two or more content silos.

I mention these failures not to dwell on the past but rather to highlight that you need to continually learn from your mistakes. Nothing is forever, and you always have the ability to adapt as you move forward.

Go Tell Your Story!

Producing factual content for a living requires having the guts to believe you can pull off miracles. First and foremost, you have to believe in yourself. Great content requires great faith to bring it to life. Your drive and determination have to come from a place deep inside of your soul and eventually extend to your entire team. The fear of failure runs high when you're inactive and not working on the solution. Once you commit to actually going about the work and solving the problem, it's easy to see the finish line. Your biggest risk isn't actually failure, it's not taking the risk in the first place. Director James Cameron once said, "If you set your goals ridiculously high and it's a failure, you will fail above everyone else's success", and that has never seemed so true. Live to dream and dream big. There's nothing quite as gratifying as seeing an idea grow from a tiny seed of inspiration into a full-fledged broadcast project. It's a unique reward unlike many others in life. As long as you have the gumption and fortitude to stay the course, anyone can do this – it's entirely possible to film your dreams and spend a lifetime creating factual content. So go out there and tell your story!

> It is not the critic who counts; not the man who points out how the strong man stumbles, or where the doer of deeds could have done them better. The credit belongs to the man who is actually in the arena, whose face is marred by dust and sweat and blood; who strives valiantly; who errs, who comes short again and again, because there is no effort without error and shortcoming; but who does actually strive to do the deeds; who knows great enthusiasms, the great devotions; who spends himself in a worthy cause; who at the best knows in the end the triumph of high achievement, and who at the worst, if he fails, at least fails while daring greatly, so that his place shall never be with those cold and timid souls who neither know victory nor defeat.
>
> – *Theodore "Teddy" Roosevelt*

Chapter Twelve

Appendix

Factual News Sites Worth Visiting

Realscreen
https://realscreen.com

Television Business International
https://tbivision.com/

C21 Media
www.c21media.net

Worldscreen
https://worldscreen.com/

Deadline Hollywood
https://deadline.com

Variety
https://variety.com

The Wrap
www.thewrap.com

Slash Film
www.slashfilm.com

Key Factual Festivals and Markets

Realscreen Summit and Realscreen West
https://summit.realscreen.com/

MIPCOM and MIPTV
www.mipcom.com/

World Congress of Science and Factual Producers
www.wcsfp.com/

DOI: 10.4324/9781003292289-12

Banff World Media Festival
https://banffmediafestival.playbackonline.ca/

Sunnyside of the Doc
www.sunnysideofthedoc.com/

Sheffield Doc Fest
https://sheffdocfest.com/

Content London
www.c21media.net/

Hot Docs
https://hotdocs.ca/

Crew Related Websites

Mandy
www.mandy.com/

Staff Me Up
https://staffmeup.com/

Working Not Working
https://workingnotworking.com/

Production Hub
www.productionhub.com/

Shooting People
https://shootingpeople.org/

Backstage – Actor Casting
www.backstage.com/

Index

Note: Page numbers in *italics* indicate a figure on the corresponding page.

9781032273235